Paul Richardson was born c   in 1963 and educated at Cambridge University. He has worked as a features writer for *Taste* magazine and the *Evening Standard* magazine. He lives in London and Spain. *Not Part of the Package* is his first book.

PAUL RICHARDSON

Not Part
of the Package

A YEAR IN IBIZA

PAN BOOKS
IN ASSOCIATION WITH MACMILLAN LONDON

First published 1993 by Macmillan London Limited

This edition published 1994 by Pan Books Limited
a division of Pan Macmillan Publishers Ltd
Cavaye Place London SW10 9PG
and Basingstoke
in association with Macmillan London Limited

Associated companies throughout the world

ISBN 0 330 33541 3
Copyright © Paul Richardson 1993

The right of Paul Richardson to be identified as the
author of this work has been asserted by him in accordance
with the Copyright, Designs and Patents Act 1988.

The author and publishers would like to thank the following for permission
to quote from copyright material:

HarperCollins Publishers for permission to quote from Janet Frame's *An
Angel at my Table*, Penguin Books for permission to quote from Laurie Lee's
I Can't Stay Long; Robson Books for permission to quote from Terry-
Thomas's *Terry-Thomas Tells Tales* and Sinclair Stevenson/Reed
International Books for permission to quote from Joan Wyndham's *Anything
Once*.

Every effort has been made to trace all copyright holders but if any has been
inadvertently overlooked, the author and publishers will be pleased to make
the necessary arrangements at the first opportunity.

1 3 5 7 9 8 6 4 2

A CIP catalogue record for this book is available from
the British Library

Phototypeset by Intype, London
Printed and bound in Great Britain by
Cox & Wyman Ltd, Reading, Berkshire

For Nacho

ACKNOWLEDGEMENTS

My thanks are due to:

the Consell Insular d'Eivissa i Formentera, who stepped into the breach with a squeaky-clean SEAT Marbella when British Leyland failed me; Smilja Mihailovich, who facilitated this and much else besides; Jessica Deighton of the Fomento de Turismo; Joan Lluis Ferrer of *La Prensa*; and Sandy Pratt, my most reliable informant and friend;

Iberia Airlines, who flew me out to Ibiza on several occasions, in comfort and without fuss; and Brittany Ferries, who transported me and a large number of my worldly goods from Plymouth to Santander;

Nick and Anne Stacey, for giving me a room with a view; Pepa and Piluca Molina, for bed and board in Valencia; Gary Cook and Brigitte; and Colette Bristow, who took my photograph;

Marlena Spieler, for her insights into food, the sixties and sheep; Vicky Hayward, an unquenchable source of expertise and news; Lisa Freedman, who read the manuscript and helped me out in many other ways; and Katie Owen, my editor, whose efficiency was a tonic;

my father and mother, for their patience; and Jenny Reed, for her hospitality and the use of her Amstrad;

and my main resource: the hundreds of people in shops, bars, restaurants, markets, offices, libraries and nightclubs; authors and journalists, people at parties, country people and city people, who gave me their kindness and candid advice – knowingly or not. *Gracies a tothom*.

Autumn

When I woke there was no one about, so I went a little way down the hill, through an unkempt orchard with a lemon tree and a fig so old and feeble its branches were propped up with sticks, past the circular dais of stones where Javier did his early-morning t'ai chi. The silence filled up with the smell of rosemary and the evening sounds that pushed their way up the valley. From the big rich-person's pad on the next hill came the dry cough of a generator; from the dairy on the valley floor, a distant clanking of machinery. Down in the field below Javier's house the first, hesitant rains had encouraged the weeds, which had taken on a weird new vigour. Rosemary and wild onion jostled uncomfortably with clumps of a baize-green, evil-smelling thing that left dark sticky marks on my hands when I grasped its stems.

I picked up a handful of earth and crumbled it in my fingers. It was the off-white colour of natural chalk, but thick and gluey like dried-out clay. Further down the slope the white was tinged with powdery orange and even further down, beyond the edge of Javier's land, it was a brick-dust brown, almost the same rich shade as my terracotta coffee cup. This was not absolutely virgin land; it was overgrown but there was no rock and rough garrigue, the slope was regular and gentle and the forest ended with unlikely suddenness, as though some hill farmer centuries before had intended it that way. What had been planted there? Perhaps almonds, or apples or citrus. They must have died or been uprooted long ago.

Or perhaps, I reflected, this sheltered space might once

3

have given forth another kind of crop altogether. An image began building in my brain, modestly at first and then with increasing detail and density; the picture of a field of green vines, bushy with leaves and with fat bunches of ripe autumn grapes hanging in their depths.

I had seen few vineyards on the island, and none in the vicinity of Javier's house on its hill of pines. Whether this terrain and this site would be good for vines I did not know, but instinctively I thought so: the field – really more of a sheltered clearing in the forest – sloped gently down the valley towards the south and there was something about the stifled hush, almost the acoustics of the place, that gave me the shiver of certainty.

Javier was shaving in his impromptu bathroom among the trees. He heard my shout and sauntered down, bringing the mingled smells of sweet black Spanish coffee and English aftershave. He looked wide-eyed and alive, exemplifying perfectly his countrymen's ability to withstand the thousand natural shocks that a life of untrammelled pleasure-seeking is heir to. It had been a manic, rollercoaster night such as perhaps only a Spaniard can appreciate to the full; a wild, careering rush from café to bar, bar to disco and disco to alcoholic oblivion.

I described to Javier my plan for his land. It would be a small vineyard, just the size to fill up this fallow field hemmed in by woodland. I would have six or seven rows running across the slope, so as to catch more of southern Europe's precious rainfall, I'd look for proper grape varieties to plant, and the vines at the top would do better than those at the bottom because they'd get more sun and they'd have the chalky soil.

The wine we'd drunk last night had been dark, thick, sweetish, musty, rustic stuff made by a farmer in the next valley. My wine wouldn't be like that – it would be proudly gutsy and authentic, but at the same time restrained and in good taste, thus combining, Javier and I agreed, the best of our two cultures.

We began a preliminary survey of the field, walking to

the clearing's lower edge where the dishevelled weeds began to give way to a sturdier flora of juniper, rosemary bushes, pine and heather. The soil was still soft from last night's shower, so that the waist-high weeds I pulled at idly came out easily. The little cave at the upper end of the vineyard, which Javier had been using as a sauna with rocks heated to whiteness in the fire, could be my cellar, my *bodega*. There the grapes would be reduced to pulp by no more sophisticated means than the pressure of naked feet, and the subsequent wine would lie undisturbed for as long as we could bear to leave it, until Château Lafite itself would have to look to its laurels.

My first day in Ibiza had begun with a flight from Gatwick, plucked from the bucket-shop lucky-dip at the back of the *Evening Standard*. The man in the seat in front was reading *A Year in Provence*. As we crossed the coast of Spain north of Barcelona the cabin was flooded with a southern light, brilliant and sweet, that made voices chatter with new warmth and excitement as though some invisible, cold burden had been lifted from them. Into my port-hole world of Quattrocento blue was creeping a small stain of green, down in front on the left-hand side, caressed by the tip of a wing. The stain took on a shape, or rather two shapes, an organic trapezium of dusty green with a much smaller wedge of land trailing from its side. And before long they had sprung to life below me, Ibiza and Formentera, the Pitiusas, named by the ancient Greeks for the pines that cover the islands' gentle hillsides.

The primary colours of Ibiza as seen from the sky are green, for the pines, the olives, the figs and the almonds, blue for the sea, and white for the houses I could see as luminous specks as though spattered from the brush of a heavenly Jackson Pollock. White, also, for the hotels which crowded the shores in forbidding ranks; and for the old town which clung to the citadel with a brightness more Cycladic than Spanish; and for the piles of something mineral – chalk, or was it salt? – that glistened on the plains as we came in to land.

Most of my fellow passengers were couples, with or

without children, with or without shell-suits. But a few were younger, hipper. Mick and Matt, seventeen and nineteen, were two blond boys from Guildford who had never heard of Provence. They were doing a work-stint in a yacht chandler's in Ibiza harbour and had been back home for a few days to see their families. Strictly speaking the boys had been working illegally, but their boss was English and couldn't be bothered to fill in the forms. They were paid in cash, and it was good money – enough for them to hit the bars every night, pay rent on a small flat in the town and still get back to Guildford with some left over for Mum. Matt told me about their summer night routine: 'I've got a friend in San Antonio who's an E dealer and we get, like, a discount. Usually we get dressed up a bit, me anyway. The birds like it. This one' – he threw his thumb over his shoulder at Mick – 'hangs out at the Café del Mar. Too poncey. Give me a nice English pub, the Geordie Lad in San An. Yeah, burger 'n' chips, half a dozen San Miguels, then, midnight, one o'clock, drop an E, sit around for a bit, chatting up the birds. Last year there was this gorgeous Dutch bird Ellen, she was with me most nights, except when she was with some other bloke, know what I mean? Yeah, so, get the woman, get E-ed up, in the car, get to Amnesia 'round two. We used to go to KU once a week, but it's shut now, innit. Roof blew off or something.'

I hired a car and drove, pausing by the roadside to puzzle over a makeshift map scrawled with the strange names of villages and the vague snaking lines of country roads. Coachfuls of tourists, one of them containing Mick and Matt, raced to deposit their cargo in the big hotels on the coast. The airport road took me straight through an off-white modern mess of warehouses, garages and shops and past a walled town on a hill crowded with ancient buildings. The signs described this, the island's capital, as Ibiza, or in places where some Catalan propagandist had been at them with the spray-paint, as Eivissa. Further along there was more indignant name-changing – San Antonio became Sant Antoni, San Miguel, Sant Miquel. On some of the larger signs with more space for self-expression there was even a stab at ideology. *'En Català!'* (in Catalan) screamed one of them next to a scrubbed-out piece of Castilian. *'Un Consell, una illa, una llengua!'* (one Council – the island's regional government – one island, one language).

As I turned off the main road, heading inland, the landscape untangled itself from the suburbs and began to unroll like a tightly patterned rug in the evening sun. It is a country of intimate scale and luxuriant detail: fruit trees – fig, almond, pomegranate, carob – herded into little orchards with a cross-hatching of dry stone walls; ancient olives, silvery green against a soil of deep rust red, the *terra rossa* of Ibiza's central plains; compact, irregularly shaped fields of wheat, barley and beans; vines, trailing in hectic profusion in back-garden plots; the occasional palm tree and cactus to remind you that Ibiza is as close to Algiers – almost to the kilometre – as it is to Barcelona. For three months this landscape had been simmering under a meridional sun and in August there had been 350 hours of sunshine, but it still wore a nonchalant look. Only a tenth of the island's surface area is irrigated, the rest being as dry and shrivelled as an old wine-skin; but the colours it wears still managed to be as fresh and luscious as new wine.

Sun and siesta seemed to have temporarily wiped out all forms of life apart from a cat, picking its way across a corn-field speckled with poppies, a hawk above the road and a hedgehog ambling trustingly across it, and two flocks of sheep lying in two shady orchards. One of the shepherds was an old lady in a wide-brimmed straw hat who turned her curious face towards the car as I passed. The other was a young boy in a red-and-green tracksuit sitting on a rock by the roadside playing with a Nintendo Game Boy. His thumbs punched the buttons. He didn't look up. Further along the road, behind a sign which said 'The Hoe Down Barbecue', were a farmer and his wife digging in a field. Both wore the same wide-brimmed straw hats as the shepherdess.

Away from the road the slopes of the hillsides nurtured the beguiling shapes of *casas payesas*, country houses in the strange and lovely Ibicenco style, all gentle curves and surfaces of coruscating whiteness. Thirty years ago, before Ibiza's tourist boom, houses like these would have been sold by their owners, whose families had often lived in them for centuries, with hardly a second thought and at knock-down prices. Now that the Ibicenco *casa payesa* is viewed as one of the glories of Mediterranean architecture, the balance has tipped the other way. Former ugly ducklings in their owners' eyes, they have become the most dazzling and expensive of swans. A house without electricity or water that in the late fifties might have cost around £500, might now fetch anything from five to forty million pesetas (£30,000–£240,000), depending on the position, the amount of land offered, and its aesthetic merit. Classic *casas payesas* are featured in glamorous design magazines and academic treatises, and at least two well-known neo-Ibicenco architects have carved out a comfortable living providing expertise to wealthy foreigners wanting to restore their expensively acquired *casas* as authentically as possible.

I bumped peacefully along a stony track for a while before plunging into a deep, cool pine forest. The narrowing track led up the hillside, squirming through the trees, and suddenly there was a dark clearing in the forest with the bright shape of a building up ahead. A sign scrawled in blue chalk on a wooden pallet read 'Sa Rota d'en Planells'. *Una rota*, I knew, was what this was, a clearing or patch of fallow ground. Planells is the surname of the Ibicenco family who once owned this hill, before the estate was split up and distributed among the sons and this mostly uncultivatable

8

woodland – inherited by a younger and less-favoured son – was sold off for a song to a young man from Ibiza town named Javier Cardona Tur.

I had seen Sa Rota once before, in the touristic dead zone of December when the island shrugs off its summer incarnation as a ludic paradise and becomes once again a tranquil, sluggish, somewhat dignified provincial backwater. But things had changed. Last winter Javier's house had been a shell of breeze blocks hidden among the trees. Now it was a pale cuboid structure with something of the solid, self-contained look of the Ibicenco houses I'd seen on the road from the airport. An enamelled Yin–Yang sign swung in the wind above the front door and solar panels glinted on the roof, both hints at the owner's character and his island's rich legacy of counter-cultural ideals.

Javier has been building houses for years, and the more he builds the more adventurous they get. Born into a conventional bourgeois family, he followed an early career as a professional builder before dropping out in a mild way, buying his bit of land in the remote countryside between the villages of Santa Gertrudis and San Lorenzo, at the island's centre, and beginning to reconstruct his life according to the ways and means of the New Age. His first effort was a whitewashed cottage on the top of the hill which now has a dual existence as rented holiday house and venue for group sessions in Rebirthing, the Californian feel-good therapy which Javier teaches when he is not building houses or earning money in various peripatetic jobs connected with the tourist industry. His second was a tiny, ravishing one-room house on the other side of the hill, custom-built for the Spanish Ambassador in Cameroon who spends a few days every year relaxing in it. For this task he consulted books about traditional Ibicenco architecture, used pine trunks from his own forest to make the beams and painted the exterior a shade of dusty New Mexico red not a million light-waves from the rust-red of the soil that covers the floor of the orchards down in the valley.

Ibiza not being a place whose native culture lends itself

to High Art, its traditional houses are its artistic masterpieces. Before tourism brought beaches and discos they were one of the island's main attractions. Walter Benjamin, the German critic and thinker, noticed them on his first visit to the island in the spring of 1932. He was particularly struck by the possibilities they offered for peace and quiet, writing to Gretel Adorno: 'The inhabitants isolate themselves from each other by means of a cunning spatial arrangement and with walls nearly a metre thick which shut out the slightest noise.'

Unlike in the other Balearic islands, Mallorca and Menorca, where building tended to be centrifugal around village and towns, in Ibiza the classic country *finca* (farm) stands in superb isolation. This is partly due to Ibiza's social structure – there were and are no powerful employer-land-owners as there were in Menorca; everyone worked for himself and was self-sufficient, like Scottish crofters – and partly due to a streak of *laissez-faire* detachment in the Ibicenco character which prefers to maintain a certain distance, physical and moral, between one social unit or group and another.

This self-sufficiency is at the heart of the *casa payesa*. Just as everything needed to build the house could be found within walking distance of the site, in the same way when it was finished the house contained almost everything its inhabitants might need to live with and by. There would be a well, a cistern for rainwater, an olive press, a wine press, and a bread oven in the form of an evocative whitewashed dome like an organic outgrowth from the walls of the house.

The *magatzem* was the granary and tool-house. There would be *corrals*, sometimes within the house itself, otherwise joined on to the house or nearby, for goats, rabbits, chickens and the all-important pig, which would be slaughtered in the wintertime and fashioned into two types of fatty, highly spiced sausage. The sausages, in turn, would be hung on racks in the kitchen or in an adjacent store-room along with cured hams from the same porcine source and strings of drying tomatoes. From the fields came cereals, broad beans, peas, lentils; from the family orchards, figs (which were dried for use throughout the year), almonds, carobs for animal-feed and for humans in hard times, and an embarrassment of fruit.

The focus and core of the house was a central room which was more truthfully a living-room than the Anglo-Saxon version because it was where most of life took place. In the *porxo* you would eat, talk, sit (in front of the fire if it was winter) and do the time-consuming necessary indoor tasks. There were almonds to be shelled and dried peppers to be threaded on strings. For those who had the skill, there was esparto grass – collected from the islet of Espardell, off Formentera – to be carded and woven into ropes, baskets and ladies' sandals. The *porxo* or 'long room' as theorists describe it, is a sideways rectangle relative to the front door. It is the first room you enter unless the house has a *porxet*, a terrace covered over with bamboo. At either end of the *porxo* are two rooms, often reached up or down a few steps which were sometimes of unequal depth so as to trip up robbers – although until recently there was so little likelihood of robbers that everyone left their houses unlocked. Decoration, external or internal, was minimal and largely unintentional. *Es tinell* was a cornice in the wall where bread was kept. There might be a hat hung on the wall. Later there were arches and pillars, First Communion photographs and calendars.

From 1000 BC until the 1960s, more or less, it was the same story. The farmer who wanted a new house built, or who wanted to add to an existing group of *cases*, announced the fact to neighbours and relations, and they all worked on the building together. There were no calculations, no detailed plans; the builders relied on a combination of instinct and cultural memory. The measures they used were human ones: the cubit, the span of the arms, the height you could reach with your hands without stretching.

The house almost always faced south. The walls were a double thickness of stones gathered from round about, sandwiched with earth or clay and *tapià* (gravel). To give the structure more security the sides of the house leant almost imperceptibly inwards. Beams of whole pine trees supported a leak-free roof of canes or sticks topped with a thick layer of dried seaweed and another of clay. The roof also inclined imperceptibly downwards towards the outside edge, where shallow runnels carried rainwater down into the cistern. The slight curve on the walls and roof gave a look of something organic and growing, as though the house had grown fat on the life inside it.

Javier's current project was a modern house that retained many of the traditional aspects of the *casa payesa*. From the outside this brand-new house had the handmade charm of a centuries-old one, even if underneath the whitewash the walls were of breeze blocks and cement and not locally gathered stones and clay. Javier had built his house around the nucleus of an old stone *païssa*, a shelter for shepherds, just as his ancestors would have done with their innate dislike of the completely new, the uninherited. Holding up the roof were pines from the forest clearing in which I had parked my car.

But there are other kinds of authenticity than the merely physical. The house was being built sporadically, slowly, lovingly, with the help of friends. Its position, hidden away in deep woodland in countryside as remote as you can find in Ibiza, seemed to me to express an age-old craving for spatial separateness. The house had an Ibicenco soul. The door was open so I pushed into the dark kitchen and sat down at a rickety table. The sun fell slantingly through the roof on to a yellow bowlful of flame-orange prickly pears, evidently gathered from the patch of rampant cactus outside the kitchen door. The prickly pear, along with the peculiar agave which leans threateningly over certain roadsides in Ibiza, was brought back to imperial Spain from the Americas. Beyond the kitchen another angled shaft of light peered into a darkened bedroom with beams, white walls, a mosquito net.

At its best the Ibicenco house has an aesthetic appeal

that is nearly erotic. The eye travels around its diffident form with lecherous concentration, greedy for these curves and textures, this Christmas-cake whiteness. Outside Javier's house, in an image that seemed to spring fully formed from some collective Mediterranean dream, a glossy green fig tree, in whose shade slept a cat, stood in a little courtyard beside a flight of gentle steps – all edges softened by design and centuries of whitewash – up to the roof. Everything that wasn't alive was as white as a snowdrift in the evening sun.

Walking up past the house I came upon a path that led along the brow of the hill. There were overgrown terraces and scraps of dry-stone wall, a few tumbledown metres of the hundreds of kilometres built by Ibiza's now extinct master wall-builders. From a bald patch where the path took its first downward zig-zag I stood and looked at the land laid out below me. To the west, towards San Lorenzo, was a rich plain stippled with fruit trees, then more hills and a thin wedge of bright blue caught between them on the horizon. In the opposite direction was a distant view of the rocky stub of Ibiza town rising like a smaller and less grim and granitic version of Edinburgh Castle between the plain and the sea. At this distance the cathedral's four-square tower and the bulwarks of the city walls, high up on the citadel, were visible where the apartment blocks and warehouses were not. Flattered by a faint evening mist and the late-summer light, this would have been the same view that country people saw for centuries on their way 'down to Vila' ('town') in their carts on market days. I waited another half-hour for Javier, then I went down to Vila to find him. It was dark by the time I parked the car beside the old market and walked up the stone ramp, under a monumental gateway crowned with the imperial coat-of-arms of Philip II and guarded on either side by two headless Romans.

For a pocket-sized capital Ibiza town has fortifications so thorough and forbidding that you ask yourself what terrible threat could possibly have occasioned them. (The short answer is pirates.) The city walls make the upper part of the town, known as Dalt Vila, into a crag. They are as thick as a London terraced house and in places three times as tall, thundering down among the low white houses that jostle round the port.

Walk up the ramp and through the gateway, follow the road's sudden twist inside the wall that makes you think of the Jaffa Gate in Jerusalem, pass the dark little cloister and turn to your left through another immense gateway, and you're in Dalt Vila. Ahead lies a paved whitewashed street, the Plaça de Vila, on summer nights abuzz with tourists like wasps attracted to the sweet delights of craft shops and restaurants serving ice-creams and milkshakes. This is as far as most trippers dare to go along Dalt Vila's breath-defying streets, unless it is for a special once-in-a-holiday assault on the cathedral of Santa Maria de las Nieves ('of the snows'). Beyond the Plaça de Vila is the dead centre of the old town – a beautiful, ancient, mouldering, empty zone where you would only go if you had a particular purpose in mind, if you were looking for a friend, visiting the Town Hall or, if it was summer and you were so inclined, cruising the handful of bars that have sprung up to cater for Ibiza's exuberant, mainly summer-seasonal homosexual population.

Follow another twist in the road to your left, and you are following the battlements along the Avenida General Franco. There is a little park, a meeting-place for dogs and stray children, and beds of municipal geraniums. In the season the *baluarte de Santa Lucia*, a flat area of rampart just over the road from the gay bar La Muralla, sees a frantic night-time exchange of cigarettes, eye-contact and telephone-numbers. It's also the place for views of the glittering yachts in the harbour, the still sea with the moon on it and, below you, the former fishing quarter of Sa Penya, now the most decadent, loudest, most sleazily glamorous *barrio* (district) in the whole western Mediterranean.

I knew where I would find Javier. As well as his other peripatetic occupations he was a member of Ibiza's amateur theatre group, which that autumn was rehearsing and performing in a converted church in Dalt Vila. The church was half-way up a precipitous street that led eventually to the Cathedral square. As I tried the door two gypsy children pulled themselves up from the cobbles where they had been sitting and tried to sell me heroin: one small bag for 1000 pesetas. 'Our sister is sick.'

Inside it was comfortably cool. Through the dim glow of the stage lights was the back view of a portly figure in a chair – the director – with a half-empty bottle of brandy and a packet of Marlboro by his side. On the stage were four more figures in attitudes appropriate to the work by Sartre that was being rehearsed; one motionless on a swing, one gazing fixedly into the wings as though in a mirror, the other two standing glumly about. One of the glum ones was my friend.

When the houselights came up he ran to the back and met me with a full southern European bear-hug. I remembered his profile, noble, almost classically so, from the winter before. It was a serious, haughty Spanish face, redolent of Roman emperors on coins in provincial museums, with a hint of sadness like a brushstroke of blue on a field of crimson. He told me he was happy: the house was going well, he had been in work all summer as a security guard in various tourist hotels and discos and, best of all, he had recently been Rebirthed.

Javier was a child in the late fifties, when Ibiza had only just moved out of the Middle Ages. Twenty years had passed since the Civil War, and still the island was miserably poor, unvisited and unblessed. By every reckoning Ibiza was underprivileged. Communications with the outside world were so bad – the mail-boat from Barcelona came once a week on a Friday (except when it didn't come) and brought a few *forasteros*, people from outside, who were gawped at as they stepped off the boat – that even the mainland Spanish knew nothing of the island.

There were two proper roads connecting Ibiza town to the island's two smaller towns, San Antonio and Santa Eulalia. Traffic was minimal and there was one tiny petrol-station where the attendants would play cards and smoke, causing it to blow up from time to time. In 1943 there were two taxis on the island; by the early sixties, according to popular memory, this number had rocketed to three. Almost more remarkable is another pair of statistics relating to private cars. In the mid fifties, remembers one eminent Ibicenco, there were 'twenty or thirty' cars on the whole island; now Ibiza has the highest number of cars per head in Europe.

A handful of ancient buses ploughed their way into town from the villages, some of which had only one service a day, necessitating long queues in village squares in the early hours of the morning. Going 'down to Vila' was a rare event that for some did not occur more than a few times a year, and in the case of women, who led much more restricted lives than their husbands, even less often. The family of a friend in Santa Gertrudis had a donkey, which was how they got about the countryside; but, every now and then, after long deliberation and longer preparation, they went down to Vila. The daughter of the family was so nervous at the prospect of the big city that she would have to run into the bushes behind the bus-stop to be sick. A friend of Javier knew an old lady, who died two years ago, who went one further: she had never once been 'down to Vila' in her life; nor did she have any desire to.

Outside Ibiza town the island in the 1950s was one of the most archaic communities in Europe. Songs and dances and rural ceremonies with roots in the Carthaginian era, a thousand years before Christ, were still being performed without a hint of selfconsciousness in houses, in village squares and around wells in the *campo* (countryside). Levels of literacy were at third world levels: in some villages there was only one villager who could read and write, and that was the priest. Between 1940 and 1955 population growth, a good indicator of economic well-being, was stagnant at around 37,000. Many able-bodied Ibicencos took the traditional escape-route of emigration, although in smaller numbers than in the period between the turn of the century and the end of the Civil War in 1939, when the emigrants had been what would now be called economic refugees and didn't expect to come back. In the 1950s they went for a season, for a few years, and sometimes for longer. They went to France and Germany for the grape harvest, or further afield, to Argentina, Cuba, Uruguay and Venezuela, where there are still Ibicenco and Formenterense communities.

The other place that offered Ibicencos a higher standard of living and better job prospects than their own island, hard though it is to believe it now, was Algeria. Cargo boats went back and forth irregularly and always took a few passengers. Until the colonial war and Independence in 1961 there was such a thing in Algeria as an Ibicenco 'pied noir'. The poet Jean Serra was born there. Much earlier, according to Elliot Paul in his 1930s best-seller *Life and Death of a Spanish Town*, there was a couple in Santa Eulalia who had lived so long in Algiers that they had forgotten the local dialect of Catalan and spoke only French.

Ibicencos divide the whole of their history into two epochs, *antes* and *ahora*, before and now. Everything that happened before the tourist boom, the way that life was lived and by implication is lived no more, was *antes*. There was some tourism *antes*, but it was small-scale and mostly Spanish. There was a market for *viajes de novios* – literally trips for fiancés, a kind of pre-nuptial honeymoon. Newspapers of the time like the *Vanguardia* in Barcelona and the *Baleares* in Palma de Mallorca advertised the island's charms showing canoodling couples alongside the legend 'Visit Ibiza. You will enjoy its eternal spring.' There were a handful of hotels. The best of them was supposed to be the Gran Hotel, now the Cafeteria Montesol, which had reopened in 1946 after a spell as a military barracks. The hotel had the only ice-maker in the city and shared its ice with fishermen. A room was 8 pesetas.

These are Javier's roots. His friend Fernando, who had been sitting at the back of the church watching the rehearsal and now came up to meet me, has a very different story to tell, reflecting in some ways Spain's vertiginous changes over the last three decades. There are only two years between them in age, but culturally it is a century. Fernando was born in suburban Madrid. At the death of Franco in 1975 he was almost a teenager, and when the dictator's death was followed in the capital by a decade of untrammelled, hedonistic self-expression he was just old enough to join the party. At fourteen Fernando was already a drug-dealer. He bought 3 kilo lumps of hash, split the lumps three ways with friends and took his lump in his satchel to sell at school. His *barrio* was and is notorious for its heroin users and dealers, and in a few years he became an addict, driving his father to distraction and his mother into a job as a cleaner. Approaching the bottom of the addict's downward spiral, however, something clicked inside him – perhaps the fact that half a dozen of his friends in Madrid had died of overdoses had something to do with it – and he fled to Ibiza. Not perhaps the best place he could have chosen, since Ibiza town in the early eighties was one of the most gluttonous, free and easy drug scenes in Europe. But at least there was the countryside, Javier, and the Cameroon ambassador's cottage.

To look at, Fernando is a dark man: he has black hair, skin the colour of uncoloured leather and eyes so dark they seem to stretch back metres into his skull, like ancient wells. Moreover there's a deeper darkness in him; an intense dark point like a black hole at the centre of him that seems to be dragging his whole psychology towards it.

How had the summer been? Not very good, Fernando thought, for the island as a whole. It *had* been a bad season – so bad that several dozen hotels had not even bothered to open their doors. But good for him.

'Yes, is great, baby.' (His English is gruff and basic, learned from rock songs and a year as a tortilla chef in London.) 'This summer I was in Space in the bar, working. I wake up six of the morning and I start to work seven of the morning when the people is coming to the *discoteca*. All the time is drugs, so much. All the time "What you want?

Extasis, cocaina, marijuana, sure, is everything." Yes! Is incredible, baby.'

The three of us went on a crawl. There was an hour to go till midnight and fashionable Ibiza was still at home in front of the make-up mirror, but already the air was thick with the promise of a good night out. The white streets of Sa Penya were lit up like a stage-set and hard House music was already thumping out of the doorways of cave-like bars. Down by the Zoo bar in the little plaza near the waterfront and all along the streets off the square people had set up stalls, as they do every night until the end of October when the summer season officially ends, selling jewellery, crazy hats and tourist bric-à-brac.

In the middle of it all an old man with long hair and the sand-blasted face of an Indian chief stood quietly behind a wooden card-table. His clothes and hair, and the table, were festooned with coloured feathers tied into bunches, like flies for fishing. They were for your soul, he explained with guru-like gravity.

Every other shop in Sa Penya sold postcards. There are two basic genres of Ibiza postcard. One is the 'art' type which envisages a culture whose costumes, dances, houses and immaculately tended landscape are all mouthwateringly 'authentic' and shot through with convention; the other is the tackier, ruder type, which flogs an equally inaccurate vision. Everywhere are tits, bums, muscles and mouths, all stretched and willing. One card I found showed a varnished pair of buttocks on a background of golden sand. The text, in a typeface that seems to drip downwards as though in sweltering heat, read, on one side of the card, 'Sex is evil, Evil is Sin', and on the other 'Sin is forgiven, Sex is *in*!' Another had an impish, epicene figure, a character from the Ibiza night whom Fernando recognized from a far-off summer, whose entire body glistened with gold paint. The picture was accompanied by two complementary clichés: 'If you are tired of Ibiza you are tired of life. The show must go on.' A third showed two scenes, both identical comic-strip images of big-titted women holding champagne glasses and men in beachwear grinning lecherously at them, except that the image is divided up into 'Ibiza by Day' and 'Ibiza by Night'.

At the corner of the port where the boats leave for Formentera we turned back into town and walked the length of the Paseo Vara de Rey – Ibiza's grandest street, rather like a miniature version of Barcelona's Ramblas, with its flamboyant monument to the Ibicenco general Joaquin Vara de Rey and his last-ditch defence of Spanish colonial rule in the Cuban War of 1898. At the harbour end of the Paseo is an even more imposing monument: the Cafeteria Montesol, known by *le tout* Ibiza simply as Montesol. The building, which also contains the hotel that was the Gran, has become as much an island landmark as the cathedral tower or the dome of the KU disco. Four storeys of 1930s neo-Rococo glory with ochre for the walls and white for the balconied, shuttered windows, it stands proudly, but with a hint of smugness, looking down across the Avenida Ramón y Tur towards the parvenu Café Mar y Sol which is supposed to rival Montesol in fashionability but cannot quite compete with its effortless *hauteur*.

The waiters at Montesol are of the old school, white-coated and efficient as hospital orderlies, and their gin-and-tonics are generous. We sat outside and whispered about the pan-European trendies and Ibicenco bigwigs on neighbouring tables. The sleek music-biz type over there, said Javier, was a wealthy German who invented the disco group Snap – the ones who had 'The Power'. At the table next to him, an Ibicenco cultural mandarin whose recent book on the taxonomy of local species of fish had been highly acclaimed. And next to *him*, at this precise moment having her hand kissed by a smart young man, was an elderly but astonishingly handsome woman, rumoured to be a Transylvanian princess, who flits from Ibiza to Paris to New York to Rome and back to Ibiza and is dear, dear friends with Roman Polanski, Julio Iglesias and the highest of European high society.

A fair number of the café's customers wore shades and of them quite a few were reading one or other of the local newspapers the *Diario* and *Prensa*. In the personal columns of the latter, which the previous occupant of our table had left behind, I read the following advert: 'Gentleman would be interested in making contact with a girl who has recently arrived on the island. I will be waiting for you at Montesol at twelve on Saturday. I will be wearing sunglasses and holding a newspaper.' How would the poor girl know which of all the Raybanned, newspaper-toting gentlemen was hers?

Over in Sa Penya the bars were gradually filling up with tanned, taut-bodied flesh, clad in exiguous and expensive designer clothes. The Ibiza look is a heady mix of Dayglo beachwear, frayed-round-the-edges hippiewear, all ethnicity and bagginess, and shameless no-holds-barred glamour. Its most urgent diktat, however, is that all this aesthetic stuff should be crammed into the minimum area of body surface. Tonight there were boys in minuscule frayed shorts with zips that didn't or wouldn't do up and the frippery was kept in place by a thin black studded leather strap over each shoulder. There were girls in the same thing minus the straps and plus a skein of something across the bosom, or alternatively a see-through tulle baby-doll dress and shiny white stilettos. And everywhere you looked there was bronzed skin. In Ibiza the news that sunbathing might be hazardous to your health has fallen on wilfully deaf ears. To be pale is to have failed.

We tried the Chupito bar, down the street from the old Fish Market, where the chairs and tables spilled out on to the cobbles, forcing everyone who went by to run the gauntlet of its deliriously fashionable clientele. Richard, from New York and here for his fourth successive summer, was standing by the door in an outrageous black and white all-in-one trouser-suit, a Charlie Chaplin moustache and hair tied back in a *chignon*. The music that filled the street was House with clanging piano riffs and a bass-line that felt like a punch in the stomach. Richard shimmied along to it on his private dance-floor in the doorway.

The Nicaraguan girl behind the bar at the Chupito was lamenting the headache she had acquired from recent excesses. '*Oh, que dolor de cabeza,*' she groaned to us, not without a slight smile, as she fixed our drinks. There had been a rash of parties the night before, including a monster fifth anniversary party at Space, the mega-disco on the seafront in Playa d'en Bossa which opens, unbelievably, at 6 a.m. and is still packed at midday. Tonight wouldn't be quite so wild, she thought – 'everyone' had been at the Space party and would be saving their strength for another mega-party tomorrow, this in honour of one of Ibiza's Queens of the Night, the DJ/personality/professional party-animal Crazy Eddie, who winters in a nightclub in Paris.

By midnight we were ready for the Calle de la Virgen. This thin, winding, whitewashed street, which formerly housed fishermen and their families, now has bars, restaurants and clothes shops on the ground floors and the large population of gypsies who have materialized in Sa Penya in the last twenty years living on the above floors. That the Calle is one of the more beautiful streets in the Mediterranean shouldn't blind anyone to its propensity for crime, which makes London's Soho look like Surbiton. The local police say that most of the inhabitants of the Calle and the *barrio* of Sa Penya in general are involved to a greater or lesser extent in the heroin trade, which is organized into 'clans' based on the extended family. Added to which there is 'protection', corruption of various kinds, and the odd mugging and murder, all born and nurtured in the bosom of the drug industry. Not for nothing is the area known as 'the little Bronx of Ibiza'. Meanwhile the glamour goes on above all the seediness, like a red carpet over a sewer.

In spite of its name, the Street of the Virgin, and the little shrine of a doll-like Mary up on the wall, which recently had a stone lobbed at it by a late-night reveller, the Calle has never been a stranger to vice, even in the innocent days 'before'. In the 1950s there were two brothels in the *barrio*, one in the Calle de la Virgen and one in an alleyway running off it. They were called Casa Rosita and Casa Conchita, and Rosita and Conchita paid rent to the Church, which is popularly believed to have owned the land. Once every few months a doctor would come and check up on the girls. Both madames were very nice, recalls one of their ex-customers, a Scandinavian gentleman who used to 'take my girlfriends there', and both establishments were as discreetly run as their landlord could have desired. The Calle starts off safely, with bijou restaurants serving things in cream sauces and *au poivre*, and gets more extravagant as it goes along. We had a rum and Coke in the Catwalk, owned by Irish dress designer Gerry Kelly. It was a tiny bar, all bathroom-pink inside. Here the music was the white Zimbabwean disco diva Rozalla with 'Everybody's Free (To Feel Good)', which had been the theme-tune record in Ibiza that summer.

Gerry was leaning against the bar at the far end, wearing a spangly waistcoat and no shirt, in deep and loud conversation with his barman about a possible business deal with the supermodel Linda Evangelista. We met the ravishing and suspiciously deep-voiced 'Kate', from London, and a girl with a bald head who had on a sackcloth dress and a paste diamond jewel the size of the Koh-i-Noor stuck to her forehead.

The talk was of discos: which were in fashion, which were holding special parties tonight, and whether you could get in free. Essentially, Javier explained, there were four genuinely fashionable, beautiful and expensive nightclubs: Amnesia, Pacha, Space, and, most fashionable and beautiful of all nightclubs in Europe, and possibly the universe, the KU. The latter had closed the previous winter after a roof, hastily erected to comply with a new noise-pollution law, collapsed in a storm, and now, to make matters worse, the club's Basque owners were facing bankruptcy. But the other three clubs were up and running, their posters competing for space and attention on walls and in shop windows all across Ibiza. Amnesia, a stunning white building on the San Antonio road with a tropical garden and glass roof like something out of Kew Gardens, was holding one of its notorious 'foam parties', in which at several points during the night five feet of foam is pumped on to a crazed and heaving dance-floor. That season the detergent in the foam had been doing damage to people's eyes, it was claimed, and the club had been threatened with legal action. But it would take more than a few cases of eye-irritation to stop the parties. In any case, with a 4000-peseta (£24) entrance fee and a capacity-crowd of close on 2000 every night that the foam was on, Amnesia's owners – disco-businessmen from Barcelona – would be the last people to burst the bubble.

The Big Four clubs move in and out of fashion in a complicated dance. Mercedes, a salesgirl in a sexy clothes shop further down the street, said she thought Amnesia had gone downhill since it was bought up last year by the Barcelona people. When José had it, she explained, real regulars were let in free as a matter of course; now, to their disgust, they were having to pay and were boycotting the place, leaving it to fly-by-night tourists with more money than style. Even worse, Amnesia had been advertising on the tacky Cuarenta Principales (Top 40), Spain's equivalent of Radio 1.

Meanwhile at Pacha, an even vaster, groovier disco-temple down by the port with a slightly older and very slightly more sensible crowd, there was a party tonight whose theme was 'Erotic Dreams'. Down the Calle de la Virgen there would shortly come a troupe of head-turningly dressed people – the Pacha dancers – whose job it was to give out free tickets to 'Erotic Dreams' and later to pose on podiums in the club *pour encourager les autres*.

By one o'clock the bars were full to bursting and the streets were on the way, everybody drinking and flirting and shouting above the music. The further we got down the Calle the more unhinged the atmosphere seemed to become, until at the far end where nearly all the bars are gay it was practically hysterical. At one point two big bars faced each other on opposite sides of the street, creating an immense bottleneck of queens, clutching their drinks above their heads, screaming and laughing above the booming Hi-Energy disco noise. Money and drugs were changing hands everywhere you looked, twists of paper sneaked into back pockets and notes pressed into hands. A barman serving drinks in the street asked us, expecting the answer 'yes', whether we wanted E. It was the best around, pure MDMA from California, 4000 pesetas a tablet. The Ibiza night is fuelled on Ecstasy, which has been around longer here than anywhere else in Spain. In the early morning session at Space, when the music is pure ferocious techno-house, unlistenable-to with a clear head, it is safe to assume that the majority of the apparently tireless clubbers have their brains and bodies brimful of the stuff.

The night had barely started, and already the gay end of the Calle had tipped into a surreal no-holds-barred decadence. Beside me, two men in black leather were kissing against the whitewashed wall, their clothes squeaking like a cageful of mice. On the other side of the street a tiny person dressed in flowing oriental robes, looking like part of the retinue of some nineteenth-century pasha, hurried past surrounded by a bevy of go-go girls in gold plastic bikinis.

It was at that point that I began to feel strangely woozy, like Alice when the White Rabbit hurries past her on the riverbank. Was it not only a few hours ago and no more than ten miles from this very spot that I had caught a glimpse of a way of life as solid and silent as a stone-built house, where straw-hatted farmers worked the land, tended their sheep and danced around wells on high days and holidays? And now here I was in the midst of this thoroughly modern madness, so forgetful of the other Ibiza, the Ibiza that's off-season and off-limits to the package-tourists holed up in their hotels in Playa d'en Bossa and Es Canar, that when a dwarf out of some Byronic fantasy and half a dozen girls in gold bikinis ran past on the cobbles I caught myself thinking there was, after all, nothing so *very* remarkable in that . . .

Next morning and every morning for the whole of that autumn I got up and showered myself in Javier's open-air bathroom among the geraniums and pine-needles, pulled on a T-shirt and jeans and bumped the car down the hill to Santa Gertrudis for breakfast. Even in late September the little roads were empty. Countryside as deep and complicated makes tourists uncomfortable.

Santa Gertrudis has three restaurants (one of them Belgian, one a pizzeria), three bars, a café, two antique shops, an auctioneer, an art gallery, a butcher, a supermarket and a bank, all in a village no bigger than Trafalgar Square. Sitting at one of the low tables outside the Bar Costa with your *café con leche* (with milk) you can easily see the whole universe of Santa Gertrudis stretching out before you: the village square parked with old SEAT vans and new Suzuki jeeps, many with German number-plates; the eighteenth-century church, white and basic, with its phallic bell-tower: the little *estanco* selling a diverse assortment of items from telephone cards to dried fish.

Before 1785, when Ibiza's first bishop, Abad y Lasierra, ordered the parish into existence, there was no Santa Gertrudis at all. The Bishop's idea was to re-Christianize and colonize the interior of the island, which was so backward that experts had to be shipped over from Mallorca to train the inhabitants in the art of agriculture. Many of the olive trees in the area, including the ones that look as though they must be thousands of years old, in fact date from that time.

But why Saint Gertrude? Every village in Ibiza apart from Jesus is named after a saint, and some are better-known saints than others. Of the males, apart from Charles and Lawrence, they are mostly familiar names: there are Saints

John, Michael, George, Joseph, Augustine, Anthony, Matthew, Francis, Vincent, and Raphael. But of the three females only Mary, patron of Ibiza town, is exactly big-time, although Eulalia is the patron saint of Barcelona.

Saints Eulalia and Agnes at least died spectacular deaths. Eulalia was a girl of twelve when she dared to criticize the local Roman judge, Dacian, for terrorizing Christians into renouncing their faith. Infuriated, Dacian had her ripped apart with metal hooks and burned alive, but as James Bentley remarks in *A Calendar of Saints*, 'Fortunately Eulalia's hair caught alight, so instead of burning to death, she was smothered by the smoke.' Saint Agnes, too, was just a teenager when she was forced into a brothel by an evil Roman governor, in an attempt to sully her maidenly virtue. Agnes stood her moral ground and refused to allow herself to be abused, whereupon she was stabbed in the throat. Beside these two the career of Saint Gertrude, an obscure fourteenth-century German abbess, seems dull.

For a century and a half after its birth the village remained little more than a pit-stop on the rough road from Vila to San Miguel. It was as underdeveloped as anywhere else on the island and perhaps a little more so. Pepe Tuells, a lawyer who grew up in the village, left the island to study law and came back to practise here, remembers a time forty years ago when there were not more than ten houses in the parish that had lavatories, and not a single one with running water. Vicente Roig owns the Bar Costa. In his father's time there were four houses, none with more than one floor. The bar, which at that time belonged to Antonio Riera, now in his nineties and living next to the fax office opposite, had a floor of white earth and an enormous chimney which filled the single room with thick smoke. On either side of the chimney were piles of carob pods, left to dry for animal feed. The bar was only open on Friday and Saturday nights and in summer it didn't open at all. Summer was the off-season.

Vicente's father was a horse dealer who tied up his foals by the *corral* at the end of the village, where the dirt road fizzled out into a fig orchard. During the week the village was empty, but on Sunday everyone came to Mass, and afterwards, showing the inborn Ibicenco admiration for horses, they would naturally wander over to see what Roig had to offer this week. The priest, who was an *aficionado*, would hurry over when he had hung up his robes and help Vicente's father make a sale or two before lunch.

That was then. In the last ten years Saint Gertrude has cast off her drab saintly robes, bought herself some expensive ethnically influenced clothes and made herself look right for the nineties. The village has been colonized again, this time by an eccentric population of middle-class people from all parts of the globe, but mainly, it sometimes seems, from Germany, who have put down roots so deep that it's hard to draw the old dividing line between 'tourists' and 'locals'. A number of the businesses in the village are run by foreigners, who send their children to local schools. The Galeria Can Daifa, a delicious converted *casa payesa* with a palm tree in the courtyard, is owned and run by a German woman. Harold and Claudia, originally from Berlin, have the fax office over the way from the Bar Costa. And right next door to Costa's is a hole-in-the-wall shop where Claire, from Belgium via Morocco, sells brightly coloured handmade stuff from Ibiza and the Third World.

In 1962 Claire and a friend were the only people she knew in Brussels who smoked dope, so they came here on holiday to find other people who did. She met a man on Formentera who played 'Ornette Coleman flute' and moved in with him. Then she fled to Morocco and fell in with a Berber tribe. She and the other village women would get up at midnight to walk the ten kilometres for wood, returning at dawn. After five years she moved back to Ibiza to raise her children and start the shop, which at first sold only things she had made herself. Now she is fifty-five, the children are grown up and completely Ibicenco, and she is getting restless. 'Maybe just another year or two here, and I'll move again,' she says.

Theo, an elder statesman of Santa Gertrudis' neo-Ibicenco community who runs the village auction house, had been in real estate in England, then in crafts in Dalt Vila. 'That was when crafts in Spain were great – you'd find potters and weavers and all that wonderful old generation of artisans.' Casi Todo – it means 'Almost Everything' – was the first shop in the village when it was opened by a friend of Theo's in 1973. Theo took it over ten years later.

For the first three years he had it Santa Gertrudis was still a backwater. 'I used to come in in the morning, sit here and think, "What the hell have I done?" Because there was nobody here.'

Then all at once the boom came along, twenty years after it happened on the coast. Santa Gertrudis became quietly hip. Now when a house comes on to the market for rent it is instantly snapped up. On a Saturday night there are cars lining all the roads into the village.

And the hub of it all is still Vicente's bar. Its nomenclature varies – it is known as the Bar Costa, 'the bar of the hams', 'the bar of the drunkards' or 'the bar of the hippies'. Its popularity never wanes. Everyone in Ibiza has spent some time here, either for *café con leche* and *tostadas* (two toasted halves of a crusty roll scrubbed with a tomato, dribbled with olive oil and sprinkled with salt – classic Ibiza breakfast food) in the slow island morning, or at night for beer and *bocadillos* (sandwiches) and an atmosphere of suppressed raucousness. It is a classic neighbourhood bar, somewhere between the Queen Vic and Cheers, neither of which, I think, have the hams from a whole herd of pigs hanging from their ceilings or serve a *bocadillo* that people will drive miles for.

If it was early we would have *tostadas*. But if we had been out the night before and were hungry for protein we would feed our hangovers with one of the Bar Costa's near-legendary *bocadillos* with ham and cheese. It was always the same, and it was always equally good, an endlessly repeated miracle. Lévi-Strauss would have said, if he had once turned his mind like a powerful beacon on to the toasted sandwich,

that its meaning *qua* sandwich arises from the binary opposition of Crisp and Soggy. Vicente and his barmen have
clearly grasped this point, because the way their *bocadillos*
play with the themes of crispness and sogginess is nothing
short of artistic. The bread he uses is the same as that of the
tostada, a flat white crusty *panecillo* which is split down the
middle and lightly toasted on the inside only, which allows
the inside to contain just enough of the filling to retain the
taste and texture of the bread, while the outside is not so
hard that it rasps the skin from the roof of your mouth. The
interior of each half of the *panecillo*, once toasted, is treated
tostada-style with tomato and olive oil. Then comes the filling:
thin slivers of salty cured *jamon serrano* and slices of mild
Manchego cheese. By the time the *bocadillo* arrives at your
table in the morning sun the cheese has begun to melt into
the tomato and olive oil and the ham, warmed by its contact
with the toast, is toothsome and sweet. On a good day, says
Vicente, some 900 *bocadillos de queso y jamon* will be consumed
by patrons of the Bar Costa.

As the morning melted into the afternoon like the cheese in
a *bocadillo* and the neo-Ibicencos drifted away to work or
sleep, I took myself on gentle jaunts through the somnolent
countryside. At the start of October the weather turned: there
were fat clouds sullying the sky, occasional rain whispering
on Javier's bamboo terrace-roof, beaches vacated by tourists
terrified by the briefest absence of sun. One day I walked all
the way from Sa Rota d'en Planells to the village of San
Miguel, struggling down the mountain through a jungle of
pine and rosemary before I hit a path that took me through
a landscape of orange groves and fields of brick-red earth. I

fortified myself with a pomegranate, late figs from the road-side and pine-nuts shaken from their cones, and when I had doubts about the way, asked a Swiss guy I met who was making for Santa Gertrudis in a tattered leather jacket and bare feet.

The season was slipping away. In a dark little hardware store near the old market, where I went to buy a rough Mallorcan hand-towel for Javier's alfresco bathroom, a neat old man gave me a run-down of the state of the towel market while his son wrapped up my purchase in a tube of crêpe paper and tape. 'In early summer we sell the most, a lot to tourists who haven't brought their own. You'd be surprised how many people lose them, on the beach, or in the hotel. But in October when there are no more tourists we hardly sell any . . . except to Ibicencos,' he added as an afterthought.

Autumn in Ibiza is not so unequivocally autumnal as it is in the North; there is none of that coppery deciduousness, more of a discreet and gradual yellowing of everything. The figs and vines are the first to register the change: the leaves, apparently bequeathing their nourishment to the sweetening fruit, are slowly drained of the vibrant green they have worn all through the summer. At the same time the grass on the orchard floor takes on a new verdancy from the first rains, like a miniature low-level spring.

The tourist industry follows the rhythm of nature. Or perhaps, in an island slowly losing touch with the land, it's the other way round. The time when the fruit is dark-skinned and beginning to pucker with ripeness is also the time when the year's last batch of sun-seekers are on their way out and the island begins to breathe a giant sigh of relief, which flows like a wave from the top of the old town, down through the suburbs of Puig d'en Valls and out into the *campo*, where it trickles into little pools of contentment.

It is a time of fiestas. The big discos have Closing Parties, and a month later when the coast is clear of tourists they have Reopening Parties for the benefit of the less frenziedly glamorous Ibicenco market. At the *torradas*, communal barbecues which are a laid-back cross between a picnic and a pilgrimage, local dignitaries can be seen in shorts eating off democratic paper plates. I came upon a *torrada* one Sunday afternoon in a pine wood near the bay of Talamanca and had a glass of wine with them. There was a *paella* bubbling on a fire, music of guitar and bongos and a pack of kids running riot in the woods. The adult members of the party all worked in the same hotel in Talamanca which had been the first in the bay to close down for the winter. This was the first time since Easter that they'd all had the same day off, and they were celebrating. From now until next Easter they'd claim the generous Spanish dole and take a long holiday. Some of them might even go to the Canaries for the winter season and earn another good salary on top of that.

A more recent tradition than the *torrada* is the full-moon party. Ibiza is obsessed by the moon and its movements, so much so that the disco Pacha markets a special lunar calendar with full and new moons clearly marked in silver. Two explanations for this obsession are Ibiza's hippie past, in which full-moon parties played the same sort of social role that dinner parties do today, and the undeniable fact that when the moon is out it shines on Ibiza with an amazing, weird fluorescent brightness that picks out colours and casts clear shadows. People discuss the state of the moon with the same enthusiasm that the British reserve for the weather. When there is a full-moon party everyone seems to know the hosts and the particular isolated *finca* they live in; strangely, however, the details always seem to emerge *after* the party rather than before. Several were planned for the autumnal equinox, the grandest and most eagerly awaited also being a celebration of the birth of Krishna, in the village of San Juan, headquarters of large numbers of Sanyassins and older peace-loving people.

Along the same line, in late September the following notice appeared on the door of the Bar Costa:

Noche Esoterica – A Night of Magic
at: Fauno
with
performances – music – dance – happenings – tantra ritual
– channelling and healing – tarot – astrology – crystals –
and more . . .

Entrance fee: 3000 ptas (including buffet and cocktails)

ENJOY THE LIGHT, DRESS IN WHITE

I saw Laura, a Santa Gertrudian from Philadelphia via Maine and Amsterdam, the day after the Night of Magic. She said it had been amusing, in fact a bit of a joke. There was some kind of introductory ritual which involved everyone going round the fire in a big circle. 'Even the serious people were laughing as they were doing it,' she said. And the dressing in white would have been nice except that it had rained the night before and there were six inches of mud in the car park. A lot of serene New Age tempers were therefore ruffled and whiter-than-white outfits spattered with finest Ibicenco *terra rossa*.

On the whole, more fun is had by more people at the *festes patronals*, the saint's-day fiestas. Every village has these every year and they vary in scale and sophistication from place to place. Santa Inés is one of the smallest villages; it follows that its fiesta is one of the cutest. In Santa Inés the raffle prizes are hams. None of your cuddly toys and Taiwanese electronic goods, just hams. Other attractions are Manolo, the friendly nutcase who sells almonds in caramel from the back of his motorbike, and a *ball pagès* (country dance) on the Saturday night; but, then, all the fiestas have that and most of them have Manolo. At the other end of the scale Vila and the quasi-towns of Santa Eulalia and San Antonio spend fortunes on concerts and ride-pasts of decorated carts and I don't know what. And Santa Gertrudis comes in between the two, with a modest programme that is neither *bucolic* hoedown nor municipal *Kulturfest*.

It is all a perfect excuse to let the hair down, or rather to tie it up. At every fiesta there are real or wanna-be *payesas* (countrywomen), stars of a thousand tourist postcards, who put on the old-fashioned *traje de payesa* and parade around the village with uncomfortable pride. The *traje* involves a long, stiff pleated dress of dark heavy material, a shawl over the shoulders, and hair centre-parted and scraped back under a headscarf. The only people who wear the *traje* all the time now, not just for fiestas and Carnival, are women in their late seventies and eighties who have worn it all their adult lives and couldn't get used to a new wardrobe even if they wanted to. Maria Ribas Marí was a country girl and now, at the age of eighty-four, lives in a modern flat in Ibiza town. But she still wears the *traje* and has a handsome plait of grey hair down her back as do all the most gorgeous old country ladies. 'She's got it all on all the time – the long skirt, the *mantén* [shawl], the *pañuelos* [headscarves], everything,' says her daughter Catalina, who speaks Castilian unlike her mother. 'The only thing she doesn't have is the *espardenyes* [sandals]. Well, she's got them stored away, but she's got a bit fat and they squeeze her feet.'

The main point of any fiesta, besides the ladies in the *trajes* and the men in proper suits and the big family parties and the wishing everyone '*molts anys i bons*' ('many years and good ones'), is the dancing. In Santa Gertrudis it happened in front of the church, on a little stage where a local band would come on to play cover versions of Fleetwood Mac songs later in the evening. The male dancers wore white high-collared Hamlet shirts and baggy white trousers, emerald-green embroidered waistcoats hung with rows of bells and multicoloured cummerbunds. On their heads they all had red felt hats which flopped limply from side to side when they danced, like roosters' combs. The women, meanwhile, were decked out in a technicolor version of the country *traje*: brightly coloured skirts and headscarves, swathes of gold jewellery across the chest, make-up that made them look like china dolls.

A drum began to beat and a flute struck up a piercing

warble. Then the dancing started. It was spectacular, odd and moving. The women seemed to glide about, immobile apart from the shuffling feet beneath their dense skirts, as though on wheels. With their steps they traced a figure-of-eight – a symbol older than the cross. Their eyes were demurely lowered, Eastern-style, in an attitude which gave off a kind of chilly sensuality. Around them the men in their floppy hats and baggy trousers energetically hopped, skipped and jumped to the drum and flute, like a Monty Python parody of folk-dance. At the end there was long and appreciative applause and everyone dispersed, dancers and audience, to partake of doughnuts and country wine – fiesta food and drink *par excellence*. Javier, Fernando and I wished each other *molts anys i bons* and went into town for another crawl down the Calle de la Virgen. A good time had been had by all.

As autumn went on I began to see the cold reality behind my first beatific vision of a vineyard. Nothing could be planted until the depth of winter when the rhythms of nature had slowed right down, from House to Blues, and there would be plentiful rain. Until then I could clear the ground and make it ready for the vines. These would be classy varieties, coming from the mainland, and would expect to be properly accommodated.

Ibiza has no commercial vineyards except for one in the hills behind San Mateo which is run half for fun by a wealthy Italian couple. Real Ibicenco wine is *vino payés*, in Catalan *vi pagès*: country wine. It is homemade, rough-and-ready, black-as-ink, heavy, heady, bucolic stuff, often delicious, occasionally unspeakable. Not to have acquired the taste for *vino payés* is to miss out on a crux of rural Ibicenco hospitality, for it is served up at every conceivable social occasion, from the village *festes patronals* to a casual drop-in on a weekday morning. It does not normally come on to the market except at certain country *tiendas* (shops) like the one in San Juan where you ask for *vino payés* and they give you a funny half-smile as if to say, 'Are you sure you know what you're doing?' before disappearing into the store-room and coming back with a plastic water-bottle full of dark purple foamy liquid. If you look particularly ingenuous or sensitive they might even add the brief admonishment as they hand you your change: 'It's strong, eh?'

The morning after the fiesta in Santa Getrudis I wandered down to the lower field, brushing my teeth as I walked. The weeds were more joyfully rampant than a month ago. But the ground was soft and the weeds were not too deep. I pulled half-heartedly at a stalk of rosemary, which left its pungent sweet-sour scent on my hand.

There were echoing voices in the valley. From among the voices came a faint barking of dogs. As I sat and listened it seemed the sounds were coming closer, until I could hear the dogs' individual barks and the whisper of their bodies in the undergrowth. Soon they began to make sallies out of the wood and then they were running all over my field, tongues lolling with exertion and puffing with excitement. They were hunting dogs, a tall, thin, old-fashioned breed of hound called the *podenco Ibicenco*, with brown and white patches and large vertical ears which suggested the hieratic, slender dogs in Egyptian friezes. Suddenly a rabbit scudded across the top of the field and the whole pack went into a hysteria of barking, converging on the unfortunate *conejo* as it plunged back into the forest. A few seconds later it must have met its fate, because the barking dramatically ceased and a terrific general panting arose from the two dozen *podencos*.

A man wearing a battered brown jacket and a straw hat and carrying a gun came out of the forest and grinned at me, flushed with success at his dogs' first kill of the afternoon.

He told me, in a Castilian thickly laced with Catalan, that his name was José Tur Planells and that he was Javier's neighbour. He pronounced his 'l's the Ibicenco way, with the tongue flat and loose against the roof of the mouth. I told him about the vineyard plan and he said he himself had some vines at his *finca* on the other side of the hill. He thought a vineyard was a good idea. 'Yes, why not? You take out all the *malas hierbas*, dig up the soil a little . . . This soil is bad for most things, it's hard and strong, but vines, they like it. They like a difficult life! You plant from now till the spring. You prune them one year in the full moon, the next in the new moon, one year for giving more grapes and the other year for giving less. Maybe not next year, maybe the year after you have wine. Country wine, *vi pagès*. You like *vi pagès*? Mine is the best in Ibiza. One day you will come to my house and we'll have a glass together, eh?' And he stamped back into the forest to find his dogs.

I set to pulling out the larger weeds, lit a bonfire and watched the flames munch their way through the pile while the dense rosemary-smoke thrust its way upwards as though from a giant joss-stick. The smoke tipped out into the valley and spread out over the gold-tinted orchards in a thin white blanket.

I was hard at work a few hours later when another neighbour came by, this time a young guy on a battered purple motorbike. This was Antonio Ramón Riera, otherwise known to his family as Antonio, and by his friends, acquaintances and enemies as Toni 'Cabrit'.

Part of the Catalan bequest to Ibiza was a baker's dozen of surnames – Planells, Tur, Cardona, Mari, Torres, Serra, Roig, Riera, and so on – which centuries of in-breeding have reproduced in a thousand permutations. The Spanish have two surnames, from their mother and father. Hence Planells Tur, Planells Cardona, Cardona Planells, Tur Tur, Planells Planells . . . And hence the *motiu* or nickname, dreamt up to distinguish between one Escandell Bonet or Ramón Riera and another. Toni's nickname meant 'little goat'.

He climbed off his bike and came over to me and the bonfire, a stalk of grass protruding from his mouth. He is stocky and thick-thighed, with artlessly layered brown hair and a wicked grin that reveals an ill-tended collection of greyish teeth. He wore a green and brown jumble-sale jumper and a pair of purple tie-dyed jeans that suggested at least a nodding acquaintance with Ibiza's ex-hippie subculture. Minus the tie-dye, he's a Mediterranean version of Albert Finney in *Tom Jones*; a rustic rogue with an impudent, swaggering charm.

Unlike most of the cosmopolitan flotsam and jetsam on the Santa Gertrudis scene, Toni was born and has lived his entire twenty-six years in the same *finca* on the road to Santa Eulalia. Yet without having been abroad (unless you consider Valencia 'abroad', which many Ibicencos would have done until the boom time gave them money and courage to travel) he has racked up more than his fair share of adventures. He was once – briefly and disastrously – married, and has a little daughter he glimpses sadly once in a while in the street. As the youngest of three sons he has a slim chance of inheriting the family *finca* but by the Ibicenco common law of *estatge* he is entitled to permanent board and lodging there.

He's a strange by-product of Ibiza's dizzying changes. By day he works the land with his parents in the deep quiet of the countryside, living on local sausages and *vino payés*, as though tourism had never happened. By night he hangs out in the village bars or, if it's a weekend, the flashier ones in town. Then he hits the big discos, chats up the foreign women, does the drugs. He is caught between *antes* and *ahora*, living all the problems and benefits of both.

He rummaged in his basket and brought out a lemonade bottle full of his own wine, made a fortnight ago by dumping the grapes in a plastic bin, jumping up and down on them and letting nature take its course. He had added nothing to it – no sugar, and none of the sulphur dioxide put into commercial wine as a preservative – but had filtered the wine through a mass of rosemary and thyme giving it a delicious, slightly resinous pungency and freshness, like a red version of retsina. Sometimes he filters the wine through marijuana or even throws lumps of hashish into the fermenting wine. The effect of this is imaginable.

We toasted our new friendship and my future vineyard. Toni dented the ground with the heel of his Reebok. It was fine for vines, he said, but if I didn't want to spend the winter digging I'd have to find a tractor and plough the whole field in one go. And another thing. If I wanted the plants to survive more than a few weeks I should find some good-quality *estiercol* (dung) and mix it into the earth below each vine. The mixing was important, so as not to shock the young roots with richness.

We picked up Javier from the house and adjourned to Santa Gertrudis's local honky-tonk, where Toni can be found most nights from midnight until it closes, which is generally when the fire has burned down low and the last drinker has fallen off his bar stool. The El Paso is not a bar for people who like beer-mats and horse-brasses and Pat Boone records on the jukebox. On the wall as you walk in is a mural depicting a lonely desert road stretching away into the distance and, in the foreground, a nearly nude woman who is bending over towards the horizon in such a way that the white lines on the road appear to pass directly under her crotch. The music is loud and defiantly rock-ist.

Toni rolled a joint and played a slow game of pool with a fisherman from San Miguel while Javier and I sat by the fire and pondered the problem of the tractor. His brother, who had a farm near San Rafael, could lend us his, although there was no guarantee it would manage to slither up the tortuous forest track to Sa Rota. The dairy down the road would let us have a plough. It hadn't rained for twenty-four hours, but we would need two more rain-free days for the ground to dry out, otherwise the plough would clog itself in the sticky earth. As for the manure, there was a stable-full of cow-dung at Javier's brother's farm which would require a Herculean labour to extract but could then be brought back to Santa Gertrudis in Javier's brother's tractor.

Next morning we drove to the farm. It was a sleepy sort

of place – big white house, orange groves, hens in the yard – but compassed about with modernity. On one side was the hypermarket where the car-park sounds of rustling carrier-bags and trolley-wheels on tarmac mingled with open-air muzak. On the other side, half-way up the hillside, its glass dome glinting in the sun, was the gigantic folly of the KU.

We found the tractor in its dusty barn, which it shared with a colony of dormant snails, clustering in the eaves and round the window-frames like a weird globular fungus. (The snails later went into an earthenware pot – asleep they were easy to pluck from their mooring-places – Ibicenco-style, with tomato, onions, herbs and an ample sufficiency of garlic.) The stable hadn't been cleaned for decades and the manure was knee-deep, its lower strata charcoal-coloured and pregnant with ammonia and heat. It was the work of one penitential day to dislodge it from the stable, another to load it on to the tractor and bring it to Sa Rota, and a third to plough the field and scatter it with fertilizer as Toni advised.

The tractor attacked the field with relish, making broad deep gashes in the earth, burying its weed-encrusted surface and throwing up clean waves of fresh soil. By the end of the third day there were seven wide furrows ascending the hillside in ordered ranks, diminishing in length from the triangular field's broad base, where there might be thirty or forty vines in each dormitory row, to its apex between flanks of pine forest, where a mere handful of luckier plants might bask in exclusive privacy.

Vines and vegetables are not the only things Toni knows about. He also knows his island's secret places and its curious dark lore. He knows deserted bays and ruined houses on hill-tops, hidden wells with cold sweet water, Moorish tombs carved out of rock in dense pine forests, and plantations of the foul-tasting tobacco *pota* that the old men used to smoke. He knows that the roots and seed-pods of *Hyosciamus albus* – the Ibicencos call it *caramel. lo de bruixa*, witches' caramel – will give you hallucinations more nightmarish than the worst LSD trip, and that rosemary tea is good for colds. Like any Ibicenco countryman worth his salt he cares about horses – he used to have one which he tied up outside village bars, where other people park their hatchbacks – and is expert with his stubby little Ibicenco knife.

He showed me places as yet untouched by the sticky hand of tourism; wild and precious places like the bay of Cala Aubarca. We took a road out of San Mateo and wound across a plain where grapes had just been harvested. Discarded bunches made gently liquefying piles at the rows' ends. A *camino* leading off the tarmac led through woods and orchards until we came to the coast, then we walked. From the top of the headland you can see the whole bay, a great green arc describing a circle of sapphire blue, with not a single house in sight, not a hint of human presence. It is a heart-quickeningly beautiful place which has somehow miraculously escaped Ibiza's thirty-year-old mania for 'urbanizing'. (So far. The town of San Antonio, which has systematically destroyed its own magical bay in the name of mass tourism, now plans to build a car-friendly – coach-friendly? – road down to the water.)

Later we went to Balafi. When the pirate menace was at its height in the sixteenth century, towers were built as places of refuge far inland. Balafi is a tiny fortified village which has two of these round towers and a tight cluster of white buildings around them, as though the buildings themselves were taking shelter under the towers. I had seen them from the terrace of Fernando's house, stuck on the side of the valley like two stone pepperpots.

You reach Balafi by another rough *camino*, along the side of the valley from the church of San Lorenzo. It consists of a handful of dwellings, two minuscule streets – flower-crammed passageways – and the towers. But like the Tardis, there is more space within than it appears from without. There is a snail-shell conception to Balafi: you have a sense of spiralling in towards the tower, of having to breach ever more 'outer' walls to penetrate ever more interior spaces. Anyone can walk around without let or hindrance though the dazzling white houses are all privately owned, all except one by old Ibicenco families. The odd one out is a house that, tellingly, looks outwards from the tower and the hamlet's social nucleus. A set of windchimes hangs above the doorway, ringing gently in the warm breeze – a clear sign of *forasteros*, people 'from outside'.

Under the tower is a smelly little courtyard where geese, dogs and chickens all seemed asleep. The geese woke up and barked at us as we passed. As at Cala Aubarca there was not a human being in sight, tourist or resident, and the place was full of a joyous, introverted peace.

Toni lives on the family farm at Ca'n Joan Ramón, just off the long winding road east out of San Lorenzo. The Ca'n means 'at the house of', a Catalan equivalent of 'chez', and Joan Ramón is my friend's father.

Señor Ramón was weeding in a field near the house, wearing an Ibicenco straw hat. We said, 'Bon dia'. He didn't know where Antonio was. 'He went down to Vila last night and I didn't hear him come back. You never know with that boy. Maybe he's still out drinking.' He shook his head and tossed another dandelion on the pile.

I found Toni's mother in the orchard, on her knees under a carob tree, scrabbling among the fallen pods. A small child was running around her, helping to collect the brown pods in a basket. Señora Ramón said the carob harvest was good this year. I picked one up and bit into it. It was a rich, sickly taste like cheap plain chocolate. But the crop was not destined for human consumption: it would go to feed the neighbours' sheep and goats.

Her Castilian was worse than mine. It sounded as though it had just awoken from a long sleep of neglect and came out clothed in the soft gurglings of Ibicenco. 'Toni? He's inside sleeping when he ought to be out here. Are you a friend of his? Well, maybe you can tell me. Why does he do it? Why? He has his room and food and everything he needs, and still he goes out every night and gets *borracho*.' She pointed at the carob basket and sighed. 'Sometimes I don't understand anything.'

At length the boy wandered out of the house wearing dirty seventies-style football shorts and his impudent smile. He showed me round the farm, telling me this was good land for growing things because it was *terra rossa* and there was water, water, everywhere. The Ramóns had not only a deep well outside the house and a cistern on the roof for rainwater, but a big square *balsa* (pond) full of bright green weed and a chorus of frogs. The *balsa* was a supreme luxury. It meant that even at the height of summer when the tourist industry was thirsty and wasteful and the water table had dropped to a record low, the Ramóns could still irrigate their melons, pumpkins, carrots, courgettes, tomatoes, potatoes, lettuces, peas, and so on in perfect confidence.

The farm was an Eden of vegetables and fruit in astonishing profusion. Everything was beautiful and fat with flavour. The non-intensive nature of Ibicenco agriculture has led to an infinite variety: in Toni's orchards there were oranges (six different thoroughbred varieties), lemons (sweet ones, too) figs, almonds, apples, pears, apricots, peaches, plums, medlars, a pomegranate and a quince. In his fields were broad beans, runner beans, red peppers, green peppers, fennel, and a whole field devoted to an expensive pepper called the ñora, shiny red jewels against their brilliant green leaves, which Toni would dry in the sun and sell in long luxurious strings. His vines were ten years old and had gnarled trunks as thick as your wrist. He also grew marijuana, and loofahs for the bath.

We went inside and he got out the *vino payés*. Two or three glasses, soaked up with sweet biscuits, while we looked at his wedding photos. The marriage was a rushed affair necessitated by the girl's pregnancy. The pictures made it look a miserable occasion. Gloomy faces, stiff poses, fixed stares at the cake as the couple cut it together, and hatchet-faced relatives in serried ranks. Terrifying were Toni's two grandmothers: head to foot in black, with the traditional scraped-back hair and a look that could outstare a basilisk. Toni looked awkward and sad, but as the photos went on and more was drunk (secret joints, too, outside the reception) he began to assume an air of faintly manic glee, and he and his bride looked almost affectionate as the camera snapped them clinking glasses. But it was all illusory and brief: they spent the wedding night apart.

I sat on the terrace with Señora Ramón, who was now sorting her way through a sea of potatoes. She talked about her life, her universe and everything the way it was *antes*. She is not one of your ultra-traditional country ladies. 'I used to have two sets of Ibicenco costume. I wore them at Carnival. But, like a fool, I sold them.' Now she wears woolly hats and long woolly dresses to sit in the *porxet* sorting vegetables. She is not a tall person and at first I thought she was rather shy, but her conversation had dark glints of wicked humour. 'Before, Ibiza was just a tiny little island. There was nobody on the beaches. Well, Ibicencos never went to the beach. You know the Punta Arabí? There were some lovely beaches around there. Now there are hotels everywhere. And on Wednesdays, is it, a strange kind of thing.' Not the famous hippie market of Es Canar? 'Yes, a market, but no fruit or vegetables, mainly clothes, hanging up in the trees' – she chortled at the idea – 'clothes, jewellery, strange little things,

I couldn't tell you what they are. What a place! I've seen people in that place like you've never seen in your life.'

Maria Riera Riera grew up in Santa Gertrudis – 'the San Rafael part', whereas her husband came from the other side of the village. They met when she was twenty-four at a *festeig*, Ibiza's graceful traditional courting ritual, long since fallen out of favour. Until tourism there was nowhere for young men and women to meet, so the *festeig* took place twice or three times a week in the house of some *al.lota* (girl) of marriageable age. The boys, all over sixteen, took it in turns to sit next to the *al.lota* while the others conversed with the family. As the Ibicenco writer Francisco Verdera describes the ritual, if the girl liked any of her suitors enough to consider marrying them she would not tell them there and then. No, she would consult her parents, the couple would agree, and the world would know she was engaged when the *al.lota* arrived at Mass on Sunday with her fingers covered in rings.

Señora Ramón has been out of the island only once (to Palma), and once asked me whether it was true that Paris was the capital of England, but she has seen enough of tourists to know what she thinks of them. She has worked at the Hoe Down in Santa Gertrudis, where package holiday-makers are taken for a 'great night out with a Western flavour', and at the New Market in Ibiza town, where she was mightily amused by the sight of foreigners paying 50 pesetas (30p) for one single fig.

'When the war finished tourists started arriving, buying plots of land, old houses, and everything changed. The tourists thought the Ibicencos were *cabrones* (idiots)! They exploited us. But, well, then things got better for the island. One of my sons is a waiter – he's done well. Sometimes when the tourists bought the country houses it meant that an Ibicenco could buy the house in Vila that he needed for the family. So you see, some things have changed for the better, and some things for the worse. The old people like us work in the country – the young people don't like it because the work is very dirty and doesn't leave you money.

Life in the country is good, in one way, but in another way it's bad. The work is very dirty, it's hard, it's tiring, and it doesn't leave you money. On the other hand, the work you do in other places, yes, you're working, but it's cleaner work, it's nicer, you earn more money.'

And what will happen to the countryside when all these stalwart old people have gone and the young people are off doing their cleaner, nicer work in offices and restaurants?

'People will realize, don't you worry,' said Señora Ramón calmly. 'People will realize, because so much food comes out of the country. These potatoes, they come out of the country. Tomatoes come out of the country. Oranges come out of the country, not out of the city! If nobody worked in the fields there wouldn't be potatoes, or tomatoes, or beans, or anything. Oh no, don't you worry. There'll always be someone to work the land.'

She may be right, but it's undeniable that since tourism the whole rhythm and regularity of country life has been thrown out of kilter. In the first place, by the disruption of an inheritance system bequeathed to the island by the Catalans in the thirteenth century. The *éspolits* were a series of legal agreements drawn up by the Ibicenco couple before they were married, one of its functions being to determine which of their future offspring would inherit what. The lion's share of the parents' property including the best land, which was usually away from the coast and in valleys where there was more likelihood of water, passed to the eldest son and *hereu* (heir). The younger sons had certain rights which were supposed to soften the blow – such as the *estatge* which gave them right of abode in the family home – and also inherited the poor land which was agriculturally unproductive, on the coast and/or on hilltops. But now tourism needed this 'poorer' land for the new sun 'n' sea resorts, and was willing to pay for it at miraculously inflated prices. Consequently it was the younger sons who became wealthy while the *hereus* struggled on in their inland farms. Ironically, now that most of the coast has been ruined and Spanish law forbids any more coastal development, the pendulum is beginning to swing the other way.

In October I flew back to London for a few days, picked up my old car and drove back down to Ibiza, taking the ferry to Santander and another from Barcelona to the island. When I got back the season had died. At night the streets of Sa Penya were virtually deserted, though a few of the souvenir shops had stayed open, not with any determination but slightly dazedly, as though they hadn't registered that nobody had bought anything for days and was unlikely to from now until next April.

When the season expires, so do all the short-term contracts in hotels, restaurants, bars, discos, car-hire firms and the rest of the service-industry universe that revolves around the *temporada*. Fortunately Ibicencos are adaptable people who do not pin their self-worth on the job they happen to be doing at any given time. Javier, my builder/Rebirther/actor friend, had finished his summer job as a security guard and gone to work as a hotel receptionist for the winter season in Tenerife. The house had been let at gratifying expense to a group of Austrian hippies, leaving me a month to find another place. Fernando followed up his experiences in Space with a new occupation as a collector of wild flowers for a Rebirthing friend of Javier's who sets them in plastic and sells them in the market.

Toni, meanwhile, had been working hard on his farm between short and unhappy bouts of dishwashing and bar work. Of his various crops the most successful had been the marijuana, which had grown into a monstrous coppice and had to be hacked down with a machete. With the money from this he bought a moped, after which he had not a peseta in his pocket. The ñoras had not found the ravenous British market he had been hoping for and were multiplying with sinister speed, their wrinkled crimson baubles hanging in garlands from the roof of the terrace while Toni wondered how best to dispose of them. When they began to invade the house Señora Ramón laid down the law: it was time he got a job.

He eventually found one as a waiter in a restaurant in San Lorenzo where he'd been trying, successfully as it happened, to sell a string of ñoras to the chef. Cana Pepeta is one of the handful of good, properly Ibicenco restaurants. It's also one of a minuscule number of decent restaurants of any kind among the thousands of catering establishments on the island. Eating out in Ibiza is not often an uplifting experience. For a good restaurant to maintain momentum through all the pitches and troughs of the tourist year is nearly impossible. Moreover Ibiza suffers acutely from the problem of mobile chefs. A more widespread problem is apathy. Many places that once had good reputations have changed neither menu nor décor for years; meanwhile standards have slipped and prices have inexorably risen.

At least, to paraphrase Tolstoy, even the bad restaurants are bad in their own way. Apart from its own splendid cooking Ibiza's greatest gastronomic strength is variety. Chinese, Indian, Thai, 'Caribbean', Argentinian, Mexican, North African, Filipino, French, Italian, Austrian and Belgian cuisines all have their proponents. There are even places you can go, if you have no self-respect, where you can eat English, Swiss or German food.

Food in Ibiza reflects the last thirty years of the island's history as vividly as any census. The hippie influx brought tofu and multi-grain bread – the latter is still baked by a German in San Miguel. Someone else makes a bread with sunflower seeds and another with rye flour. The tourists and foreign residents, unadventurous and nostalgic respectively in their eating habits, brought exotic tastes and specialities undreamt of in the Ibiza of *antes*. The French, with more urgent gastronomic requirements than the rest of us, have set up their vital supply line of croissants and baguettes in an all-night café-bakery in the old market square, and a couple outside Santa Eulalia who produce foie gras from their own ducks find themselves besieged at Christmas by French residents who find the festive season meaningless without it. There are excellent hamburgers at Can Sans, fresh pasta at Casa Andrés, good Italian pizzas at the Pizzeria in Santa Gertrudis. Not least, Werner Salewski's *metzgerei* is a flourishing business that supplies the German community with a terrifying selection of authentic *würst*.

Like the rest of its traditional culture Ibiza's own cuisine has been marginalized and eroded by the boom but is now showing signs of a revival, along with the dances, the music, the stories, as the Ibicencos realize what riches have been lost in the rush for prosperity. The only two books exclusively about Ibicenco food both came out in the early 1990s.

Cana Pepeta, where Toni worked as a waiter, was a new restaurant in an old house on the road to San Juan. Toni, wearing an unusually clean white shirt, black trousers, black shoes and a serious expression, showed me to my table and brought me country bread and mineral water, whispering to me when the *maitre d*'s back was turned that he'd come straight to work that morning from Amnesia's final foam party of the year and had had to borrow the shirt. He would bring me a few small things *para picar*, to pick at.

It was all delicious, fresh and simple. There was a *guisat de peix* (fish soup) with saffron and vermicelli; little fried fish called *gerret*; and two salads. *Enciam* is the classic Ibicenco salad of tomato, onion, green pepper and chopped garlic (correctly no lettuce), all sluiced with olive oil and a few drops of vinegar. Ibicenco tomatoes, sweet and firm as apples, also played their part in a dish of *crostes* – biscuity chunks of oven-dried bread, fat squares of tomato, and a dressing of puréed tomato and more olive oil.

Like all old-fashioned cuisines, but more so because it

developed on a small island where communications with the outside world were poor, Ibicenco cooking is all about self-sufficiency. It is a celebration of availability. The only major ingredients not produced at home are sugar and rice. Otherwise, nearly everything can be found within a few steps of the kitchen door. In the inland country the annual *matanza* (pig killing) is the power behind the pantry. From the pig come many and good things. First, the meat itself. Next, the twin pillars of Ibiza's charcuterie: *sobrasada*, a thick, rich sausage of cured raw pork meat spiced with deep orange *pimentón* (the latter is a powder of finely ground dried ñoras like the ones at Toni's) and *butifarra*, a sensational black pudding using the pig's blood, plenty of fatty bits and a variety of spices. Then there are the hams, lard, *tocino* (fatty bacon) and in the old days – a special delicacy this – *greix vermei*, the fatty scum from the surface of the water in which the *butifarras* were boiled, which would be removed with a spoon and spread on toast for breakfast.

Other meats are lamb, chicken, rabbit, turkey, all kept within the grounds of the farm. Ibicenco men are great killers of wild animals, so there will always be rabbits from the *campo* even if there are none at home. At one time a great rustic treat was hedgehog, which, according to the culinary expert Joan Castelló Guasch, has a delicate flavour 'reminiscent of sucking-pig'. Most dubious of all Pitiusan specialities is the *virotada* or seagull stew. The *virots* were hunted by night on the cliffs of La Mola in Formentera. The next day, plucked and skinned and drawn and with beaks and feet removed, the birds would be cut into chunks and stewed with tomato, onion, garlic, parsley, nutmeg, bayleaf and *pimentòn*. Castello Guasch advises boiling them in salt water for 'a good while' before adding the rest of the ingredients to soften their hard flesh and take away some of their shellfishy flavour. Even with this precaution, he admits, the dish is 'strong'.

Ibicencos on the coast eat a little less meat and, naturally, a lot more seafood. Two of the island's most common fish dishes are *arros amb peix*, rice with fish, and *borrida de ratjada*, a simple soup/stew of ray with potatoes, garlic and parsley. Otherwise most fish and shellfish are served 'a la plancha' grilled on a piping hot metal surface or in *paella*. Dried fish is big in Formentera, less so in Ibiza.

The proof and glory of all Ibiza's natural wealth is its most famous dish, *sofrit pagès*. The name translates roughly as 'country fry-up'. I first had *sofrit* at the restaurant Cas Pagès, on the way out of Santa Eulalia towards San Carlos. It is a real Ibicenco place run by a family comprising Antonio Marí Marí, his wife and cook Maria Ferrer Ferrer, and their daughters Carmen and Lucia Marí Ferrer who help in the kitchen and front-of-house. Cas Pagés has been running for twenty years and has not changed much in that time. Every day they serve the food of their forefathers: *arros de matances*, a rice dish made with various cuts of pork, traditionally on the day of the *matanza*; a salad of grilled red pepper and potatoes; and always *sofrit pagès*.

Many versions of *sofrit* exist and every version is naturally thought by its maker to be the original and best. Basically it is a rich, oily stew of various meats, potatoes and as many herbs and other flavourings as the dish will take. Lamb and chicken are the usual meats; you can also use rabbit (seldom pork). Maria Ferrer disapproves of the practice of adding vegetables, but Señora Ramón, for her part, she cheerfully slings in as many celery tops, peas, red peppers, ñoras, as she feels like and the *finca* provides, to make a dish whose colours are as various as its flavours. Somewhere in there, too, according to taste, there might be slices of *sobrasada*, *butifarra* and *tocino*, masses of garlic, parsley, cinnamon, cloves, bayleaves, saffron. The meat is boiled in stock, then cooked up with everything else in two or three tablespoons of lard.

It is not a dish for the faint-hearted or people on diets. At Cas Pagès a single serving would feed an average Protestant family. Whether there are vegetables in it or not, there is no point in denying that *sofrit* is a glorification of the two most highly valued elements of traditional rural cuisine: meat and fat.

Shopping one October day in the market in Santa Eulalia I stopped at a tiny stall crammed between two greengrocers. It was a *lecheria*, one of that odd species of Spanish shop which sells not only milk, butter and cheese, as you'd expect from the name which means 'dairy', but pastries, tea, dried fruits, sweets, sometimes wine. Behind the counter was a lady whose face I thought I recognized, clear-eyed and smiling a smile that couldn't make up its mind whether to be angelic or mischievous. I told her I lived near San Lorenzo and she said she, too, was from there originally.

She grew up near the river, she said, on the way up to Santa Eulalia. From her parents, who worked on the land, she had received her first name, Maria Teresa, and inherited her two surnames, Ramón and Riera. Suddenly the smile made sense. By spring I wouldn't have been surprised, because Ibiza gets you used to such serendipity. But my friend Toni, the little goat, was Maria Teresa's little brother, and her mother was the mistress of the *sofrit pages*. They all had the same wicked-cherub grin.

Maria Teresa showed me what she had that day: a home-made goat's cheese with parsley and garlic that she said I would love, and something else, '*muy especial*', that she had made herself. Not only her name she had got from her mother.

The cheese was bright-flavoured and tangy with garlic, effortlessly eclipsing the only commercial Ibicenco offering, which is pleasant, medium-hard, almost as dull as Edam, and made at the dairy in the valley below Javier's house. *Antes*, every country *finca* made a mild ewe's or goat's milk cheese, occasionally with herbs like the one Maria sold me, or a creamy *queso fresco*. Now good, truly local cheese is a threatened species.

The very special thing that Maria Teresa Ramón Riera had made herself came from Ibiza's surprising repertoire of puddings. If the eater of an Ibicenco meal can survive the *sofrit pagés*, he or she has treats in store. There is *greixonera*, sweet and soggy, made from crumbled day-old *ensaimadas* (sweet soft pastries), eggs, milk, sugar, cinnamon and lemon-rind. There are *bunyols* – glorified doughnuts, sometimes with orange peel and aniseed. There is *flaò*, an unbelievably delicious sweet pastry tart filled with eggs, cheese, sugar and speckled with mint. And the greatest of these is *flaò*.

As with *sofrit*, what and who makes the best *flaò* are matters of debate. Maria Teresa sets great store by the *hierba-buena* (mint) which she plucks from a bush outside her house. The more mint the merrier, she believes. Another theory suggests that everything depends on the cheese. Catalina Tur Torres in San Miguel, whose *flaò* sits seductively on the counter in the little post-office-cum-bar by the church, produces her own cheese from the milk of her own goats, which she says makes the difference. (She also uses her own hens' eggs, which should go without saying.) Better cheese, and more of it, says Catalina Ribas Marí of San Rafael, whose mother made 'the best *flaò* in Ibiza. In the shops they put in less cheese because it's expensive. Instead they put in other things, I don't know what and I don't want to know.'

Eggs, cheese, mint and sugar, yellow as a cornfield in the centre, brown on top with a crust of more sugar. It is always eaten cold, in a generous wedge. Vicente Ribas, a learned gentleman who is an expert on most facets of Ibi-cenco culture, thinks you should leave alone the prim little fork that's always provided and eat *flaò* with the fingers, the better to appreciate its crumbly delicacy. 'Which is the best *flaò*?' is a question to which Vicente gives a philosophical answer. It is all to do with fidelity to the past, to the way they did things before Coke and burgers became the culinary norm.

The only real criterion is memory. 'The best *flaò*? That's simple. It's the one that is nearest to the way it was made in the countryside by country people when I was young. No more, no less.'

On a rainy autumn day in a provincial town, if the shops are shut and the cinema is showing the last-but-one Schwarzenegger, you can always try the local museum. Ibiza has two of them – one up near the Cathedral, housed deep inside the Renaissance city wall, and another one in an undistinguished thirties block in a street in the modern part of town. Both are archaeological museums, because Ibiza is currently fascinated by its own history. The Ibicenco cleric Isidoro Macabich is one of three historians to have a street in the town named after him, and a foot and a half of shelf-space in the Municipal Library is devoted to his frighteningly learned multi-volume History of Ibiza, a magnum opus which some Ibicencos consider unreadable. The two local papers, the *Diario* and *Prensa*, vie to produce lavishly illustrated weekly Histories of Ibiza and reproductions of vintage photographs which are then plugged endlessly in radio ads featuring jangling Ibicenco folksongs.

Even more visibly, any or all of the island's many names under successive imperial powers – Ibosim, Ereso, Yebisah, Eivissa – as well as the names of historical personages and deities, can be found wearily serving as names of bars, laundries, car-hire companies and ugly purpose-built apartment blocks. It is as if, wrested violently out of their own past by the tourist boom, the islanders are now doing their best to squeeze themselves back into it.

The more modern of Ibiza's two museums is called the Museu Puig d'es Molins after an archaeological site of the same name, which extends up the hill behind the building in an ancient jumble of rocks, grass, olive trees and wild flowers. This was the necropolis where during their one-thousand-year stay on the island the Carthaginians buried their dead in ant-like cells burrowed into the hillside. From the second century BC until 1906 it was an unremarkable patch of unproductive countryside, unknown except to the campesinos who grazed their sheep and harvested its meagre olive crop once a year. In the paradox familiar to archaeologists, it was only the discovery of its extraordinary importance that allowed it to remain in this humble state, while blocks of flats were flung up all around to house the newly prosperous population of Ibiza town.

Considering the fuss that is made about the Museu Puig d'es Molins and its expensive interior – all polished marble floors and back-lit exhibits – the museum contains surprisingly little of any great aesthetic, as opposed to purely archaeological merit. Or perhaps the Carthaginians were better at farming and fighting than they were at sculpture. Either way it is hard to form any impression of them as a people from these strange primitive images with their rigid attitudes and over-sized heads, except that they all seem to have had a rather pinched, sharp-nosed look like the face of someone sucking on a lemon.

Ahead of me as I walked into the second room was a bewitching exception, properly given a showcase of its own in the middle of the floor. Tanit was a goddess of love, death and fertility, the most worshipped and glorified of all the Carthaginian pantheon and Ibiza's own special deity. In this bust of her, an unknown sculptor has achieved a degree of Hellenistic beauty to which his colleagues never came close. The goddess comes across as a strong, worldly woman, perhaps in her mid thirties, of the sort that if she were around in the 1990s might be running her own travel agency or a small PR company with two or three household brands on its books. Her face wears the confident, no-bullshit expression of a career woman, but there are old-fashioned, feminine touches too – her medusa-style Big Hair is tied in front with a bow of thin ribbon, and on her head is a demure little pillbox hat more appropriate, one would have thought, for Covent Garden than Carthage.

There was little else of much interest, and after a while I began to find the signs themselves more absorbing than the objects they described. I noticed they all took pains to mention the digger-up of the object in question and to give the date of its discovery, as if this information were of more weight than anything about the nature of this fragment of rust-red clay, its provenance or possible use. It seemed to confirm that Ibiza cares almost more about the recovery and dissemination of its past, about the fact of having *had* a past, than about the intrinsic value of that which is dredged up by its tireless archaeologists.

Tourists are only the most recent of the hordes that have invaded Ibiza, colonized it more or less enthusiastically and left their more or less permanent marks. Just about every civilization in Western history, large or small, enlightened or barbaric, has set foot on the island at one time or another. To the sheer number of invasions and consequent cultural influences, the Ibicencos attribute their nonchalance when it comes to hippies, gays, lager-swilling Englishmen and other modern phenomena.

The Carthaginians first directed their attention and their navy towards the Pitiusas in 740 BC. Under their rule Ibiza was possibly richer and happier than it has been ever since. In the third century BC the Roman commentator Diodorus of Sicily wrote that the island was a cosmopolitan place 'inhabited by people of all countries'; he was impressed by its 'memorable ports, the ample construction of its walls' and by its agricultural produce, which he compares with the best of Greece and Rome. Hannibal may have been born here. The people of Ibosim, as they themselves called it, were superb farmers who irrigated the valleys and understood how to graft olive trees. They cultivated the palm tree, the fig and the vine. They fished, produced salt in the salt-flats and mined for lead which made the pellets they fired from their lethal slings. When not farming or fighting they built up a Mediterranean-wide industry based on the precious purple dye secreted by the sea-snail *Murex brandaris*. Since it took 10,000 of these unfortunate molluscs to make a gram of dye it was an expensive commodity, but, purple being the favourite colour of Rome's upper-classes, there was always a market for it. Above all the Carthaginians were businessmen.

For the Carthaginian's Ibiza was a holy island, sacred to Tanit, whose very earth was thought to radiate positive energy. Poisonous animals were (and still are) unknown and the clay was thought to have curative properties. The necropolis had a waiting-list. There were temples and sanctuaries in caves like the one at Es Cuieram near San Vicente. Apart from Tanit, the gods were Bes (fecundity and the continuance of the life-cycle, hence the massive phallus with which Punic sculptors always endowed him), Melkart (travel), Resef (thunder and lightning) and the terrible Baal. The latter had a cult following which, as in the pagan rites disapprovingly described by the prophet Jeremiah, involved pacifying the god's wrath with offerings of oil, wine, birds, goats and children.

After the Third Punic War of 146 BC, Ibiza fell into the orbit of the Roman empire. It had held out valiantly against Rome during three Punic Wars, even rebuffing an attempted invasion in 217 BC, but with its twin town reduced to ashes it must have seemed like a good time to give up the struggle. By ceding voluntarily to the power of Rome the island managed to avoid the fate of Carthage as well as preserving a measure of independence and it became a *civitas federata*, a Roman confederate city. Coins were minted bearing the head of Augustus, Claudius or Caligula on one side and the god Eshmun on the other.

For the first few hundred years of Roman rule the islanders were left in relative peace. Punic culture and religion were given free rein and the island benefited from aqueducts, roads, harbours, and all the mod cons of Roman civilization. Ibosim received a brand-new, thoroughly sensible new name: Insula Augusta, after the Emperor. In the year 70 AD things were going so well that Ebusus, contemporary Ibiza town, was elevated to the rank of Municipium, signifying the end of its marginal status within the Empire.

But as the island became increasingly Romanized its

atmosphere of tolerance evaporated. First the Romans began to impose their own religion. In 283 AD the emperor Marcus Aurelius rebuilt the Punic temple of Eshmun that had stood on the Acropolis of Ebusus, dedicating the new building to Mercury. And when Christianity became fashionable they imposed that too. With the help of the Jewish community who had their own *barrio*, synagogue and cemetery in the town they demolished the pagan sanctuaries and the new religion established a tenuous hold. Meanwhile Tanit transmuted herself painlessly into the Virgin Mary.

After the stability of the Roman years there was a dark and complex period in which successive waves of Vandals, Western Goths, Byzantines and others swept, in the way that marauding minor civilizations are supposed to sweep, across the western Mediterranean and on to Ibiza. The next great colonizers were the Moors. Under their benign rule the island enjoyed an affluence it would not experience again until tourism. The Arab geographer Al-Makkari gave this glowing assessment of its economic health:

Yebisah is thirty *parasangas* long and almost as many wide, and it supplies a great part of Africa with wood and salt. The island is highly populated, and its inhabitants are industrious; it produces all sorts of grain and fruits, but cattle do not multiply there . . . Grapes, almonds and figs are the things which the natives cultivate and export to the nearby island of Mallorca. Olives do not grow in Yebisah; they are not known there, and oil comes from Andalucia. Since there is much woodland in Yebisah, the islanders' main industry consists in making carbon which they take in boats to Barcelona and other Mediterranean ports.

The influence of the Arabs on Ibiza was deep, subtle and evanescent. One catches impressionistic whiffs of it in the domed bread-ovens at the side of the classic *casa payesa* and in certain Ibicenco dishes such as the sweet, thick soup of ground almonds called *salsa de Nadal*. Beyond the impressions there is a scattering of facts. Thin books on sale at the Museu Puig d'es Molins document the Moorish remains on the island, which consist of a few crumbling walls, a tomb or two and a handful of inscriptions, blurred by time. A few resonantly arabic place-names have survived where Catalan and Castilian failed to eradicate them: Benirras, Benimussa, Alqueria. Among the two or three sub-dialects of Catalan on the island there are still a few Arabic and Berber words. In one type of traditional song, the *porfedi*, the woman looks downwards as in the dance, covers her face with her hand and punctuates her song with quavering wails (properly called ululations) that have a strong spice of North Africa.

Islam as it existed in tenth-century Spain was a confident, sophisticated ideology with none of the paranoia-driven severity of its modern counterpart. In Ibiza, as much as in the great city of Cordoba to whose caliphate the island at first belonged, tolerance was the main theme of civic life. Muslims, Jews and Christians lived and worshipped side by side. When Cordoba collapsed and Ibiza and Formentera passed to the small Moorish kingdom of Denia, King Mudjehid munificently allowed the Bishop of Barcelona to keep control of all the churches in the Balearic islands. In 1058 this privilege was confirmed by his son Ali.

The population grew and prospered. In the town of Medina Yebisah there were new schools and mosques; in the countryside there were new and more efficient irrigation systems called *norias*, employing water-wheels turned by mules, which were still in use until the middle of this century. Near the disco Pacha, off the road that leads around the harbour, you can still see the remains of this Moorish high technology. The Arabs' most enduring legacy, however, is their organization of the island into six administrative regions to which, with a few changes, modern-day Ibicencos still reluctantly pay their rates.

Not content with sharing equal status with idolaters, it was Christianity that disrupted Ibiza's brief Pax Arabica and pitched it again into the ebb and flow of warring dominions.

Pirates based in the Pitiusas had been more and more successful in their raids on merchant ships from the city-states of Florence, Pisa and Siena, enraging the Christian world which in 1113 decided to retaliate by mounting a mini-crusade against the Balearics. With Pope Pascual III's approval, a fleet of 380 Pisan and Catalan boats set out from Barcelona and laid siege to the town, which they captured and pillaged. A year later the Moors were back under caliph Ali Ben Yussuf, the buccaneering raids continued, and a century after that came another Christian invasion under William of Montgri, later archbishop of Tarragona, and Don Pedro of Portugal. The 'ample construction' of the city walls had been rendered less so by the battering they received at the hands of earlier invaders, and the island was easily taken with only 1500 men. A legend perpetuated by modern guide-books – probably because it reinforces Ibiza's sex 'n' sin image – suggests that the Christian war-effort was indirectly assisted by a gorgeous, pouting white slave-girl belonging to the brother of the sheikh of Yebisah. Licking his lips at her Occidental charms the sheikh took her off to his personal harem, whereupon his vengeful brother let the Christians into the citadel via a secret passageway under the walls.

The islanders' recompense for the loss of the Moorish good life was a constitution and a Universidad – nothing to do with education but an independent Government – both of which claimed to have their best interests at heart. The Carta de Franquicias, a kind of Bill of Rights, can still be seen, though not by the public, in the municipal archive as part of the medieval Book of the Chain. In it are enshrined the Ibicencos' inalienable rights to possess their own houses and orchards 'as free properties and without sanctions', to graze their sheep on the meadows and take fish from the sea.

When the Town Hall announced a transcription of part of the Book of the Chain in order to make life easier for students of the history of the Pitiusas, it wasn't just the off-season scarcity of news that got the story into the *Prensa de*

Ibiza. Among the colonizers the Catalans' stock is rising. If you made a hit-parade of the island's historical sympathies it might look something like this:

1. Carthaginians (9 out of 10. Still number one for their sexy deities, and because of their high opinion of Ibiza)
2. Moors (8 out of 10 for tolerance)
2=. Catalans (8 out of 10 for autonomy and the constitution)
4. Romans (6 out of 10 for their sensible but boring culture)
5. Tourists (5 out of 10. They made Ibiza rich but stole its soul)
6. Hippies (4 out of 10 for amusement value)
7. Vandals/Normans/others (2 out of 10. All they ever did was sack and pillage).

Out of the Catalan period came Ibiza's mellifluous language, a dialect of Eastern Catalan which is now under threat from Castilian and English – much to the fury of the island's intellectual Catalanists. Less than half of the population now speaks Eivissenc, only ten per cent write as well as speak it and, according to the sociolinguist Bernat Joan i Marí, the language/dialect is heading for extinction unless Ibicencos 'take an active part in the defence of their own sense of identity', in other words speak it more. Joan i Marí complains that the Church, which continues to hold services mainly in Castilian, is guilty of a 'lack of respect' towards the decisions of the Second Vatican Council, which specifies that the language of the liturgy must coincide with that of the people. Castilian, he writes, is still the basic language of culture, as it was under Franco when Catalan poetry could be published but not Catalan narrative or non-fiction.

In effect Ibiza is still going through a process of Castilianization which began in 1714 with the Decree of the New Plan when Castile imposed its own language and institutions on the whole country after the War of Spanish Succession. When Philip V's troops moved into Ibiza after the Castilian 'occupation' they sent back to the king that the inhabitants 'only talk in their native language', and Ibicenco was officially forbidden by Royal Decree in 1768. Castilianization took place at an administrative level as well as a linguistic one: out went much of the democratic sophistication of the old systems. The Catalans had determined the right of ordinary Ibicencos to a share of the profits from the salt industry. Profits were now diverted directly to the Crown. In 1784 Bishop Abad y Lasierra ordered the church to fall in with the new order. And the island was finally named Ibiza.

None of this has much interest for the vast majority of rural Ibicencos, who consider the Catalans almost as foreign as the Germans. But the intellectual Catalanists of Ibiza town have strong opinions about it all. As the writer Mariano Planells puts it, 'It was an obligation by force, an imposition which came from a war that had been lost. But it didn't succeed. The problem they found was that the houses were very far apart, and *antes* there weren't cars. The speed that news could be transmitted was the speed of a horse, and a slow horse at that. So they tried to go round the parishes giving everyone the Christian doctrine and making them speak Castilian. The people they met just nodded their heads and went home. Two hundred years have passed, more than two hundred years, and you could say that absolute colonization still hasn't happened.'

Apart from cultural and political questions, the most important thing that happened in the 479 years between the Catalan conquest and the Decree of the New Plan was that piracy and plague together dragged the island into poverty. Pirate attacks began when dispossessed Moors who had fled to the North African coast came back from time to time on pillaging visits, but over the next four hundred years the visits became more and more frequent, so that the whole economy was sapped. In 1392 there were only five hundred families in Ibiza and the entire population of Formentera had vacated the island, terrorized by pirates. (Formentera was only repopulated in 1697.) In the fifteenth century plague cut such swathes through the populace that new cemeteries had built to accommodate the dead. Illa Plana, the island connected by a thin spit of land to Ibiza harbour, became an impromptu plague-pit.

The situation called for drastic measures. With typical inventiveness the islanders took up contra-piracy, often recovering from North African harbours what Moorish pirates had stolen and, in revenge, bringing back Arab slaves to work the land. From the late seventeenth century until the early nineteenth were the glory days of the Corsairs: Ibicenco bounty-hunters who set sail in *xabecs*, nimble wooden boats made out of local pinewood to a unique design, to plunder the high seas with the backing of the Crown.

In 1830 the French began to stamp out the piracy industry in their Algerian colony, and since Algerian pirates were the Corsairs' principal quarry, buccaneering soon became an unsuitable job for an Ibicenco.

Slowly the island began to lose its isolation, becoming part of the Spanish province of the Balearic Islands in 1833. Connections with the mainland took longer – like the mail which as from 1852 was delivered once a week by boat from Palma. By the end of the nineteenth century, at last there was a regular ferry service to and from Barcelona. After the First World War the island's economy began to pick up and in the 1920s and 1930s there was even some early tourism. But the light at the end of a long, dark historical tunnel was snuffed out by the Civil War, which plunged Ibiza into greater misery and isolation than it had known for centuries.

My birthday fell on the same late-October day that the last straggling package-tourists came to the end of their holidays and the whole island seemed to echo with relief. In the morning Toni and I took to the deserted lanes on his moped, stopping for beer and olives in a terrace bar by the church in San Lorenzo. The landscape glowed with quiet contentment. At home Javier fixed up a picnic on the roof – Menorcan cheese, as nutty as a ripe cheddar, a loaf of three-seed bread from the German baker in San Miguel and a cheap white wine that sent us all to sleep.

In the evening at Can Ramón, Toni's mum gave me a birthday *butifarra*. Ushering me into a dim store-room she pointed up to a serpentarium of sausages hanging in fat coils on a rack from the roof and made me choose one, clambering up on one of her squat little chairs to hook it down with a scythe. It was an evil-looking homemade blood-sausage, halfway between a haggis and Hell. In the kitchen Toni sliced it up for me, cut some bread and the family sat down to watch me carefully unpeel the skin from the *butifarra* and sink my lips into the rich brown greasy mulch inside. 'It's good for the heart,' said Toni.

Though the days were still bright the evenings were suddenly cold, and Señora Ramón pulled her flimsy cardigan tighter round her shoulders while her husband knelt on the ground to puff at the faltering fire. They told me about their winter, how it comes on quickly and seeps into your bones with damp and mists. 'I remember the last time it snowed here,' she said. It was in 1982. In Santa Inés there was a good dusting, like the icing sugar on *ensaimadas*. 'We used to say "What are those big sheep over there?", but they were just trees covered with snow.'

At night in town, the wind rattled along darkened streets that a month before had overflowed with sexuality and noise. On the Calle de la Virgen a gypsy child pulled along a bright green plastic anaconda, and there were no high heels for it to get entangled with. Life seemed to have moved indoors. Through a doorway at the harbour end, a glimpse of domesticity: two moustachioed men arranging the cushions on a sofa near the door. Just one bar was open, imperturbably blaring its summer soundtrack into an empty street.

Winter

Even in November the Ibicenco countryside is alive with colour and light. Autumn lingers on, like a late dinner-guest, in the coppery brown of vines, the dark indigo of juniper-berries and the 'sere and yellow leaves' of fig trees on which a few dusty, shrivelled but perfectly edible fruit can still be found. But hardly a month goes by in the *campo* without at least one new flower event, and now it is lavender – the same exhilarating pale blue as the sky – and heather in banks of delicate pinks that change subtly with the location and the light, from caster-sugar white-pink to a bluish pinky-violet when the flowers are out of the sun.

At the close of the year I was living in a holiday house on the rugged northern coast near San Miguel, far from my friends in Santa Gertrudis and even further in time and space from the sangria-swigging, suntanned Ibiza of the tourist season.

My new home had things which Sa Rota d'en Planells did not. It had conventional electricity, and comfortable chairs, and a bath with hot water which seemed an almost obscene luxury. But it was a summer house, with cupboards full of beach-mats and sun-tan oil, and winter gave it a melancholy air. Casa Luisa is part of an *urbanización* – a word that is just beginning to take on the negative associations in Spanish which 'urbanization' would have if it existed in English – begun with zeal and good intentions, but never completed. Shells of half-finished villas crouch along dirt roads, like a post-nuclear Beverly Hills; and across the track from Casa Luisa is a monstrous skeletal structure my English landlords had christened the Grand Hotel. All around the landscape, as if unperturbed by these eyesores, glitters coldly like lizard-skin. Behind this scene can be glimpsed the figure of the wealthiest and most powerful man in Ibiza, and one of the least popular. The extent of Abel Matutes Juan's wealth and influence can be judged by the fact that he runs the family bank, the Abel Matutes Torres Banco de Ibiza. A complete mythology has grown up around Matutes, whose nickname is El Padrino, The Godfather. He is the man the Lefty intellectuals of Ibiza love to loathe, and the island's favourite subject for gossip. Most of the stories told about him centre round allegedly suspect financial deals, political string-pulling, wolf-like cunning and sheer greed, and none of these stories, needless to say, contains the merest fraction of truth.

What is undeniable is that the Matutes family is by far the biggest employer on the island. It owns hotels, agricultural and real-estate companies, as well as the bank, which has branches in Madrid and Barcelona. It has substantial shares in at least forty other businesses, including the company that owns the dairy that makes the cheese in Santa Gertrudis. And it is one of the distant outposts of this economic empire that owns, and wilfully neglects, the Urbanización Isla Blanca.

It's an unusual place where from one window you are faced with two storeys of concrete, each column topped with the rusty crown of metal spikes familiar from building sites the world over, and from another with a perfect arrangement of sky, cliffs and pine forest tumbling down to a rocky *cala* where the sea boils and roars. The house faces west, so that while the drinkers in the Café del Mar in San Antonio oohed and aahed over the sunset over the sea, in my rural urbanization I had a private nightly showing of Technicolor splendour. Then when the sun had gone and the wind came up the Grand Hotel began to emit a deep bass howl, like an immense harmonica.

The weather grew chilly and changeable. Sometimes it would rain for two days and nights and the dirt track through the *urbanización* would become a roaring torrent that period-ically flooded the Danish holiday-villa at the end of the track; but then there might be four afternoons in a row whose incandescent clarity almost tricked the eye into believing it was summer.

This is the fallow time of year: tourism is on ice until April and nearly all the resident *forasteros* have flown, either further South with the sun or North to where they came from. Things are not always easy for those who decide to stay. In the summer it sometimes seemed there was money whirling about in the air and if you just put out your arm you would catch as much as you needed. Now the neo-Ibicencos' favourite sources of easy income – markets, bar-work, English-teaching – have mostly dried up. The one great compensation of Staying On is having the island, in all its serene winter beauty, practically to oneself.

Life grows simpler, more old-fashioned. Because central heating is a novelty on Ibiza, the main source of warmth and conversation is wood. Sophisticated *forasteros* who had never given a thought to this substance when they lived in the big city suddenly become great specialists. The following is a typical exchange for a November evening around the fire-place in the Bar Costa: 'Hey, I've heard there's some great stuff up near Portinatx – it all blew down in a storm last year. It's perfect, really dry. Whaddya say we take the chainsaw up there this Sunday?' 'What kind of wood is it?' 'Pine.' 'Oh, I'm not into pine anymore. You know that apricot log I found? It burned all night and most of the next day. Now *that*'s what I call good wood.'

I too became an expert, scavenging in the abandoned orchards above the Grand Hotel for fallen fig trees which I sawed into porous chunks. The rarer the wood, the better the fire. When the orchards were exhausted I found a perfect larder of old pine planks in the Mad Max interior of the Hotel itself, where at least the wood was tolerably dry even if it was encrusted with cement.

People who have moved to Northern Ibiza from the south

of the island or from Northern Europe like to think they have found 'the real Ibiza'. Like in Britain, but unlike in France, Italy and the Spanish mainland, it's the North that's less built-up, poorer and more beautiful while the South is believed to be more 'civilized'. From Santa Gertrudis northwards the countryside is rougher and wilder, there are fewer and worse roads and fewer buildings, and hardly any tourism apart from a couple of hotels in Puerto de San Miguel and – the exception that proves the rule – the holiday-complex of Portinatx, thrown down on a deserted stretch of coast at the forgotten north-east tip of the island.

But it's not only the landscape that's different. Because of the absence of sheltered plains such as there are in the South and centre and the greater average height above sea-level, the weather in the North is less temperate and stable than elsewhere. In winter the temperature plummets after sunset, bringing freakish mists and dews that have cars choking reluctantly into life the next morning. The wind can whip across the land with incredible ferocity and force. Going out after a storm I would find the terrace swept shiny-clean as though by a TV housewife, and garden-furniture in strange positions where I was sure I'd never left it. One morning there was a plastic chair upside-down on the roof; the clothes-frame had jack-knifed and reformed like an Alexander Calder mobile, in a remote corner of the terrace.

In Rubió, as my *barrio* was called, I soon learned that surreal occurrences – to paraphrase Alice B. Toklas's description of hashish – were to be complacently expected. Another morning I opened my front door to find a flock of sheep corralled within the white wall of the front garden, quietly munching the cacti.

Doubtless it was a *barruguet* that had stage-managed the chair, the clothes-frame and the sheep. This possibility was suggested to me by Mariano Planells, the writer and connoisseur of Ibiza's secrets, who grew up in Rubió 'surrounded by ancient customs and superstitions'.

The *barruguet*, whose ancestry is thought to stem from the Carthaginian god Bes, with whom he shares a scraggy

beard and lascivious nature, is a little devil with clear family
ties to the leprechaun and poltergeist. Residing in wells,
cisterns, holes in the wall, and the like, he emerges to wreak
havoc on the household and torment women with obscene
suggestions. Mariano Planells retells the story of the *'barruguet* de San Lorenzo'. Once upon a time a woman was walking
back to her *finca* from Ibiza town and saw a baby sitting at
the side of the *camino*. The child was bawling its head off
and in need of comfort, so the woman gave it her breast to
suck. She was alarmed to discover that the baby had a full
set of sharp teeth. 'You've got teeth!' she cried. The baby/
barruguet replied, *'Tenc dentetes i dentasses, per menjar faves i
favasses.'* Literally this means 'I have teeth and big teeth, for
eating beans and big beans,' but as Planells points out the
word *fave* is also country-speak for 'cock'.

On my first solitary days in Casa Luisa I simply walked,
allowing my whim, the weather and the path itself to take
me where they would. Far below the house I discovered the
secret bay of Portitxol, known only to the fishermen that
have built their huts there and a few beach-lovers who guard
the secret with jealous enthusiasm. The path turns discreetly
off the *camino* that descends to another bay, known as Sa
Punta de l'Aguila after a hulking rock that, if looked at with
an open mind from a certain point, might almost be said to
have the shape of an eagle in flight, and winds through the
woods and along the cliffs, passing the bleached stone dome
of an abandoned charcoal-oven. Naturally there was no one
on the beach; but a motorbike was parked among the trees
above it, and one of the fishermen's huts stood open and
empty.

When I began to take Rubió for granted I got in the car

and drove. The days were as silent and empty as the roads. The island seemed to be full of Mrs Bennets, 'whose solace was visiting and news', and life slipped into a Jane Austen-ish rhythm of tea at six and wine at nine and evenings in front of the fire. Acquaintances became friends, or occasionally remained acquaintances.

Once I met Javier's friend Pepa in the health shop on the Plaza del Parque, a drop-in centre for half the hippies on Ibiza. (She had her finger on the pulses.) Come round, she said. The next day, surprised by loneliness, I took her at her word and searched out her house in the deep countryside outside San Lorenzo. I had looked before and never found it. This time I followed my nose, looking out for patches of white among the dense rust-brown and green. I passed a tiny *casa payesa* with a rainbow painted on the wall and a little boy on a bike dressed in a yellow smock. I recognized the boy, and followed him down the tortuous *camino* to his house.

Pepa was looking radiantly motherly, beaming and heav-ily pregnant, like a cross between the just-Annunciated Madonna and Hope Steadman from *thirtysomething*. Being a Rebirther she was intending to have the baby at home accord-ing to Rebirthing principles, which would mean leaving the umbilical cord uncut for twenty minutes to allow the child to adjust to the trauma of birth. Had she ever considered an underwater birth? She said it had never appealed to her, 'even though I'm a Pisces'.

It was lunchtime and Pepa's husband wasn't yet back from his surgery. Where other doctors do medicine, Juan does Health. This means he provides, along with the cough linctus, individual Rebirthing classes, acupuncture, Bach flower remedies and sessions on the MegaBrain, a Fritz Lang-style machine which when wired up to your head claims to remove stress, anxiety, depression and the whole pande-monium of modern mental life. Pepa handed me a leaflet for a course he was running in the 'art of being healthy, joyful, full of life and energy'. Just a few of the desirable states you could attain by following the course were 'Abundance and prosperity', 'Creativity in your work', 'Harmony and peace in your emotions', 'Pleasure and love in your relationships', 'Relaxation: efficiency without effort' and your ideal body weight. All this and more for 14,000 pesetas – around £85.

Pepa and I stood in the sun for a while looking at the sunset and the view of orchards and woodlands daubed with the Regency pink of heather. 'For me winter is the prettiest time of year in Ibiza,' she said, stooping to remove a Ninja Turtle from the mouth of her daughter. Around us was an Orientalist fantasy of mosaics and terraces interspersed with bushes of the herbs that Pepa uses for her plastic pictures and tisanes. A kind of magic throne made from a single upright stone was, she said, the ideal vantage-point from which to gaze on the full moon. We went inside and I looked around the house while Pepa put on the kettle and a New Age tape, of the kind that sounds like choirs of angels singing in some distant bathroom.

Juan came home and swept the children up in his arms. He was trim, sensibly dressed, his hair short and neat, with the contented air of a successful, but by no means rich, provincial doctor, which I suppose is what he is – though far removed from the Trollopian image that he conjures up. The couple grew up and met in Madrid, fled the city and bought a patch of ground from an elderly man up the hill who lives in a stone shack and blows all his money at the discos. They built the house themselves, to their own specification. It's a solid, country-style construction overlain with their own taste, which is whimsical and romantic.

On the kitchen wall Juan showed me a photo of himself and Pepa, bronzed and dazed with sunlight, in each others' arms on the beach at Benirràs – once Ibiza's hippie beach *par excellence*, the site of orgiastic full-moon parties, now calmer, more accessible and full of families. Their history, I realized, reflects that of the beach. They are What Hippiedom Did Next, when it also got calmer, more accessible and produced flower children of its own.

The advantage of having been in Ibiza for a decade or two of winters, as Juan and Pepa have, is that you know what to expect and you take precautions. People lay on parties, happenings, lectures, courses in Tarot, massage, Reiki, Rebirthing, Rolfing, reflexology, past-life regression therapy, De Silva mind control, crystals, kinesiology, colour healing, herbalism, anything to fill up the long winter days and nights and, in the case of the lectures and courses, to scrape together a few pesetas.

The next night there was no more firewood and nothing on the radio, so I drove to the village of San Lorenzo for a session of 'Ecstatic Drumming' at Can Pou, the ancient bar which was one of the first to cater to the tastes of the colonists of the 1960s. Drums are hippie Ibiza's favourite instrument, so a three-day seminar in the art of drumming, with the suggestion that it might involve reaching undreamt-of heights of exultation, was guaranteed a healthy turnout.

When I arrived at Can Pou two women, one French, one Spanish, were sitting in the doorway talking in fractured English about the time the event was supposed to start. The French woman, wearing purple cotton trousers and a Moroccan multicoloured shirt, was complaining about unpunctuality. How annoying it was, she said, that the drumming always started half an hour late even though on the poster she had seen on the door of the Bar Costa it said '7 p.m. prompt'. She had to pick up her children after the session and get up early the next morning. The Spanish woman replied that it was her own fault if she didn't want to get up late like everyone else.

I got myself a Coke and sat on the floor in the main room, a big white farmhouse *salon* with cushions and antique mirrors. Drums of various sizes were lying around, many of them homemade in traditional Ibicenco style from the hollowed-out trunks of trees. People were beginning to gather and chat, and soon there was a quiet Babel of European voices. A friendly long-haired Frenchman shared my Coke.

I looked around the room. Apart from me and my friend and a sexy girl in a black velvet top, black velvet hat and patched jeans, almost all the drummers were in their thirties and forties. Many had brought children in designer hippie-wear who sat looking restive beside their parents and had to be shushed into silence.

Gilles was the man in charge, or as he described himself, the leader. In dress and demeanour Gilles was unlike the others. He had sensible trousers and a sensible collared shirt, and flattened his Rs in his French-accented English in a way that made him seem boffinish. He also differed from the rest of the group in that he could actually play the drums, finding impossible subtleties of timbre and, when he showed off as everyone implored him to do, struck up intricate interlocking rhythms whose precision mocked our incoherent mess.

What he had in common with the rest was that he had travelled – to Asia, Africa, South America. He reprimanded us for squatting on the floor with our drums between our thighs. 'In Africa you never play the drums sitting down. Always standing up, with a belt round your body to hold it, like this.' He gave a little paradiddle on a double-headed tom-tom. 'Well, in *most* of Africa they play the drums standing up. In North Africa they play them sitting down, but that's because they're lazy.'

First Gilles wanted us all to compose our own songs and sing them with a drum accompaniment provided by the rest of the group. The composition was supposed to have a simple chorus that everyone else could sing along to. First off was the girl in the hat, whose song set the words '*Musica y ritmo en mi corazón*' ('Music and rhythm in my heart') to a doleful two-note melody. She had forgotten the chorus, so we all chimed in with '*corazón*'. There was a break while Gilles badgered us to volunteer – 'You mustn't be shy, this is all about *contributing*'. After an embarrassing silence when it seemed the evening might be about to come to an abrupt halt, a timid hand went up and we all breathed a sigh of temporary relief. This contribution came from a long-haired Spaniard whose lyrical style seemed to have been influenced by those seventies posters bearing droll *sententiae* like, 'You don't have to be crazy to work here, but it helps', or 'What would happen if they held a war and nobody came?' His text was, 'Today is the first day of the rest of your life.' Chorus: 'Yeah, of the rest of my life.'

This phase over, Gilles split us up into groups, informing us that in Brazil drum troupes are organized in families: the son plays the woodblock, father the bass-drum, and so on. He tried to give each of the members of the group a rhythm in turn and build up an authentic Latin jam, but no one was picking up the rhythms and the sounds that give the rhythms their meaning: 'open' sounds where the hand rebounds, 'closed' ones where it cups the sound above the skin, thudding dead ones at the centre of the drum. While he was giving attention to the flagging ensemble of one group, the other groups were losing their patience and trying to join in, whereupon our leader also appeared to lose his patience, demanded silence (the rain of feeble drum beats trickled to a halt) and asked us sternly to be 'auto-disciplined'. All at once the figure of 1200 pesetas – the price of admission – seemed to hover over Gilles' audience of would-be Ecstatic Drummers like a small grey cloud.

The first twelve days of December were an auspicious time to plant vines. I knew this because Heinz, who lived a little way down the hill from Javier, had told me so. Heinz himself knew because he had looked up the dates in his Rudolf Steiner Calendar of Biodynamic Agriculture, which tells you in which constellation the moon will be and whether the root, flower, or leaf is favoured by the heavenly bodies on any given day of the year. Heinz came to Ibiza more than twenty years ago from a little town in the south of Germany but his Spanish was still more Baden-Baden than Barcelona.

Heinz had a small but unimpeachably ideologically-sound business making organic compost, with the assistance of a strain of worms with the unlikely name of Tennessee Wiggler and a voracious appetite for household waste. The compost was a product tailor-made for neo-Ibiza, yet so far turnover had been minimal. This is because the only way neo-Ibicencos could have heard about it, short of hearing the news from Heinz's own lips, was if they had caught sight of the minute advertisement he had stuck on the door of the Bar Costa. The company logo printed on this advert showed a tiny tree-like form with sinuous branches enclosed in a circle. Heinz said he'd chosen the image because it looked 'like a mandala'.

On a grizzled rainy afternoon in Hay-on-Wye, I'd found a strange little book, *The Science and Technique of Wine*. Half technical treatise, half layman's guide, it had some pretty pictures of vines trained in different shapes and diagrams showing the structure of the vine-leaf and the correct way to prune. Then in the studious hush of the pale-blue-ceilinged British Library, I sorted through the pile of books which a grumpy woman in horn-rimmed glasses had just dumped on the desk in front of me. The available literature was of three kinds. There were impenetrable highbrow French guides to viticultural practices in various regions of France. There were tomes from the University of Western Australia in Perth, full of gripping essays on 'Problems in Clonal Selection' and the incidence of grey rot in the Margaret River area. And there were cheaply printed booklets by retired army colonels documenting the nightmare of producing wine in England. For my purpose there was nothing but a slim volume promisingly entitled *Practical Viticulture*, which when I rang up the Wine and Spirit Education Trust, an organization that trains the wine trade in matters oenological, they said they could supply if I went along to their headquarters in the City.

Practical Viticulture is not for the faint-hearted. It is short and grey and dreary, like an English winter day. At first I pored over it dutifully and translated relevant chunks to Toni, who pooh-poohed them with the hauteur of experience. Vine roots should be prepared for planting by dipping them in a solution of ammonia, the book suggested, in order to kill off 'nematode worms'. My friend retorted that this was a waste of time, since commercial nurseries were not in the habit of supplying their customers with worm-ridden plants. Almost everything in the book seemed either redundant or misleading or both, which was not surprising since its author clearly had as much hands-on knowledge of vine-growing as I have of Formula One motor-racing. I lost it in the thick grass of Javier's orchard soon after we started planting, when its contents began to collide with rude reality.

Back in Ibiza I made a round-trip of every nursery on the island. The only varieties anyone knew about were basic red and white, anonymous breeds that Ibicenco agriculture had been growing for generations without a second thought. If I wanted to aim any higher than *vino payés* I would have to look to peninsular Spain. The nearest proper vine-nursery was in the town of Xativa, near Valencia. I took the ferry over one morning. I would buy Tempranillo and Garnacha, the two classic red grapes of Spain, which together go to make the vanilla-sweet wines of Rioja.

From Valencia to Xativa would be an easy two hours' drive; but I had reckoned without the rain, which was merciless. Lorries had toppled over every few miles in the flooding. Valencia's famous orange orchards, now full of uniformly bright fruit, not like the grubby organic specimens in Ibiza, looked like a giant lake of muddy water with a thousand green-and-orange islands.

The puddles had slowed me down, and when I eventually found the nursery, a kind of hangar in the light-industrial suburbs of Xativa, it was apparently shut for lunch. It looked a dismal place in the grey light of the mainland winter, and most unlike the sort of nursery you see in post-agricultural societies, where couples go on Sunday mornings to buy smug-looking pot plants that have been cosseted under acres of glass.

I went away and sat in a nearby bar where they served me beer and slices of *tortilla* made with aubergines and garlic. An hour later there was an old Citroen van in the car park of the nursery and the iron door of the hangar stood ajar. Inside was a concrete floor, a corrugated-iron roof, and a complete absence of plant life unless you counted several stacks of twigs in a distant corner of the hangar. To one side, eyeing us curiously, a row of employees who looked like dwarves, thanks to the child-sized chairs they sat on, were eating their lunch from plastic boxes. The men were in flat caps, the women in headscarves. They reminded me of stand-in Munchkins from *The Wizard of Oz*.

The owner, Manuel Lorente, was a small stubby middle-aged man in a tweed jacket and cap. I'd been standing about for a few minutes before he emerged from his office wiping crumbs from his mouth with a handkerchief and strode towards me with a businesslike *buenas tardes*. He looked me up and down with understandable suspicion. What could someone wearing shorts and a pink-and-yellow T-shirt want that he might be able to supply?

I told him what I'd come for, and Señor Lorente propped his chin on his thumb and forefinger and frowned. His suspicion was increasing. A foreigner in shorts and a pink-and-yellow T-shirt and a large quantity of vines, both destined for a tourist island notorious for its moral laxity – not to say decadence. He had seen stories in the papers about Ibiza, and vaguely recalled a scandalous TV item some years ago.

He asked me all sorts of questions – about the soil (was it calcareous or clayey?), about the root-stocks I needed

(*Viniferax berlandieri* or *Ripariax berlandieri*?), about the climate – and I bluffed creatively. Apparently satisfied, he then clicked his fingers and one of the Munchkins sprang up from his baby-chair and disappeared towards the far end of the hangar. There was a distant rustling.

What the man returned with gave me a start. Vines, surely, were green and sinuous and graceful. These things looked like dead sticks: no greenery at all, a dark little fist punching its way out of one end and a Rasta tangle of roots at the other. And all tied together in four tight bundles, like four old-fashioned brooms.

'These are your *parras*,' said Señor Lorente, introducing them to me with an expansive movement of his arm. All had been grafted on to special root-stocks enabling them to survive whatever it was about Ibicenco soil that Señor L. thought was a problem. They were all in the prime of their youth, guaranteed worm-free and a bargain at 6op apiece. But with their unruly mess of earthy roots they wouldn't all fit in the back of my car. Could they be pruned for me?

Señor Lorente clicked his fingers again. Three of the Munchkins immediately put down their lunch-boxes and picked up their secateurs. Dragging their baby-chairs across the concrete floor they deposited themselves near the piles of *parras* and set to work, snipping away with dexterous fingers, counting the vines out as they went. I knelt down beside an elderly lady in a black headscarf and watched her at work. Her fingers were as sinewy and brown as the woody stalks that she snipped. She glanced at me and winked. As she reached the end of a bundle of fifty she motioned with her hand that she had something to tell me. I bent my head towards hers and heard her whisper mischievously, 'Don't tell the boss, but there's fifty-three in this bundle!'

When the Munchkins had finished with them the vines looked even more dead than before. Or maybe they were simply more primitively alive. They had just a root-stub at one end and a branch-stub at the other – earth and air – and a foot-and-a-half of wood in between that seemed almost to vibrate with potential energy. From the diminutive pruners they were passed to a man in his thirties – Lorente Junior – who wrapped up the bundles in clear plastic and sturdy industrial tape, telling me as he did so that he himself had some vines at his house in the hills. He dangled the newly packaged bundle from one hand and made a vague gesture towards the end of the room and beyond, towards the open country to the west of Xativa. Here in the *pais valenciano*, *parras* like these grew well and made good wine. But *Ibiza*, that was a different matter. Did they even make wine there? If they did, it couldn't be good. The trouble was about the Balearics, that people nowadays spent too much time on the *turistas* and not enough time on the land. The best he could do was wish me luck.

Toni, Fernando and I planted the vines a few days later, when the ground was soft and manageable. The rain was over. By midday the sun had fought its way through the morning mist and was creating a passable impression of heat. For a while the sky was lavender-blue and the pines filled the air with spice. Half-way through the morning Toni appeared with a load of oranges from his *huerta*, which tumbled out of his rucksack like treasure. We ate two each, gorging in silent shock at their icy sweetness. The field being ready-ploughed and dug, the work required less struggle and sweat than we'd feared.

Practical Viticulture said the plants should be set 1.5 mètres apart. Toni said it didn't much matter. He found a length of old metal tubing on a tip down by the dairy and decided it would make a perfect template. It was just a little longer than my two outstretched arms. With this makeshift measure, laid on the ground successively from one end of the row to the other, Toni determined the position of the holes and Fernando and I pulled out forkfuls of loose soil from the tractor's furrow, while Javier followed along behind, sprinkling each hole with a lining of manure from his brother's farm.

Practical Viticulture suggested the *parras* should be planted up to their shoulders, with only their stubby heads and 8 centimetres of stalk protruding from the earth. This was to obviate 'frost damage'. But in a Southern climate where the temperature barely drops below 5 degrees and frost is a meteorological freak, vines can be allowed to emerge less tentatively from the protective earth. We held them in their holes at the half-way point between bud and root, scooping the soil back into the hole and patting around the stalk in a gentle mound. By the afternoon of the second day the hillside was bristling with a delicate army of slender twigs, their tight little stubs as cutely defiant as babies' fists.

It was lunchtime. We downed tools and hunted for cigarettes. Javier went off to one of his stone-built outhouses and came back with an iron *paella*-pan the size of a lorry-tyre. He stood it against a tree, rubbed it with olive oil on a scrunched-up newspaper to clean off the rust and wheeled it through the woods, setting it up on a flattish patch at the top of the vineyard.

Paella is not an Ibicenco dish. It came from Valencia, the nearest mainland city to Ibiza, spread all over the east coast in the 1960s and is now practically a nationwide dish. *Paella* occupies a unique place in Spanish life and has no equivalent in Britain, unless you count the Great British Sunday Roast, which shares something of its affirmative, celebratory quality, though it's hardly a culinary event in the same way. Every sentient Spaniard from nine to ninety understands its significance, if not the art of its making, and it's a traditional dish in as much as one generation learns about it from another, often on holiday afternoons when Dad builds the fire and Mum constructs the dish while the rest of the family works its way through the Rioja.

There are certain things about *paella* that need to be grasped. In London a Spanish friend once made a reasonable one in a frying pan on a gas stove, with pudding rice and Sainsbury's plastic-wrapped prawns. This sort of thing is perfectly permissible, but falls very far short of the ideal. It is less a question of morality than of aspiration. The Platonic *paella* is one made in a proper broad, flat-bottomed *paella*-pan with handles like miniature wings on either side. Size does matter. It sometimes seems that the pan produces good results in direct proportion to its diameter. A *paella*-pan for two is a slight embarrassment. However convenient, it smacks of meanness. Conversely, a *paella* for two dozen is commodious and welcoming, an object of pride.

The other thing that experts say about *paella* is that it's best made outdoors over a wood fire. This is for reasons of atavism and romance as much as culinary excellence, although the smoke that curls over the lip of the bubbling pan does lend an elusive fragrance to the finished product. The analogy is with the barbecue, picnic, and other outdoor meals; the closer to nature you are, the better it tastes. In the case of *paella* it's also fun, the hunt for wood and the complicated architecture needed to support the pan on bricks or stones, not to mention the anxious vigil as the fire threatens to burn out before the saffron-gold *paella* is ready.

Fernando must have watched carefully and gone easy on the Rioja at all those family picnics. His post-planting *paella* was a classic of its kind – rich, simple and substantial, and extra-special in that every ingredient apart from the rice, a fat short-grain type from the paddy fields of the Ebro delta, had their origin within a few miles of the meal. The chicken was a *pollo payés*, a country chicken which had spent its uneventful life pecking and clucking in the *corral* on Toni's farm. (The red peppers and garlic were Toni's too.) The prawns and mussels were bought that morning at the old fish-market in the shadow of the walls of Ibiza town. The saffron came in a fold of paper stapled at both ends, from the *tienda* in Santa Gertrudis. The salt, all the way from the salt-flats in the south, came in big crystals like fragments of windscreen.

Even the music was homegrown – sonorous, repetitious House with a beat like a dancing giant, left over from last season in the clubs. Pounding out of a ghetto-blaster into the quiet countryside, it had an odd solemnity. 'El Sonido . . .

De . . . Verano', the sound of summer, the DJ announced portentously, while the music loped and clanged in sad exhilaration. Clutching his cup of wine Toni frugged his way through a disco-routine between two rows of infant vines.

Paella begins with a rough-and-ready stock, the *caldo*, boiled up from the chicken carcass. It continues with fried garlic and chunks of chicken tumbled sizzling in the hot oil. The Valencianos then add two or three types of bean. Fernando added chopped red pepper, which sweltered and popped as its skin began to blacken; then the stock and saffron; then rice, pouring it from the bag in a long wall across the diameter of the pan – an old trick for judging the proportion of grains to liquid. The smells of the garlic and olive oil, the cooking chicken and sweet red pepper and pungent saffron came successively and together, billowing out of the pan in one intoxicating wave.

In half an hour the *paella* was a great glowing circle of Buddhist yellow dappled with dim red and the brown of frying. The rice had risen from the bubbling depths and there were puffs of steam escaping from little blowholes that had formed in the surface. It was almost ready. Fernando laid out the prawns and gaping fat-fleshed mussels on top of the rice. Then, suddenly, he ran off into the woods, leaving Javier and I to wind cloths round our hands and lift the pan, with salivating care, from the fire.

There was one last trick to come, a stroke of genius probably undreamt-of in *paella*'s Valencian heartland. Fernando came out of the wood with an armful of rosemary-twigs, laid them across the pan and covered the whole thing with a layer of newspaper. Five more minutes and the rosemary, activated by the last gasps of unabsorbed chicken-broth, was sending out a wild, delicious fragrance. It was late afternoon and the winter warmth had gone out of the sun. The paper and twigs were thrown aside, and we ate in grateful, noisy silence.

Toni had found himself a new girlfriend. She was English and almost exactly twice his age. The week after I got back from Valencia they both came round to my house on the clifftop. Toni built up the fire and we talked all night.

The more joints she rolled the more intriguing Monica became. She grew up in an old-fashioned upperclass family. Her father was a priest, her mother an old-fashioned upper-class woman who said 'stuff and nonsense' and disapproved of doctors. She was expelled from schools and ran away to London, embarking on a picaresque string of experiences that would put Moll Flanders to shame. 'I've just always kept on moving. I mean, the way I always used to look at it is, if I stopped moving I stopped living.'

Her first job was as a croupier at a Mayfair Casino. She was soon sacked because the management thought she talked too posh. Shortly afterwards she became a prostitute's maid. Her boss was a ladylike character who never actually had sex with her customers ('What do you think I am, Monica, dear, a tart?') but gave them tea and Discipline instead. 'One day she pretended I was her student. "This is Monica, I'm training her." I had to whip the guy, and after I'd had a go she did the same thing to him. Afterwards she said to him, "*Now* can you tell the difference between the pupil and the master?"'

Monica lived in Barbados for five years with a Rastaman, did a bit of soft porn and stripping, was in prisons in England (where she learned how to knit and crochet and 'met some really interesting people') and Morocco (not so nice), did a bit of dealing to get her daughter through school, got qualified in Reiki massage and hung out in Brighton, and at last, a few years ago, wound up in Ibiza.

Two years ago she bought her eighteenth house in succession, in a remote valley in the north west of the island near Santa Inés. It is the land that Time, or at least the late seventies and most of the eighties, forgot. If you walked up the *camino* from Monica's house you would come to a magnificent, tumbledown Ibicenco *finca* where the inhabitants make their own carob cake and hold parties where the adults get into ecstatic drumming while the kids boogie down to their own disco next door.

'We like living this way,' says Simone, who is French and looks as if she's stepped out of a Godard movie, apart from her clothes which are coloured and baggy and come from developing countries. She and Paco and their three children used to share their house with another family which consisted of a man, his three wives and twelve children. Strangely this ménage didn't work out. So now Paco and Simone live out a slightly more conventional existence. They have no light or running water, but they live luxuriously without either. Being French, Simone is a natural cook, and makes truffles out of carob pods. The kids do their own washing. Every so often they have 'exchanges' – you couldn't call them 'sales' because no money changes hands – where people bring unwanted clothes and spread them out on the grass. Afterwards there is always a party (they are great party-givers and -goers) where Paco plays the flute like the Pied Piper and all the kids dance along behind him.

The black hair on Paco's head and his black beard seem to join seamlessly, stranding his gentle features on an island of expressivity. He grows vegetables in an abundant *huerta* crowned with a Shinto archway. In the house he keeps a big boomy drum he made himself from a hollowed-out agave. It is for ceremonies – parties, birthdays, plantings and harvests.

When I first met Paco and Simone they apologized for the lack of dope. They had smoked it all over the last three days at a shamanistic rite at Benirràs beach. They'd made a 'spirit lodge' out of bamboo canes and stones and sat inside it for a while; later there was some blindfold running. 'It's all about conquering your fear,' said Simone.

Their friend and neighbour Monica is into some of the same things as them – herbal medicine, acupuncture, astrology – but takes it all with a handful of sea salt. We laughed about Stuart Wilde, the wise-cracking greed-is-good New Age guru who boasts about taking money out of beggars' bowls. According to Wilde, he's doing the beggars a favour. 'I mean, most of those guys probably haven't actually *given* anything to anyone in their lives.'

Toni and Monica lived Ibiza's sparse winter nightlife for just over a month, until the difference in their energies finally exhausted her and he got bored. He would present himself on her doorstep, propping himself up against the lintel, at the conclusion of a drinking binge that had lasted all night and most of the next day, and ask to borrow her car. There were tensions. They both spoke Castilian as a second language, which made communication tricky. Neither had much money, which made nights on the town a strain. And the age difference was the final straw. But it was fun while it lasted. He brought her bottles of his own *vino payés*, bags of his own grass, sweet homegrown tomatoes and onions, potatoes and carrots still dusted with the iron-rich earth of Ca'n Joan Ramón. When the olives were in fruit we spent a day shaking them out of her trees and bottling them up with water in clay pitchers to take away their awful bitterness. A few weeks later, in the correct way, we replaced the water with salt-water and added garlic, lemons and thyme. The smell that wafted from the jars and the sight of them bobbing darkly in their brine were exciting and *echt*, but when Christmas came round and they were as bitter as ever Monica went into a sulk of disappointment and almost threw the whole lot away.

Ibiza's olive trees do much for the look of the landscape but their stone-hard fruit, mean-fleshed and sour, is an acquired taste. Similarly the island's olive oil seldom attains the heights of flavour you find in the very best mainland Spanish oils. Mariano Costa Bonet, down the road from Monica's, runs the only press for miles around. People bring their olives from Santa Inés, San Mateo, San Antonio, even San

Agustín and San Jorge, in other words the whole western half of the island. If the olive tree is well cared-for – and most are not – the oil can be clean and fruity. Mariano thinks the best trees grow on rocky white soil, like the top of my vineyard, not on *terra rossa*. He finds only two problems with his job. One is the appalling 5.45 a.m. winter wake-up time. The other is the olive-fly which afflicts much of the crop and makes it unusable. Ibiza never gets cold enough to kill the fly and Ibicencos don't like using insecticide on trees under which animals will graze.

Every other week Monica and I would visit the herbalist in Sa Penya to stock up on Ibicenco herbs and herbal lore. The Herbolaria Colom is a hole-in-the-wall place in the Calle de la Cruz with a green hand-painted wooden sign hanging aslant above the door. Push inside, and a Mrs Tiggywinkle figure with twinkling eyes is ministering to a variety of people: a nun in a wimple, a couple of lowlifes with bad skin, a lady in the all-black country *traje*. Among elderly folk who have always trusted local remedies and younger alternative types fleeing from conventional medicine, Señora Colom has a reputation for something approaching genius when it comes to healing with the pharmacopeia of the Ibicenco countryside.

The walls of the tiny shop are lined with brown paper bags bearing mysterious abbreviations, as in an old-fashioned chemist's: Tom., Salv., H. Buena; and there is always a delicious exhilarating smell redolent of hay, aniseed and dried flowers. On the wall behind the counter is a black-and-white photograph of a distinguished-looking, professorial man surrounded by the same brown paper bags. This is Señora Colom's father, who handed over the reins of his business to her seventeen years ago. He came from Valldemossa in Mallorca, near the monastery where Chopin and George Sand stayed one famous dreadful winter.

Though the shop has been there for as long as anyone can remember, Señora Colom says not many of the herbs she sells have actually been used, medicinally or otherwise, in Ibiza for all that long. Parsley, yes, and *frigola* (a local variety of thyme) – 'on the top of tomato salad. In the old days there weren't lettuces or endives or any of the things that you find here now, so an *ensalada ibicenca* was just tomatoes, peppers and onions, with *frigola* sprinkled on top. *Nada mas*.'

Señora Colom doesn't think she can cure anything but she'll have a pretty good go. In the winter most of her business seems to be in *frigola*, which she prescribes for coughs and colds and the bunged-up feeling the Spanish call being *constipado*. She recommends making a tea, or, for an even more efficacious cure, breathing in *frigola*-scented steam from a vapour-bath with a towel over your head. She wraps up the fat little faded purple flowers in brown paper, giving her advice in a loud, confident but comforting voice, like a scaled-down Hattie Jacques.

Apart from the miniature white castle of its church and the cluster of old houses that spiral down the hill, San Miguel, or Sant Miquel de Balansat to give it its full Catalan name, is a thoroughly modern village. In the last fifteen years it has been transformed from a pretty, rural hamlet into a dully functional mini-town, with a laundry, three banks and a supermarket, that serves as a stop-off point for tourists on their way to and from the slab-like hotels of Puerto de San Miguel. You can tell how much it has grown by the sign proclaiming 'Sant Miquel 1km', which has been swallowed up long ago by the expanding village.

Where Santa Gertrudis has courted the eccentric end of the expat scene San Miguel has remained solidly, resolutely ordinary. There are no funky neighbourhood bars; only neighbourhood bars. The phonebox doesn't take phone-cards, and bleeps throughout the call to tell you it is making an exceptional effort. There is a gift shop, but it has none of the sixties-influenced finery of Claire's in Santa Gertrudis. And it sells *postcards*, which people in Santa Gertrudis, who believe they are not tourists but *really live here*, would never lower themselves to buy.

A few yards down the road to the Port, though, is one of hippie Ibiza's great institutions, the café/bar/gallery/commune of S'Hort. S'Hort (it means 'the orchard') took root in another counter-cultural adventure, Can Tirurit in San Juan – which began, in turn, when a group of sixties freaks got into story-telling sessions every Thursday. (It was always the same story, 'Mushkil Gusha' by Idries Shah.) From this grew a fully-fledged community with workshops, meetings, art-shows and a crèche. When Can Tirurit fell apart, as com-munes do, some of its disgruntled members left to set up S'Hort, and for a while there was the same buzz of creativity and spiritual DIY in San Miguel that there had been in San Juan. But then this too began to go wrong: there were rows over money and organization, or lack of it, and people couldn't 'get it together' any more. When I lived nearby it had been shut for a year or two, only opening reluctantly on special occasions.

S'Hort is still a beautiful rambling building, whitewashed inside and out and furnished with cushions and carpets and paintings by Ibiza people. Ethnicity is everywhere. There is a bar serving herb teas and carrot cake. It is all you would expect of a place that has been a *point de repère* for people in kaftans. There were no kaftans here tonight, though there were some flat multicoloured Tibetan hats, a long-established fashion accessory, and a smattering of smocks. The place had been shut for weeks, and there was a feeling of social cob-webs being blown away. People were meeting and stereo-kissing who had not seen each other since the end of the autumn when the cold set in and they became more pre-occupied with fixing holes in the roof and making sure they had enough dry wood than large-scale socializing. I sat down with Fernando on the floor with my back against a rough white-painted wall. Petra, a lesbian glass-blower from San Carlos who was here with her son, took a break from joint-rolling to light a joss-stick.

Opposite her a straight-looking woman in a sensible skirt was drawing a poster for a mystical dance-event she was organizing in a sports centre. As she drew she chatted to her friend in cheery American. 'Well, I was on the phone to Mallorca the other day, and all of a sudden I just felt these amazingly strong vibrations coming down the phone, and I just felt sooooo great . . . you know what I'm saying?'

Through the fug of social sounds, almost inaudibly at first and then more clearly, came the twanging of a sitar. The instrument had been lying under an ethnic drape on a table in the corner of a far room, but I'd never considered the possibility that anyone would actually take it up and play it. And yet here was a sound, sweet and plangent, to which twenty-five years ago Ibiza must have echoed.

The reason we were gathered together at S'Hort was to listen to some New Age evangelism. We'd all seen the posters in the Bar Costa and the health food shop on the Plaza del Parque, and from the well-designed look of them this was an evangelist who meant business, not one of your everyday spiritual peddlars with their photocopied ads. But as to the product, it was mystifying. 'Human Design System.' 'The Rave Ephemeris.' 'Ra Uru Hu.' What could it all mean? Tonight's 'free chat' – Ibiza loves a 'free chat', especially if it suspects there might be a Free Drink thrown in – would enlighten us.

We sipped on a sweet milky cinnamon tea while he talked at us. He was a tall grey-haired person with a Tibetan hat and wide, intense blue-grey eyes. He spoke rapidly and with pre-ci-si-on in the kind of voice that hits some kind of pleasure point in your head and makes you woozily compliant.

Ra Uru Hu (for it is he) was once a Canadian with a

normal name. 'Since I came to Ibiza in 1983 my life was always fairly unusual, but since 1987 it has become even more unusual.' This is an understatement. On 3 January 1987 Hu was coming home to his ruined *casa payesa* in San Juan ('near the gas station') when he experienced a Channelling. He opened the front door to find the light in the centre of the room wheeling round and round and the place feeling 'like a pressure chamber'. For the next eight days and nights he neither ate nor slept while a voice – The Voice – revealed to him a complex and audacious system of belief which Hu, in turn, was to take out and explain to a startled world. He'd had to take notes. Though what it had to say was profound and occasionally perplexing, The Voice showed that it had at least a rudimentary sense of humour, even when it was pouring scorn on Hu's human frailty. 'At one point I said to The Voice "You treat me like a dog", and it replied, "That's because you *are* a dog".'

After the Channelling Hu was, by his own admission, 'mad for three years'. His theory was of great complexity. Plainly The Voice had a passing acquaintance not only with astrology, the I-Ching and chakras, but also with the latest developments in physics. Mr Hu was much taken with the idea that there were 'three million million neutrinos hitting us and everything on the earth every second – think about it, *three million million*,' and, to him, the fact that these neutrinos come from stars made sense of the influence that the heavenly bodies appear to have on our lives.

It's hard to condense the intellectual apparatus of the Human Design System into a few words or to reproduce Mr Hu's rapid-fire delivery (imagine a New Age Robin Williams, but without the jokes). Its central characteristic was a certain uncompromising determinism. 'It's in the program,' he kept saying. Raves, which is what The Voice called human beings, 'don't ask me why', can have no power of change over themselves or the world; all we can do is know and understand and follow our 'program'. What about pollution, war, oppression and the world's generally disastrous state; could humble Raves such as ourselves not effect any kind of change over these things? Apparently not. Mr Hu shrugged his shoulders with an indulgent smile, as if to say he was sorry, but it was beyond his control. 'The world, my dear friend, is what it is. It's in the program.'

When Mr Hu came to the end of his expatiation and we all resumed our buzz of chatter, with refills of cinnamon tea, I walked around to look at the paintings and talk to people. In general it seemed as though, in spite of having been revealed in Ibiza and being clearly aimed at Ibiza's soul and pockets, the Human Design System did not pose any great threat to Christianity, Buddhism or horoscopes as a world-wide system of belief. For people weaned on 'positivity' the HDS has a whiff of nihilism which many of the S'Hort congregation found, as one woman put it, 'a turn-off'. Petra, the German dyke, later told me she had been to see Mr Hu and he had told her that since Raves ultimately have no control over their actions, there can be no morality of any kind, and therefore 'Hitler is the same as Mother Teresa.' This she found a very deep turn-off.

But more to the point, people were saying, the advantages of studying the System were not clear enough. If you couldn't have any influence over the flux of your life, the only advantage of knowing more about the System would be a kind of glum satisfaction that every time something went wrong or right or you felt happy or sad, your stall in the hippie market was a success or a failure, you'd know there was only one reason for it. 'It was in the program.'

The New Age culture of Ibiza is merely the latest chapter in a thirty-year history of turning on, tuning in and dropping out. Before about 1960 the foreigners on the island were a leisured class of predominantly British and American extraction. There was also a multi-national handful of artists, some of whom set up their own gallery, El Corsario, in 1959. (It's now a hotel.) Among the earliest and most discerning Ibizaphiles were Walter Benjamin and his friend the art critic, Jean Selz, who both came in 1932; Le Corbusier and his Catalan follower, Josep Lluis Sert, and, famously, the Berlin Dadaist, Raoul Hausmann. During the thirties Hausmann spent long periods in the Pitiusas, became fascinated by Ibicenco architecture and culture and documented both with an almost visionary acuity.

Eminent among the few pre-1960 pioneers still on the island is the architect and writer Rolf Blakstad. Originally Norwegian, he had been travelling restlessly in North Africa, the Middle East and Asia before stepping off the Barcelona ferry in 1956. 'I thought it was the promised land. There were thirty or forty foreigners on the island, and about thirty Spanish. And I don't mean "Spanish" as a joke, because everyone else spoke Ibicenco. The place looked like a garden – and in fact it was a garden, because it had 50,000 gardeners tending it. There was no garbage anywhere.'

In the early sixties the artists/intellectuals and retired people were still the majority of the new immigrants, but as the decade went on more and more of them were young people with flowers in their hair. By 1965 Ibiza had become an important stopover on the Grand Tour that also included San Francisco, Greenwich Village, Amsterdam, Goa and Katmandu, with optional stops in London and the Greek Islands. India was supposed to be the ultimate destination, the end of the trail, but many people never made it beyond the Mediterranean. The ones who came to Ibiza and stayed for good make up just under a fifth of today's neo-Ibicencos.

Pedro Planells, who has a leather shop in Ibiza town, remembers an early wave of beatniks that flowed into later waves of longer-haired people. What set them apart from any invaders Ibiza had ever had before was their attitude to life. 'They were artists, intellectuals. It was, today's today, yesterday's gone, tomorrow I don't know if it will come. Life was difficult, but it was in a way much easier than now, because no one was in a hurry.'

At first the funkiest people all lived around Figueretes, a beach near the town. There were a lot of jazz musicians around: the clarinettist Pony Poindexter, the trumpeter Larry Kayson, and a bass-player called Titi – 'thin as a whistle, black as Coca-Cola' – who once posed for Dali. Titi and another seriously hip black 'beat', the painter Jesse Richardson, were known as the Black Panthers of Figueretes. There would be all-night jam-sessions with a flute on one balcony, a sax in another and a bass in a third.

Pepe was one of the few Ibicencos to get involved in this incipient hippie scene. Not surprisingly he and the other *peluts* ('hairies') caused some perplexity. 'When the hippies came there were some conservative people who thought, "Oh, they're bad, they've got long hair, they don't wash." My parents looked at me like it was a bit strange, but it was more my other family and friends of my parents who thought it was a *disaster*, you know, like being a junkie today. "Oh, I'm so sorry for you, your son, he's a hippie." What they didn't realize was that people like that brought charisma to the island. In those days, to have four or five people in the same room was illegal. So we used to go to Benirràs and make a big fire, and have drums, and make a jam, all naked, with joints . . .'

Ibiza was the perfect site for the counter-cultural dream. There was little traffic, no industry to speak of, and hardly any modern buildings. Contemporary photographs of the view from the top of Dalt Vila show the town fizzling out into countryside just beyond the fishing-boats of the port, just where the banks and blocks of flats start nowadays. You could rent a *casa de campo* without bourgeois amenities like water and light from a farmer for a few pesetas, or live in a cave or in the open air. Food was cheap or free and drugs were everywhere. There was nobody on the beaches.

The novelist Joan Wyndham spent eight months on Ibiza in the 1960s, when she became 'that ludicrous creature, a fifty-year-old hippie'. Her friends were French longhairs who dressed in outrageous gowns, had 'OM' tattooed on their foreheads and dusted their faces with glittery powder. She passed her time playing mother to a houseful of homeless hippies, cooking up vegetable soup and pancakes, drinking white wine and listening to Santana records.

The drugs of choice were hash, heroin and LSD, supplemented in hard times with Dormedinos and Romilan from the chemist. Joan and her friends drank at the Tavern and danced at Lola's. One day they all dropped acid on the nudist beach at Las Salinas. She wrote in her autobiography *Anything Once*: 'The sun was shining, the sand was firm and damp to the touch, but Speedy was metamorphosing into a devil, an angel and finally a woman with a face of radiant beauty like the moon goddess who rules over Ibiza.' Later she visited a *finca* called Strawberry Fields where she remembers dancing to drums when it was not only a full moon but a full moon *in eclipse*.

'The huge courtyard was lit by flares, and by children who ran around like fireflies waving torches. All around were black bearded freaks banging away on African drums and Tibetan bells, while in the centre of the square the rich French poseurs gyrated slowly in their ethnic robes . . .'

Encuentro en Ibiza is an unassuming privately printed volume written in 1969 by Margarita Gomez Espinosa, a Madrid woman who had recently moved to the island and described the impression made on her by people like Joan Wyndham. The tone of her description hovers between disapproval and a fascination bordering on envy. 'In caves, and in dwellings as unconventional as their inhabitants, are crowded together groups of people eager for freedom who will not submit themselves to rules and regulations alien to them, but only to those marked out by their own wishes . . . Opposed to the family and society, they stroll around careless of the mocking, admiring or indifferent looks directed at them by passersby; they live purely in order to enjoy the moments they spend reading, painting, getting drunk, dancing or loving.'

Generally antics such as these were looked upon by Ibicencos with extraordinary sang-froid and the *peluts* felt the benefit of the island's traditional xenophilia. Even heavy pot-smoking was tolerated: some Ibicencos already knew about opium, which was grown for 'medicinal' purposes. Still-vivid memories of the isolation that followed the Civil War meant that anyone who came to the island in the early sixties, however long their hair, was treated as an honoured guest. Drinks would be paid for in bars by anonymous strangers. Shopkeepers would insist that you paid later, tomorrow, next week, or when you next came to Ibiza. This trust was less readily offered when, inevitably, it began to be abused.

As more and more travellers arrived on the island, there was friction. There were more and a greater variety of hard drugs. In the seventies the cults moved in: there was a Buddhist temple in San Lorenzo, the Bhagwan built up a following in San Juan, and the Hare Krishna people could be seen doing their thing – bald and be-robed – on the streets of Ibiza town.

By Spanish law under Franco public meetings and large late-night parties were forbidden unless you had permission from the police, which of course few party-givers bothered about. This was the cause of much of the trouble. In June 1967 there was a series of 'Disgusted, San Antonio' letters in the local press denouncing the hippies' 'drugs and dirtiness', their nudism, their orgies, and the threat they posed to public morality. There were discontented mutterings that the *peluts* had been robbing grapes and figs from the orchards, causing damage by sleeping on building-sites and starting forest-fires with their candles. One letter-writer suggested it was time to 'fight against fashions and conditions foreign to our own tradition'. Another fulminated against 'long hair and outlandish beards, clothes as threadbare and dirty as the people . . . God knows they live in complete sexual promiscuity; they eat badly and drink to excess. What little money they have they spend on "stimulants" . . . If when they set foot on the harbour or in the airport we were to send them back to their places of origin, Ibiza would be cleaned up without any harm being done to the tourist industry.'

By the end of the summer the authorities had taken up this winter's suggestion that *peluts* should be ejected from the island. In August 1967 Guardia Civil were drafted in from the mainland and twenty-seven hippies were expelled from Spain for 'Antisocial Conduct and Economic Irresponsibility'.

Apart from the police and the Press few could summon up much outrage about these young people. The strongest emotion most Ibicencos felt was probably amusement. At times there was even a kind of complicity. There were instances of hippies and *payeses* trying on each other's clothes. One farmer in San Carlos – with San Juan, the main freaks' centre – 'employed' hippies to build a house for him in return for vegetables and spices.

Occasionally the 'alternative' cause received powerful allies against the reactionaries, such as in July 1971 during the famous battle between police and three hundred freaks that ensued in Santa Eulalia after the police had moved in to evict one hundred of them from a *finca* in nearby San Carlos. The priest of San Carlos made it known that he supported the *peluts*, not the police, even though the *peluts* were reportedly guilty of defecating in wells used by Ibicencos for drinking water and various other outrages. Incidents like these were quickly forgotten. In any case, most hippies had better things to do than quarrel with the police – like hang out and play guitar in Anita's and La Tierra. Both these famous sixties bars were run by formidable women. Arlene, from New York, had La Tierra, while the great Anita, an Ibicenca, ruled at her eponymous bar in San Carlos. Erwin Bechtold, a German painter who has lived in the village since 1959, spent happy days and nights at Anita's. 'She was a wild woman.'

Everyone in San Carlos knows Anita's story, which is full-bloodedly romantic and ought to be considered by Hollywood. As a girl she fell in love with a local boy of whom her parents disapproved, so they eloped to his parents' house and were married. During the Civil War her husband fought on the Republican side, and when the Nationalists reconquered the island did time in the concentration camp on Formentera, where she went to visit him. When the war ended he was still active with the Republicans and decided it would be prudent to leave. He took the boat to Algiers, where he stayed until the Algerian war broke out. He fled to France and found another woman. Meanwhile Anita worked away in the bar, which officially belonged to her brother-in-law.

The years slipped by, and it seemed he was gone for good. Then, one fine day more than thirty years after he'd left, he sat down at a table in front of the bar and ordered a *café con leche*. Anita was still devoted to him and took him back unhesitatingly, to the annoyance of her family. Anita is now a widow living quietly nearby in Figueral, on the coast near San Carlos. Erwin Bechtold sees her from time to time. 'Yes, she was a wild woman then, with her black hair. Now she's very distinguished. I last saw her in the cemetery, at a funeral. That's where you see people these days.'

At Las Dalias they have a special 'hippie market' in addition to their regular Saturday-afternoon event, a few weeks before Christmas. One evening I hitched a lift with my German neighbour Heidi, the only other off-season inhabitant of my desolate *urbanización*, in her four-wheel-drive Japanese juggernaut.

There was not a lot of business at the market. Heidi's theory was that fewer and fewer of the sort of people who might be attracted by the kind of wares on offer actually opt to stay on the island the whole year round. Rising prices and the general environment of affluence have frightened them off. One stall-holder seemed to be in a trance. Perhaps he was meditating.

Las Dalias offered a favourite Ibiza combination of classic hippie style – tie-dye T-shirts, leatherwork, the Ethnic Look, items for smoking through and with – with Club Med holidaywear. Much of this stuff you could have found without looking too hard in the Rastro in Madrid, Clignancourt in Paris or Camden Lock in London, or indeed in almost any street-market in the western world. There was so much overlap it was tempting to imagine a central depot where vast quantities of snake rings and little wooden boxes (surely they could only be intended for one thing) were mass-produced to satisfy world demand.

Occasionally at Las Dalias you will hit upon something truly original and different, but not very often. There was one stall where a lanky guy with black frizzy hair and a woolly beret stood behind a collection of objects that turned out on closer inspection to be musical instruments. The instruments ranged from the recognizable to the downright Martian. Most of them appeared to be of African inspiration, though they were made of native Ibicenco woods – olive, apricot, apple. The most beautiful was the oddest: it had a row of metal strips, fanned out in a row like the fingers of a hand, which you twanged with your fingertips and they resonated over a shallow box of polished olive-wood, making a satisfying *thunnggg*, like a violin plucked in a wardrobe. A few stalls further on was Helen with her icing-sugar-sweet paintings of Ibiza – flower-strewn *casas payesas*, churches and landscapes – and her big motherly smile. Helen fled from Streatham and now looks after her two little boys in a flower-strewn *casa payesa* outside Santa Gertrudis. She told me she goes to the same Rebirthing group as Javier, which in Streatham would be like saying you drink in the same pub. Heidi took me up to Mora's stall, a temple of every conceivable colour and texture of wool, where I tried on some of

Brigitte's crazy woolly hats, nobbly brown and grey with spatterings of colour, sort of Granny Goes to Woodstock.

Mora and Djin, her lover, are enormous, gentle people, all six foot six of both of them swathed in coloured woollens that are the height of hippie glamour. He, especially, towers above everything; he has immense muscular thighs, wears skintight woolly leggings and frayed suede mini-shorts that suggest a cross between Conan the Barbarian and the Green Giant, and sports a weird moustache that wanders around his face before finally arriving at his sideburns. They lived near Isla Blanca, in a stone house on a hill.

Mora was knitting away at something pink, fluffy and complicated – a *Jersey-kleid* – while Djin wound a skein of brown wool into a ball. Everywhere you looked were theatrical clothes with shoulder-pads and glittery bits worked in. Mora takes two days, knitting from sun-up to sundown, to complete a jersey (longer for a *Jersey-kleid*). I wondered whether her colour scheme was influenced by Ibiza, because the flamenco dress that hung above my head was just the colour of the heather that was kindling the landscape into purple fire in the *campo* between her house and mine. But she thought for a while, looked down at the knitting in her lap and said no, her favourite colours were *these*: an Afro palette of black, yellow, orange and green.

I nearly bought a Christmas stollen, a plain silver ring, a bottle of homemade Hierbas Ibicencas – Ibiza's own syrupy homemade herb liqueur – and a Tarot reading by the legendary Renée Cohen, self-styled Queen of the Ibiza scene, who was sitting at a table wrapped in a veil of shocking-pink chiffon surrounded by her press cuttings from the local papers. Her throaty Brooklyn rasp was clearly audible as she gave the low-down on a client's future. 'Well now, honey, this is reeeal interesting,' she said, leaning forward over the table. 'Didja know you're gonna be going through big, and I mean *big* changes this year? Well, the cards are telling me you are. We're talking about a whole new ball-game, honey. Are you ready for that?'

Renée had a rival Tarot-reader in Noëlle – flame-haired,

friendly and French – who sat at her table by the garden door. Noëlle was one of the most passionate apologists for Ibiza I had ever heard.

'The world has always needed pockets of a different kind of reality,' she told me. 'A place where there is relative peace and relative freedom. A place that's available for freedom of the spirit. In Ibiza people are outlaws – they are living out their fantasies of freedom.' She thinks nothing much has changed since 1974, when she crashed into Ibiza from her world travels, except that everyone has got older and if you wanted to do today what she did in 1974, 'you would have to have your material trip much more together'.

She is one of Ibiza's famous party-givers. 'Parties are very important. I mean, you see African tribes having parties, and every so-called primitive people have their fiestas, don't they?' Noëlle's ingredients for a perfect party are:

1. 'The right spot. In a country house, away from neighbours.'
2. 'People with heart.'
3. 'Great music. Lately there has been a return to drumming . . .'
4. 'A good moon.'

I was walking away from Noëlle's stall towards the bar when I noticed a poster I had also seen in that Piccadilly Circus of Ibiza's neo-hippie scene, the health food shop on the Plaza del Parque. AURIC CHAKRA MASSAGE, it said in handwritten letters superimposed on a bulbous organic shape suggestive of something amoeba-like and growing, or possibly an extremely fat and featureless Buddha. 'Around the physical body', it continued in Spanish, 'there exists an energetic field or aura. Massage of the aura allows one to obtain a deeper understanding of oneself. Susie, Can Bernat, San Carlos, 4000 pesetas.'

Beneath the poster was Susie herself, a thin, pale New Zealand woman in purple leggings who sells Bach flower remedies as a sideline to her main profession as an Auric Chakra Masseuse. She seemed friendly, and I figure everyone's aura needs a check-up every few hundred lives, so we fixed a time. The price was a little steep, but New Age people are open to barter, especially in the winter. Besides, it would be my Christmas present to myself.

In Ibiza as in the rest of Spain, Reyes Magos, the feast of the Three Kings on 6 January, was once much more energetically celebrated than Christmas Day itself but has now been relegated to second place, largely owing to the commercial possibilities inherent in trees, toys, tinsel, and the whole panoply of the Anglo-American Christmas. In Ibiza the week before the big day there are Teutonic carols – in Catalan – blaring across the Vara de Rey, and turkey-with-all-the-trimmings is now a popular choice for the Christmas meal, although the meal itself is still likely to be on Christmas Eve rather than, UK-style, on Christmas Day.

Out in the *campo* some of the old traditions still cling on, and none more tenaciously than *salsa de Nadal* or Christmas sauce. The idea is to combine the most highly valued, rare and delicious products of the land into one luxurious mixture. Ground almonds, honey, chicken broth and spices all find their way into the pot along with copious amounts of fat. The resulting golden sludge, the consistency of school custard, is a great delicacy, and would have been even more so in times when the diet of people in the country was mainly characterized by monotony.

There are really only two possible attitudes to *salsa*: you either get excited about it during the first two weeks of December, gorge yourself on it for the second two and find it an ambrosial experience, or violent waves of nausea course through your body at the very mention of it. At C'an Joan Ramón they start shelling almonds in mid December. I drove up to see Toni one afternoon. He was sitting in the kitchen in front of a blaring television, restlessly zapping back and forth from a promotional programme about the Seville Expo to a Catalan-dubbed version of *Indiana Jones and the Temple of Doom* while his mother and father sat by the fire cracking the hard almond shells with little hammers.

A thinly veiled competitiveness surrounds the making of *salsa* and, like any good local speciality worthy of the name, the exact method and quantity of the ingredients used vary from household to household. Señora Ramón could not possibly tell me how she made hers – that would be to sell its soul – but I could rest assured it was 'the best in all Ibiza'.

A fortnight later she was sitting in the same chair by the fire, but there was an addition to the scene in the shape of a giant cauldron, half the size of herself, on the floor in front of her. It was full of a thick liquid which she was stirring with a stick. The steam which filled the kitchen was heavy with a cinnamon sweetness.

The revelation that I had never tasted *salsa de Nadal* was received by the Ramón family with horror. It was as though I'd just confessed that as a child I had been forcefed with a diet of bread and water. Such deprivation would have to be remedied immediately and abundantly. A large soup bowl was fetched, filled to the brim with freshly made *salsa* and presented to me with a slice of *bescuit pagès*, a cake spiced with aniseed, balanced on its rim. From what I knew about the Spanish mania for dipping biscuits, cakes, bread and *churros* into coffee, hot chocolate, soup or whatever liquid happens to be on hand – it's a dunking culture – I deduced that the *salsa* was to be conveyed to the mouth soaked up in the spongy *bescuit*.

Salsa is intensely sweet, rich and cloying, and strangely delicious especially when consumed in small quantities. You cannot taste the chicken. Almost the point of the whole concoction is what wine-tasters call mouth-feel, which is to say its thick, smooth, sticky fattiness. The cake is a good idea in that it gives the teeth something to bite on, but with or without it a few spoonfuls of the liquid are quite enough. More than that and you are likely to turn an interesting shade of green. *Salsa* is the culmination of the Ibicenco Christmas meal, occupying the same position and arousing roughly the same passions, both for and against, as Christmas Pudding. In fact pudding and *salsa* go extremely well together, and after all *salsa* is only slightly more unhealthy than brandy butter. Before that, if you live in the *campo* you have *arros de peix* (fish rice), and *sofrit pagès*. The urban bourgeois of Ibiza town, typified by Javier's family who have a large gloomy flat overlooking the necropolis of Puig d'es Molins, enjoy a different, but not necessarily superior, menu. Their meal opens with a salad of sliced raw cabbage eaten with a vinaigrette made with ground almonds. Then they have *sopa de menudillos*, a soup of giblets, chicken blood and tapioca. The third course is simply a large chunk of meat, often taken along to the bakery to be cooked because many Ibicencos, even the urban bourgeois ones, lack an oven of sufficient size. This also provides an opportunity for the baker to show gratitude for his clients' loyal custom throughout the year.

After the meat the townies rejoin their country cousins and demand cups of Christmas sauce – a case of 'everybody salsa'.

My own Christmas that year was as Ibicenco as I could make it without alienating my family, who predictably wanted their festive season more or less *à l'anglaise* apart from the weather. I would have liked to have *sofrit pagés*; but cultural absorption and tolerance can only go so far. There would have to be turkey, and Señor Ramón had already agreed to provide the bird.

Whenever I'd been at the farm I had seen his three big *pavos* strutting among the fruit trees of the *corral*, like ostriches on the African savanna, with the magnificent arrogance that comes with true stupidity. The Ibicenco turkey is a venerable bird, closely related to the American wild variety as it appears on the label of the famous Kentucky Bourbon – and its pedigree shows in its clear black-and-white markings and proudly upstanding tail-feathers. The three at Ca'n Joan Ramón had their palatial headquarters in a clapped-out Renault 4, minus engine and wheels, that is gently decomposing under an orange tree. They roosted on the back seat and in the boot, as though leaving the driving-seat for an eternally absent chauffeur.

The Ramóns had decided not to have a *matanza*, a pig-killing, this year. It was a shame, said Señora Ramón, but everyone apart from Toni was grown up, her husband was getting on and the business of pig-killing requires the strength and agility of a younger man. Anyway it was all too much trouble these days. They would be getting their *sobrasadas* and *butifarras*, their lard and bacon, from friends in Santa Gertrudis. I hoped it was some small consolation to the family that this winter they would be slaughtering a turkey instead, even if they were doing it for someone else's benefit.

We pitched up on the night before Christmas Eve and, on the Macbeth principle that if it were done, 'twere well it were done quickly, downed our *vino payés* in one difficult gulp and let ourselves be led to the scene of the crime. Toni's father shone a torch into the Renault 4 and we peered inside with incredulous gasps. There it was in the gloom, immense and white, feathers puffed up against the cold, occupying the entire boot of the car. It was a monster. Who knew how it might react when its sleep was rudely disturbed by a man with a knife?

We cowered in the shadows as Señor Ramón advanced on the open boot, grabbed the turkey's powerful legs in one hand and shoved it into a sack in such a way that its head and neck protruded from a small hole in one corner. The bird's face registered an expression of the most profound outrage, but the shock seemed to have rendered it speechless. There was a beating of wings, but not the merest gobble, not the slightest squawk, even when the sack was secured around its legs and suspended from a carob tree at a more convenient distance from the stove and Señora Ramón's pot of boiling water. It was an operatic scene: the victim swinging pathetically from its scaffold, the knife glinting in the light from the kitchen door, the local *tricoteuse* brandishing her plastic bowl, the cringing crowd.

In a few moments it was all over bar the plucking. At the moment of truth Señora Ramón had rushed forward and caught some of the torrent of turkey-blood in her bowl, and now she was thrusting the luminous red jelly under my turned-up nose. I had to take it home, she urged. Didn't I know how good it was, how nutritious and delicious when cut into quivering slices and fried in plenty of oil, for breakfast? She pushed the bowl nearer my face and shook it so that the blood slapped hotly against the plastic.

When stripped of feathers, innards, and head, the *pavo* which, before its brutal assassination, had been lord of the orchard, weighed in at a mighty 14 kilos. It was almost more imposing in death than it had been in life. It was of a dimension that would make Bernard Matthews, the East Anglian agro-businessman renowned for his 'bootiful' ways with turkey-meat, sell up and go into quiet retirement with half-a-dozen chickens in his back yard. Moreover, when it arrived on our plates at Christmas lunch its flavour was far from the spongy tastelessness of factory-bred poultry. The meat was as dense and dark as game.

If in the matter of the Christmas meal I had ceded to British tastes, in other areas I stood my ground with Ibicenco tradition. After the Midnight Mass in the Church of Santo

Domingo, the baroque church just below the walls of the old town, there were Caramelles. Nothing to do with sweets or sugar, but a type of song which is associated with Christmas and only heard in public around that time of year.

We walked around in Dalt Vila before the service and got briefly lost in its dim maze of silent streets. On the corner of two grimy alleyways that met in the centre of the old town, a gypsy street party was letting its hair down in the style to which Spanish gypsies are accustomed, their faces lit from below as though by Caravaggio by a blazing brazier. A bottle of 103, Spanish lowlife's favourite brandy, was doing the rounds. As we stood watching like spies from a doorway one of the older men brought out a guitar and struck up a spine-chillingly raw and guttural flamenco.

caramelles are something else again. The historian Isidoro Macabich describes them, noticeably steering clear of excessive enthusiasm, as 'the oldest musical numbers of our singers as well as among the oldest compositions of the country'. Elsewhere they are called 'archaic', 'enigmatic' or 'intense' – but that is as far in the direction of praise as any commentator gets.

Despite that, the church was full. It is not usual to have music at the Mass, and this one had not only a choir in smart black-and-white costumes who were to sing the ubiquitous carols, but a three-piece band of instrumentalists playing three traditional Ibicenco instruments: *flauta*, a recorder made of oleander wood; *tambor*, a hollowed-out pine log with the skin of a rabbit or baby goat stretched over each end; and the strange *espasi*, a metal strip that makes a gentle clanging sound when struck. The young man who played the drum also sang.

Together this *esquadre de caramelles* made a sound which was fascinatingly monotonous. Each song was made up of a single endlessly repeated vocal phrase, after which the singer made the gobbling sound known as *sa redoblada* (the redoubling) and the flute resumed its warbling melody. Musicologically speaking *sa redoblada* is a chimera not found in other folk traditions. But at the time it seemed to me that I had stumbled on its true significance. It was clearly nothing less than a droll imitation of a Christmas turkey's death-rattle.

When I saw Susie again she was driving round the corner in a pale yellow Renault 6 to meet me in Anita's Bar. Susie is tall and tired-eyed, and today looked like a stork that had accidentally been dyed purple. Her long thin legs were encased in purple leggings and her top half swathed in a thick homemade purple sweater. The only punctuation of the purple was a big complicated brown belt.

Susie apologized for the crumbling car in her soft hooting New Zealand accent. 'The other day the floor fell out. My friend had to put fibreglass down.' She had a kind, lined face and long thin blonde hair. On the back seat of the car was her son, a twelve-year-old with a blond bowl haircut and transatlantic accent who begged his mother to take him fishing. 'Aw, c'mon mom, everybody's going from school. C'mon . . . Just for an hour or two, *please*.' She kept her eyes on the bumpy *camino*, blinked her tired eyes and weakly agreed. He seemed the tougher of the two. She had been in Ibiza for thirteen years – or was it fourteen, she couldn't remember. 'I was travelling and I'd been living in Greece with some people who told me about Ibiza. The first place I lived was a little house that the shepherds used to sleep in. Of course there was no electricity, but there was a well. I really got the bug. A few years ago I went away and swore I would never come back. So I went to Australia, but a year later I was back here.'

Her house was beautiful and as expected. An old white farmhouse among orchards where a few early lambs were playing in the green-gold afternoon. Inside were carpets, cushions, low tables, low ceilings, low everything. On the walls were charts and poems and prayers, one by Rebirthing queen Louise L. Hay, which was about loving oneself. Between the kitchen and the sitting room was Susie's New Age consulting room. There were thick white walls and a skylight to let in the warm January sun. A large, low bed enveloped in a purple drape; at its head, a kind of shrine with Oriental bowls artfully arranged and a row of bottles of liquid of various colours, many of them shades of purple. I took off my shoes and Susie lit what she called a 'smudge stick' made of four different herbs – she pronounced the word the antipodean way, 'hirbs'. 'These are hirbs which the Tibetans use, and the American Indians also use. They're to take away the negativity and let the positivity, beauty and harmony come through. One of the hirbs only grows in America, but there's a woman in England who sells it; I'll have to write off soon and get some more.' So saying she waved the smoking bowl around my body. It smelt strong, rich and bathroomy, and I did indeed begin to feel a dozy quietude begin to take the place of watchful scepticism. 'Exercises' followed – Jane Fonda meets St Ignatius – and then I went to lie down in the consulting room while Susie said a little prayer. There were wisps of sound: a lamb in the field outside; a breath of wind through the small square window just above my head.

In the kitchen before, over tea and toast, I'd wondered aloud what Susie meant by 'auric chakra'. She said it meant different things to different people, but the chakras were the energy points on the human body and the aura was exactly as it sounded, a kind of force-field extending outwards from our physical selves into space. A third pole of her personal therapy was 'colour healing' as practised by Vicky Wall, a woman who teaches that colours are closely bound up with mental and physical well-being. I would say, but Susie might not agree, that there was a fair dollop of psychoanalysis in there somewhere too. Whatever its ingredients, she arrived at her technique after a year in Ibiza when she 'did a session' every week with the same friend. The friend soon became a close friend.

My eyes were shut but I sensed her sit down at my side and her hands begin to hover above me, perhaps getting the measure of my aura. 'OK, I think I'm getting something from the teeth, the teeth are kind-of locked and tight, also something in the throat, not so much the throat, more just under the chin. Is there some kind of lack of expression there, some kind of inability to express something? Let's concentrate on that thought. Is anything coming out of that thought? If there's anything you want to say about that thought, let it out.' And she started tapping lightly, repetitively, around my chest and shoulders, letting out little moans which increased in anguish and volume while I tried to let a suitable thought come to the surface.

For the next two hours I could sense her hands weaving and fluttering around my body and occasionally feel them exerting a slight pressure on it. Meanwhile, as she talked she would identify – from the feel of my aura – areas of what she thought were doubt or anxiety; she would propose an image and ask me to do something with it, to reject or accept or manipulate it somehow. Sometimes I felt it was easy to express myself and that she was leading me skilfully towards doing so; other times I knew I myself was being manipulated.

Even while Susie's moaning and groaning was reaching new heights of intensity – at one point there was even a gurgling noise in her throat and she spat something into a plastic bowl at her side – in a strictly emotional sense I felt nothing. All the same, there were moments when I saw things, visions almost, impossible to say whether an effect of deep relaxation combined with something similar to hypnosis or a genuine manifestation of my aura. I saw fountains, oceans, islands floating in the air like clouds, and other images from seventies album-covers. It was an experience simultaneously profound and tacky, magical and banal.

By the time it all ended I felt as exhausted as if I had just taken a five-mile run. Susie had to pick up her son from school, so she whacked on a tape (the choice was between Waterfalls of Light and Eternal Pipes) and left me lying on the bed until the music irritated me into life. Outside the afternoon was turning the grass speckled with yellow flowers and the mantle of bougainvillea that covered the white dome of the old bread-oven in the courtyard and the triangle of sea, caught between two nearby hills, into fields of psychedelic colour.

What my aura really needed now, though I doubted I would find it in Susie's larder, was a cold beer.

That evening in Santa Gertrudis, there were rumours of a full-moon party. Fernando and I were installed at a fireside table in the Bar Costa when a tall bony man with straggly hair wearing faded purple-cotton Gandhi trousers sloped up to warm his hands at the fire. A decade ago Txiki had dropped out gratefully from a wealthy family of Basque industrialists into a life of leisured penury in Ibiza. His girlfriend, similarly straggly-haired and purple-clad, was an American dancer from Marin County, epicentre of Northern California's post-hippie scene. Txiki's and Debra's lives revolved around parties: planning them, publicizing them, attending them. Debra began telling me about her birthday party last June, when she'd had a whole room given over to wall-painting and there was 'just the most powerful atmosphere' until a group of local kids showed up and began scrawling the names of English punk bands, and the whole atmosphere was ruined as well as the painting. She thrust into my hand a half-sheet of photocopied A4 covered with a mishmash of proto-religious symbolism and New Age folklore: pyramids, hearts, an Aztec priest doing an awkward knees-up, an elephant-headed Indian god, the CND logo, the Yin-Yang sign, and a series of moons in various stages of waxing. On the back was a map tracing a serpentine *camino* that crept through the countryside, beside *casa de Jacques* and *casa de Stefan y Helen* and past the Falcon Blanco, a New Age retreat where an Argentinian shaman had recently staged a *succès fou* with his course in getting to know the Universal Being, before finally winding up at the party venue.

Twelve full moons a year, multiplied by thirty years is 360, plus in the past you would have had several big parties going on at the same time in various parts of the island; which makes more than 500 full-blooded full-moon fiestas since 1962. Over the years the Ibiza party has evolved into a creature of some sophistication. Innovations, hit upon in a moment of wild inspiration, have mutated into traditions. Skeins of silver tinsel glittering in roadside trees are a reassuring sign that you haven't lost your way on the endless dirt tracks. When you arrive, there will always be a fire outside, often in the centre of a circular space like Javier's dais; inside there may be drumming and/or a DJ who plays at least one Bob Marley record at some point during the night. More often than not you will be able to buy sweet milky tea, a taste acquired on the Asia trail where it is practically the only thing safe to drink.

At midnight we pulled off the road that runs from San Carlos to the sea. The long *camino* was lined with crumbling cars. Walking to the house, a big gleaming white *finca*, we heard the thrum of drums, louder as we came nearer, as though we'd stumbled on some tribal ceremony, which in a way we had. Everything was lit up, by candles in cutaway water-bottles all over the *terraza*, by a bonfire in a grove between the fruit trees, and by a gaping full moon, bright enough to pick out cobalt-blue sea, ferrous-red earth and the unearthly titanium-white of the *finca*. Out on the terrace by the light of a candle the eye picked out a mysterious clump of bodies at the centre of which, like a mast in a storm, stood a big dark man with curly black hair whose hands clasped the shoulders of another figure, part of the human swarm clustering quietly around him.

Further in, there was dancing around an over-arching carob tree. The DJ, who stood behind a mixing desk next to the Indian tea stall in the porch, was saving his Bob Marley for later, for now regaling the party with African pop, bits of old rock 'n' roll and disco, and other unconsidered musical trifles from the last thirty years. A tall man in Eastern robes was spinning in tight circles on the stone dancefloor, whirling around him a long pink silk scarf which if he kept on gyrating would shortly turn him into a spinning pink mummy. I remembered him as a Tarot reader whose palm I once crossed with silver in a nightclub in Ibiza town. Screaming over the music, he'd foretold my immediate future as a dizzying series of life-changes, all to do with the Moon, the Tower and the Traveller.

Inside the house the living-room was a freak-out of drumming. All around the fireplace were half-a-dozen bearded figures, the elders of the San Juan/San Carlos scene, sitting on the floor with drums. Paco from the house above Monica's was the Identikit hippie in straw hat, printed baggy trousers and open-toed sandals, his special-occasions drum between his knees. He banged away furiously all night, from eleven till seven, with only the occasional pause to take a drag off a joint while one hand continued drumming. It was done on the run, like a Tour de France cyclist. Dancing in the central room, under an ornate Indian lamp that cast ecclesiastical shadows on the wooden floor, was a barefoot woman in a long coloured East-European-peasant dress, shimmying rapturously with her eyes closed while a funky blonde in sequinned hot-pants and black stilettos tried not to step on her toes. And there, directly under the Indian lamp, were Txiki and Debra, alternative Ibiza's most inexhaustible hosts, he resplendent in tasselled leather American-Indian garb with parrot feathers in his hair, she in red leggings, both of them doing a flat-footed shuffling Indian dance, whooping in time to the throbbing drums. In the kitchen a girl from San Lorenzo was serving fruit cocktails: Apricot Cooler, Pisco Sour, Pina Colada and milkshakes. She wasn't selling anything and was not in a party mood, but we decided this was not after all a very promising constituency for cocktails. Most people were sticking to grass and beer. By her stall I talked to a cartoon punk with chick-yellow hair and a battered black leather jacket with the word PEST painted on the back in Tipp-Ex. This person, Javier whispered to me later, was the offspring of one of the most respected figures on the British stage.

Moving out into the back garden, where there was an old-fashioned hippie jam session involving a concertina, a flute and a violin played between the knees, I met Sid from Paros, with long flaxen hair and an expression of extreme geniality bordering on the idiotic, and his friend David, who was wiry and moustached and talked continuously in a low voice, almost inaudibly, so that in order to converse with him you had to interrupt him with a loud question, which he would appear not to have heard but would invariably come round to answering in the course of his rambling discourse. He and Sid were in Ibiza for a three-day course in 'Healing the Flow of Life' which had ended that afternoon. 'I really see this party as, like, not just a full-moon party but, like, a real celebration of the whole healing experience we've been through over the past three days,' said Sid, producing for my benefit a crumpled leaflet which explained more about the course. The man in the picture was Frank Natale, founder and president of the Natale Institute for Experiential Education and 'a prominent figure in alternative education for the last twenty-five years'. His CV included a stint as a researcher on *Self-Actualized Personalities*, 'the first-ever study of healthy personalities'. 'Through lecture, trance dance, guided adventure and individual healing', the blurb went on, 'Frank will create the opportunity for the participants to have a "direct Experience" of their far memory. They will Know that being human is no accident but rather the end result of millions of years of evolution.' The capitals on 'Experience' and 'Know' appeared to have been used for emphasis, in the eighteenth-century manner.

Txiki had stoked up the fire in the orchard with old almond wood and the flames were flooding the cold moonlight with warmth and colour. Behind a circle of dancers Sabine, in a blue and yellow overall, was sitting on a table with her back against an olive tree, a beatific smile wreathing her rosy cheeks. 'I jumped it earlier on,' she told me proudly, pointing to the fire. Here was another classic party trick. To jump a fire is thought to have the same kind of effect on the spirit that a raw egg in fresh orange juice has on the body. Perhaps that explains Sabine's energetic smile, and the way she then lowered her voice in awe to murmur as she stared fixedly into the glowing core of the flames: 'Explain it. Where does it come from, and how does it go on?'

The pipe of peace was passed round, arriving in my hand via a middle-aged Ibicenco lady wearing a thick woollen cardigan pulled tightly around her ample frame. She sat on a folding chair flanked by her husband, who was of the same size and age, but seemed, surprisingly, to be in the process of constructing a joint in the palm of his hand. They both gave me toothy smiles as I took a cautious puff on the pipe. 'We're the neighbours. They always ask us to their parties, and I'm sure they hope we won't come. But we always do!' said she, and then, noticing my struggle with the pipe of peace, 'You've got to take a big drag, right down to the chest.'

I did as she suggested and the rich smoke hit the bottom of my lungs like a lead weight, making me cough and splutter like a neophyte. As if in explanation the owner of the pipe, an elderly hippie with multicoloured feathers tied in his hair and a broad grin which made his grizzled cheeks crack up like dried mud, passed around the circle a screw-top jar half full of a pinkish-grey powder. When it reached me I took off the lid and breathed in the aroma. It smelt of lavender and Earl Grey tea.

'It's peyote. A friend sent it to me from Mexico,' said the man with the feathers, showing his teeth at me. I later discovered that this man's main claim to fame was his unique collection of several hundred plastic cigarette lighters, every one a miniature artwork of fantastical beauty, decorated by his own hand in enamel paint, glitter and tiny metallic shapes during each of several hundred acid trips. He had once given Fernando a guided tour of the collection and even allowed him to take one of the lighters as a gift – which precious thing I'd subsequently seen occupying pride of place in a kind of curio-cabinet in the Cameroon ambassador's cottage at the head of the valley. That one, an early example from the mid seventies, was painted in mysterious shades of dark green, orange, yellow and black, in flames that licked up the sides of the lighter and exploded into gold and silver sparks around the flint. Here and there were mini-constellations of silver stars, or a word or phrase risen like a bubble from the depths of the artist's hallucinating mind. Fernando's lighter bore the word 'Enciende!' ('Light!'). Others he remembered had, 'Quien eres, Ibiza?' ('Who are you, Ibiza?'), 'Te amaré' ('I will love you') and, inexplicably, 'Tiempo es para' ('Time is for').

For a while the peyote seemed to do nothing but make me feel weary and bored, but after half an hour I suddenly felt I had five-league boots on. I skipped and jumped around the terrace, or stood still and stared at the candles while the music surged and swelled. By five o'clock the party was in full swing. The drums had reached a pitch of frenzy and there were exuberant yelps from the house; meanwhile in the garden Debra and friends were busy reclaiming an old military bunker for peace, painting the interior with spiritual graffiti and figures traced around their bodies. Finding myself a space on the white wall, I drew a huge thick-rooted, over-arching vine and painted it with deep green leaves and drooping clusters of purple grapes. 'Hey, y'know, that's really strong, man,' said Debra. 'Well, war is strong, so I guess creativity has got to be strong too.' She had taken off her top and painted coloured circles around her breasts, which bounced as she talked. A French friend of hers, expensively clad in a black silk hippie dress and clanking with ethnic jewellery, took time out from filling in a large purple love-heart to describe to me her plan to arrange all four elements in her back garden: earth in the form of a mud bath, water in the form of a fountain, fire in a specially designed ceremonial fireplace, and air in the sea breeze that drifts up to her house from the bay at Aguas Blancas.

At six o'clock the disco played some laidback blues and finished for the night, and everyone moved back into the drumming room for a last frenzied hour. The sound seemed relentless and one-dimensional, but as your ears grew accustomed you heard new things, as your eyes grow used to a moonlit landscape: mysterious harmonies, discreet melodies within the ebb and flow of deep, pure rhythm.

Shortly it began to rain, snuffing out the candles on the terrace, sticking slick black puddles on the former dancefloor. The dawn was beginning its slow fade to grey, so that from the edge of the terraza I could just make out a pewter-coloured patch of sea, cradled in a V-shaped valley as if in a pair of fur-grey hands. I sat alone in the porch listening to the drums, watching the rain and the morning. The man in the pink silk scarf was handing round oranges from the orchard, cold from the rain and as sweet as acid-drops. Mine seemed the most delicious thing I had ever eaten, a luxury more rare and excellent than caviar. Astonishing, that taste, that dawn light and the magnificent drums beating out along the valley.

Spring

I had a brown rusting Mini, brought from England, which took Ibiza's network of treacherous *caminos* in its stride. There are hundreds of kilometres of 'roads' on the island which have more in common with dried-up riverbeds, yet my small brown car nonchalantly bumped and scraped up and down them all. It seemed happy here; perhaps because it was a child of the sixties and felt at home with all the sixties resonances; or perhaps because of the attention it received by virtue of its strange number-plate, the strange position of its steering-wheel, and the fact of being a car of real character on an island crowded with mediocre motors. Apart from the flash open-tops containing Gucci-wearers that you see parked outside Montesol in the summer (a girl I met was once driven home from Amnesia in a pink open-topped Cadillac by a man called Fairy) there are only really three kinds of car in Ibiza: the Toyota/Suzuki *rus in urbe* jeep-look estate-car (Germans and richer Ibicencos); the squeaky-clean SEAT Euro-hatchback (thousands and thousands of ordinary Ibicencos) and crumbling superannuated versions of the latter (crumbling superannuated hippies and impoverished foreigners).

But the island's winter nights have the kind of damp chill that spells death to old cars, and as spring came over the horizon slowly 'el Mini' began to fall apart. Rust ate its way around the headlights until they threatened to fall out, like monocles from an Edwardian's eye. The left indicator light was pulped by an unknown assailant in Vara de Rey. One week I lent it to Toni – an example of trust triumphing over common sense – and it came back with a headlight switch that fluttered limply between On and Off.

Worst of all was the sudden death of the petrol-gauge, which thereafter stuck obstinately on Empty. Every journey became a battleground of complacency and fatalism, and it was the latter which was, naturally, vindicated every time the car juddered to a halt on some country *camino* miles from anywhere.

Yet I found even this, a road-user's nightmare, had hidden benefits. I was forced to walk, to watch the hawks circling in the air and the lizards on the *camino*. And I met people like the Petrol Lady. It was a dark January night when my fuel-tank showed itself to be empty on a country road just outside San Mateo, a village whose half-a-dozen dwellings are served by a disproportionate range of amenities including two *tiendas* or bar/shops, a tennis-court, a telephone exchange and a massive whitewashed church, optimistically large for the size of the village. One of the *tiendas* is the only place you can buy 'Pep Daifa', the island's single example of sparkling wine, made by Italians in a nearby house with a Tuscan garden. The only thing San Mateo lacks is a petrol station.

I'd heard rumours about a ninety-year-old lady who sold petrol from her house and I felt I was fortunate to have broken down where I did, less because she might be able to get me out of trouble than because I now had a tailor-made opportunity to meet one of the last living examples of a dying species. Eulalia Marí Torres lived by the side of the road in a big house with an arched front in the classic form of Ibiza's country *tiendas*. She beckoned me into her lair, a cross between a shop, a bar and a front room. She was a creaky old lady, but in fairly good shape, though there were lines on her face that seemed to go down to the bone, and around her nose were ancient blackheads, so ingrained that it would have taken wire wool and sulphuric acid to remove them. As she leaned over a table scratching with a pencil on a piece of paper to see how much I owed her, her whole person seemed to reek of petrol. But she had good clean, strong-looking teeth – perhaps the effect of her daily gargle with the gas.

Eulalia must be one of the last people in Europe selling petrol privately. 'I've been doing it for forty-odd years.' She prefers not to reveal her age, but she has three married daughters who all have children, and one of her grand-daughters is old enough to be studying, 'oh, what's it called, it's *moderno*, something to do with computers,' at the University of Barcelona.

It was a disappointment to discover that she buys her petrol from the *gasolinera* like everybody else. I imagined her cutting out the middle-man, having barrels of crude oil delivered to the house by a friendly North-Sea oil rig and making the petrol up herself in her bathtub. No, she has a friend in the village who picks it up for her at the Campsa petrol-station in a big metal drum. She pays him for his trouble, but since her mark-up on the Campsa price is roughly 100 per cent she can afford to.

Whether all this is illegal she isn't sure, but there has been the occasional snooper. 'One day a man came in a big foreign car, maybe a Mercedes, and he asked me, "Are you the woman who sells the petrol privately?" Now, I believe if you tell lies you don't have a good life, so I answered him "Yes". Then he bought just half-a-litre, and I never saw him again.'

Legal or not, she knows she provides a useful service and she enjoys the gratitude. A lot of her trade comes from ingenuous foreigners such as myself who forget that despite Ibiza's recent arrival in the twentieth century there is not yet an all-night petrol-station around every corner. One man, she says with a small smile of satisfaction, had been pushing a large motorbike for 4km in the summer heat and was nearly dying of exhaustion when he chanced upon her *tienda*. 'He almost fell at my feet.'

She took me round the back in the moonlight, unlocked the door of her petrol-store and busied herself with a long rubber tube and a watering-can specially adapted for her unusual purpose with an extended spout clamped on with a piece of rag. Adjusting her headscarf she bent down unsteadily and sucked on the tube, then stuck it in the can and in a few seconds the clear liquid began to flow. 'Sometimes it comes up into my mouth,' she chuckled. 'But I'm used to it now.'

A few weeks later it happened again. This time I broke down just outside Santa Gertrudis on a Sunday morning, so I left the Mini under a palm tree by the roadside, walked to the village and sat outside the Bar Costa with a *café con leche* wondering what to do next. Steve and Hanna don't go out much, they just come to the village now and then to pick up their mail from the post room by the church, so it was another piece of Ibiza synchronicity that we met when we did. Steve is a painter. He is unusual among the island's brush-wielding residents in two ways: he's under thirty-five, and he's good. During an earlier stage of his career he painted murals. His is the brilliant *trompe l'oeil* of Renaissance arches, gardens and what-have-you on the side wall of a tennis court at Pike's, the rock stars' hotel near San Antonio. He has done a city-scape in a disco and a sea-scape in Hanna's son Sean's bedroom. Probably his most famous work, though, is in London: an express-train that seems to be powering its way over the road and into the shopping centre at Shepherd's Bush Green.

After the mural period there followed a dramatic change of style, partly as a result of decline in demand for murals, and his current paintings are as different as can be imagined: large, fluid, expressive abstracts suggesting the interplay of elemental forces. Paint is flung and dripped and poured and scraped, as though the medium itself as well as the personality of the painter have been unleashed from the constraints of painting to order.

On the next table at the Bar Costa was Hanna, beautiful and Germanly cool, but smiling the unmistakable feeling-groovy smile of a long-term neo-Ibicenco. The nearest *gaso-*

linera, she told me, was the one outside the city. Too far to walk, and no fun to hitch. But maybe Steve could help. He came out of the bar having paid the bill, wearing white shoes, white leggings, a white T-shirt, white teeth. The only things that weren't white were his left-over suntan and short blond hair, which were both the colour of cornfields. Sure, he could help. There was a full tank in the bike. He left me with an empty wine-bottle full of petrol and an invitation to lunch.

The two of them and Sean live in the hills outside San Mateo in a house that sits on the borderline between simplicity and glamour. There are clear signs of a hippie past – Hanna's macramé wall-hanging in the bathroom (macramé never went out of fashion in Ibiza) and her vegetarianism, which is repudiated by Sean, who disgraces himself by wanting *bratwurst* and Westphalia ham – but even clearer signs that in the nineties what is more important by far than all the back-to-nature pseudo-primitive stuff is comfort. The house, a restored *casa payesa*, has electricity, running water, and a TV in a prominent position on the floor of a living room whose walls are hung with Steve's paintings. Sean watches Bond films on the video in his room.

Despite the long journey Ca'n Vinyes has made between its earliest incarnation as a basic sort of farmhouse, little more sophisticated than a mud hut, and a modern dream home with its own art gallery, its architecture is more or less unchanged. You walk in through a cool white *entrada*, still with its olive press in the corner, and into the rectangular *porxo* which would have seen most of the day-to-day activity of the household and where its products would have been displayed, as they still are. Leading off the *porxo* up a small flight of steps at either end of the room are a bedroom which looks out over the courtyard through two arched windows, and a kitchen with a fireplace and a parrot in lollipop colours who squawks so noisily that Hanna has considered silencing it in the manner of her forebears at Ca'n Vinyes when they needed a chicken for the pot.

It's said that there are more artists per square metre in Hackney than anywhere else in Europe. If this is true Ibiza must give London E8 a run for its money, because every other person you meet on the island professes to do something with a brush, a pencil or a chisel. This may be due as much to the indisputable fact that Ibiza attracts artists as to the idea, which most neo-Ibicencos would probably subscribe to, that deep down we are all artists and that all it takes is Ibiza's liberating atmosphere for us to be able to describe ourselves as such.

According to Elena Ruiz Sastre, director of Ibiza's Museum of Contemporary Art, the reasons they came here in the first half-dozen decades of the century, blazing the trail later to be followed by hippies and package tourists, are more or less the same reasons they are still coming: it is peaceful, it is beautiful, and compared to Paris, London or Frankfurt it is still relatively cheap as long as you are prepared to forgo meat, cheese and nights on the town.

The museum is housed in a collection of buildings within the town's Renaissance fortifications, among them the ancient armoury, the gunpowder store and cavalry stables. It grew out of the Biennial exhibitions of Ibiza art, begun in 1962, which had begged and borrowed various sites including the old convent of Santo Domingo and the then unfinished Archaeological Museum of Puig d'es Molins, until 1968 when it found permanent lodging in the city walls. As a site for a museum it's nearly unbeatable. The main gallery is a fine four-square stone building, whitewashed and cool inside, high up on a bulwark. Just across the courtyard, perched on a dizzying corner of the walls, is the Director's personal office in the miniature pyramid of a watch-tower.

And below the main gallery, deep inside the walls, are the echoing vaults where nowadays the Museum shows the work of individual artists. From every vantage point there are postcard views up to the old city and down to Sa Penya and the port, which are a good deal more attractive to the eye than many of the paintings on display. In 1984 the museum fell victim to economic problems (it is funded entirely by the Town Hall) and political squabbles about its future. For five years it remained shut, to wails of 'cultural suicide' from Ibiza's chattering classes, and is now undergoing what its director describes as a *recuperación*. Evidently it has suffered from clumsy management in the past, to the extent that until this year there was no detailed inventory of its collections.

Elena Ruiz is an elegantly dressed, serious woman of thirty-one whose hairdo, tied back in the Spanish style, reinforces the impression of brisk professionalism. She studied History of Art on the mainland, married an Ibicenco eight years ago and came to Ibiza 'for sentimental reasons'. The works of art in her charge have little in common beyond the fact that all of them are donated, not purchased (although in special cases there may be a *'precio simbólico'*); also the fact that almost all were created by artists who were born in Ibiza, have lived here, or at least dropped in from time to time. There are representatives of 'different tendencies, different schools, different styles', says Elena Ruiz, therefore it is difficult to generalize, but the museum has always supported abstraction and its collection of abstract art is 'strong'.

Of all the painters represented in the museum not many are well-known outside the ranks of specialists. 'Historically the great names are very few, very few,' admits Elena Ruiz. There has been no Matisse, no Pollock, no Hockney (although he would appreciate Ibiza), and in some respects the island seems a poorer place artistically than Mallorca, which was home to Joan Miró and has recently turned out the wunderkind of the Spanish art world, Miguel Barceló. Poor communications, and the absence of New York's or

Paris's network of agents and galleries, have meant that most ambitious artists tended to consider Ibiza as a place of refuge and inspiration rather than as a permanent home.

If not always for quality, then for quantity and variety the island is assured at least a paragraph or two in the history of art. At the turn of the century a tightly knit group of mostly local painters, led by Narcis Puget, specialized in inoffensive landscapes. The Café Bohemia – speciality: absinthe topped up with water and syrup of lemons – was Ibiza's equivalent of Les Deux Magots and a favourite haunt of then-famous figures such as the writer and painter, Santiago Rusiñol, and his friend, José Costa Ferrer, known as 'Picarol'. This first wave of artistic visitors was mainly Catalan-speaking.

The thirties brought a welcome breath of internationalism. Man Ray and Le Corbusier passed through, and it's pleasing to speculate on the influence of the *casa payesa* on the latter's own cool, plain, white forms. By this time the Café Bohemia had been supplanted by another artistic hangout in the shape of an old windmill converted into a makeshift nightclub, the first in Ibiza's history, which brought Weimar decadence to the olive groves of the *campo*. Later on there were visits from Tristan Tzara and Walter Gropius.

Among the pioneering generation of neo-Ibicencos one of the most distinguished was the Swiss Hans Hinterreiter, who had his first exhibition in Ibiza in 1965, under the aegis of English gallery owner Ivan Spence. Spence, as much as Hinterreiter and the rest, was a part of Old Ibiza, the naive and wild Ibiza that still existed in the fifties and early sixties when the island was not yet, as he put it, 'devastated by the winds of touristic change'.

Spence was born in Berlin in 1902 of a Russian mother and a Scottish father and had spent most of his life as a respectable lawyer when in his late fifties he turned up on Ibiza. He lived in Dalt Vila in a big house with two pistachio trees in the courtyard, and took trips to the country in a cart drawn by his donkey Emma with his three dogs running behind. He was a grey-bearded, good-humoured giant whose unconventional nature was conventional among his circle.

He shared his house and life with Heidi Rheistahl, a German weaver who, said a friend, 'knew about colour and understood artists'. Ivan, too, understood artists. His gallery ran from 1961 to 1975, during which time it staged 142 individual shows by artists from more than thirty countries. More than Ibiza town's artistic centre, the gallery was the nub of its social life, at least among *forasteros*. There was a different exhibition every fortnight in the summer, which meant there would be two opening nights a month, and Ivan Spence opening nights were the best fun in town. People fell over themselves to be invited to these wildly fashionable free-form events that had more in common with hippy happenings than conventional glass-of-dry-white-wine gallery-openings. When the gallery died a chapter in the island's social history came to an end.

'Whoever we were that arrived on the island during those years,' Spence reminisced shortly before he died, 'we found ourselves stripped of elegance and dirtiness, of beliefs and customs. No longer were we tinkers, tailors, soldiers, sailors, bakers or candlestick-makers; no longer were we poor man, rich man, beggarman, thief; no longer doctors, lawyers or architects. From then on we were "minimal people"; we were ourselves, each one of us free in our own nakedness and fascinated by each other . . .

'In those days there were "minimal people" who wrote books, played music, sang, wove, cooked or painted. Everyone did "their own thing", enjoying their idleness and making love. Then the message went around the world: "There is an island that is lovable," they said. And some people came to love the island. But many more arrived, elegantly dressed, as if Ibiza were no more than a famous brothel. How the gods of old would have hated them!'

If you didn't get your big break as an artist from Spence you got it from Carl van der Voort, an American whose eponymous gallery is a few steps away from the Museum of Contemporary Art in Dalt Vila. Carl's gallery was once a guardroom for the town's Roman fortifications and is now a cool stone arched space, a perfect backdrop for the severely chic abstraction in which it specializes. At the far end of the gallery can be seen the equally chic and severe figure of Catalina Verdera, a former director of the Contemporary Art Museum and now director at Carl van der Voort.

Van der Voort was part of the second wave, the post-Second World War art crowd who were fleeing less from war and repression than from *urbanización*, stress and the cost of living. In a sense, he suggests, it was the memory of the first wave that produced the second. Among the pre-War art scene in Ibiza had been people who now occupied positions of strength and influence in the international art world. These people now told their protégés that if they wanted a good, cheap place to live and paint they should do what their elders had done and move to Ibiza. When Carl first arrived in 1954 'the place hadn't changed for probably hundreds of years. The town was still the Ibiza town of the 1890s, except that there was a little electrical plant which functioned intermittently. In the fifties and early sixties there was no money-economy here, so anyone with any money at all, francs or marks or dollars or pounds, was rich. You could rent ruins or *corrals* in the country for nothing.' He remembers monumental parties of 500–600 people – 'artists, actors, musicians, deadbeats' – in remote country *fincas* in the very early sixties. 'A lot of the people who went to the real legendary parties ended up in San Francisco. So you could say those parties were the start of the whole hippie movement.'

One of Ibiza's greatest sights is a natural wonder so eye-catching it probably causes car crashes. You see it almost wherever there is greenery, even in patches of land long since swallowed up by suburban sprawl, though its real centre of operations is the idyllic valley of Santa Inés. It begins surreptitiously in mid-January and, for a few giddy weeks, tricks you into thinking the year has done a forward somersault and ended up in late spring.

When the almond-blossom comes, dusting the bare boughs with a sugary whiteness that occasionally blushes demurely into Laura Ashley pink, it is an emotional event. Not much more of the damp and dark and the endless empty winter evenings, it seems to signify. We're in the home straight. For these few weeks, *las flores de almendro* become a kind of benign social cult, like a small-scale version of the cherry blossom mania that sweeps Japan in spring. As soon as it arrives, blossom-freaks scour the countryside for branches blown down by the wind (to gather from the trees themselves would be to go against an unspoken ethical code). It is the done thing to comment on the flowers when they emerge, and then more and more excitedly, as they turn the valley of Santa Inés into something resembling a gigantic bridal showroom, for people to ask each other: 'Is your almond blossom out yet?', or, rhetorically, 'Isn't it just the most incredible sight?'

And it is. By moonlight, on walks with Monica down the hill from her house, the landscape had the supernatural ultraviolet brightness of an Alpine valley after a snowfall. And driving down towards Ibiza town one early morning it was as if a vast cloud of pinkish smoke had drifted out of nowhere and settled on the plain.

'Urban Leisure: War On Boredom' was the headline in
La Prensa on 11 February. The town was making nothing less
than 'a declaration of war' on the habitual tedium of the off-
season, the newspaper claimed, in order to liven up the
remaining months before the collective madness of the *temporada turística*. Chess-games in the warmth of a bar, basketball
in the playground of Sa Graduada college, Visconti's *The
Leopard* at the Cine Cartago, the artier of Ibiza town's two
cinemas, or a bracing walk through Dalt Vila, 'a veritable city
within a city', were a few of the distractions proposed for
those who chose to rebel against the dire soap-and-game-
show fare dished up nightly by Spanish television. Outside
the city however the cultural stagnation was total, so when
a new gallery was due to open one evening in Santa Inés the
news spread through the countryside like wildfire.

I went round to Steve and Hanna's for dinner beforehand. Nearly everyone there was German, and so was the
food. There was goose fat in a plastic pot which was to be
spread on thin slices of rye bread, and rubbery Bavarian
cheese with a smell of bad plumbing.

Steve was working up a one-man show for a gallery in
London and needed some words for the catalogue. He had
got in touch with Elena Ruiz Sastre at the Museum of Contemporary Art, she had come to his house and spent a long
time contemplating the paintings with their panels in mul-
tiples of three, the studio outside with the old millstone still
in place and the stone floor spattered with paint; then she
had gone away and written rather gushingly about it all.

In Santa Inés the Toyotas were filling up the village
square. The new gallery, called Cap Quadrat after the Ibicenco nickname for Germans (it means 'square head'), was
a tiny room sandwiched between a restaurant under a palm
tree and a shop selling leather goods. It was a candidate for
Smallest Art Space in the Universe, which meant that while
half-a-dozen people stood swigging *vino payés* in the gallery
itelf another hundred were spilling out into the square where
someone had fixed up a fire in a rusty old wheelbarrow.
There was a clatter of Northern European voices.

The first artist to put his work on the postage-stamp-sized walls of this brave new venture was Jean Willi who has lived and worked in Santa Inés for years and has written a book set in the village. In the eyes of locals however he is still a 'square head' despite the fact he comes from Switzerland. For the Cap Quadrat gallery's inaugural show he had produced one big murky painting of beams in the roof of a *finca*, which occupied an entire wall, and a number of fine blue-and-brown prints, somewhat Japanese-influenced in their restrained use of colour and line, and suggestive of rural themes. By the time we arrived one of the prints had already been snapped up and bore an orange sticker to say so. It was a familiar image: on a field of wisteria blue, a single almond-tree decked out in white.

Another of the prints, as yet unsold, was a delicate piece of work Jean explained was intended to evoke a pile of vine twigs at the edge of a field. I thought guiltily of my own vineyard, which I had been neglecting for months and would have to be rid of any precocious weeds in time for the rising sap and temperatures of spring.

By the drinks' table was a tableau of artists. One of them, an Englishman called Timothy, had shoulder-length white hair, a black suit and satin scarf, and an accent redolent of Old Chelsea. 'I haven't painted for eight months, you know, I'm going through what you might call a *dormant* phase,' he announced to no one in particular.

Beside the wheelbarrow with its cargo of coals I talked to Katerina, a dead-ringer for *Eastenders'* Pauline with the same weary smile and nicotine hair, but with the addition of a long Indian-cotton skirt and a thick line of kohl around both eyes. There was a commotion over by the drinks' table, and shortly the crowd parted to admit Timothy, who was complaining bitterly about the cold. Still clutching his glass he lay down on the ground in front of the wheelbarrow and rested his feet on the edge, within inches of the fire. He was wearing black espadrilles. The cry went up: it was a happening! A piece of free spontaneous expression, just like in the sixties! 'No no no,' shouted Timothy protestingly from his position on the ground. 'It's not a happening – I'm simply warming up my feet.'

In the midst of the Santa Eulalia English-speaking crowd, who hang out at M&M's bar and gossip about each other, lives Barry Flanagan, one of the handful of living 'Ibiza artists' who are genuinely internationally reputed. Others, arguably, are the Germans Heinz Mack, Erwin Bechtold and Rainer Pfnur, who according to an interview, 'paints almost nude amidst Grecian vines with music from Beethoven, Bach or John Cage'; and the Chilean, Andres Monreal, whose brilliant blend of Breughel and Surrealism adorns the walls of the Bar Costa in Santa Gertrudis.)

I met Barry at a sunny table outside M&M's. He was tall and white-haired with a friendly freckly face, and sartorially bohemian in a bottle-green cord jacket, collar and tie. He was sitting alone, being a little early for a rendezvous with the man he calls his 'spontaneous fixer', an unpublished author of three novels including one set on Ibiza in Roman times.

Barry Flanagan is not very keen on small talk. When I rang him at his studio there were silences so long and dark I thought the line had gone dead. And now at the table he shook hands politely, grunted something and continued to sip his coffee while the woman on the next table talked at him about her five-year-old daughter's precocious talent for dress-designing. When eventually our conversation ground into life I asked him why he had come to Ibiza. He leant forward in his chair and opened his eyes wide; then he said, in a conspiratorial near-whisper: 'I came here to be a father.'

And was it a good place to be a father? This time he almost shouted: 'No!' And then, whispering again, 'It's a good place to be a mother.' At this the woman next to us leant across and asked him if he, like her brilliant daughter, had had an early talent. He turned to her and said civilly that no, by no means, he'd had to go through school and endure architecture college and realize he couldn't do Calculus – 'you know, the simple things' – before he discovered . . . (he paused, then opened his eyes wide again and made a gesture that suggested 'making things with the hands') . . . 'This!'

We went to the Museum to see Élena Ruiz. We were late and she had gone to lunch, so we looked round the exhibition in the old gunpowder room where Barry was to have his show in June. He paced up and down the room and said he'd have them paint the arched stone ceiling white and put a dark green carpet on the floor. 'It's mostly work I've done here. I've got about forty drawings; also some things in hessian, or sacking, which hang on the wall. They've all got this big hole in the middle. It has a religious sort of overtone – the thing it reminds me of is those vestments, the ones that priests wear. Do you know what I mean? Also there's a sort of Zen connection there.'

While we dawdled past the paintings he was quietly damning about the derivative nature of most Ibiza art and the lack of a real support-system for such artists as choose to live and work here. What was the difference between Mallorca and Ibiza, I wondered aloud, that allowed Mallorca to have Joan Miró and a dozen galleries? Barry stopped in his tracks and said in the same half-whisper he had used to answer my earlier question about why he was here: 'Ibiza's got no middle class.' It's the middle class which provides the buyers of the work, the public for the galleries that show it and the intellectuals to arbitrate over its quality and create taste, and Ibicenco society has only a very small sophisticated bourgeoisie. On one hand there are farmers and country people who don't care a fig for *haute culture*; on the other there are the *nouveaux riches*, drug barons and summer jetset who, if they were buying art would buy it in Barcelona or Milan rather than Ibiza.

We stopped in front of a big op-ish canvas in peculiar

shades of orange and green in complex bold geometrical patternings. It was signed H. Hinterreiter, 1975–77. Hans was a neighbour of Barry Flanagan's. 'The important thing is that he came here with all his intellectual stuff worked out,' said Barry gnomically, tapping his temple. As I understood him, he meant you have to have some project, some kind of momentum, or else the island sucks you in and you never reach your full creative potential. In Barry's case he was already well on the road to fame, if not fortune, when he came here six years ago and seems to have had his 'intellectual stuff' worked out at least since his famous bronze Leaping Hare. So he can arrange his creative life between London, Ibiza and wherever else they want his work – which now includes Barcelona where he was taking part in a Homage to Miró, and the Reina Sofia museum in Madrid.

His studio is a big, slightly dilapidated house near Santa Eulalia. It was hard to find, but Barry had drawn me an immaculately detailed map in purple ink, showing individual dustbins by the roadside and a *corral* of Butane bottles outside his local *tienda*. If I hadn't known it was *casa* Flanagan I could have guessed. On the wall by the front door was a Jaws-sized leaping hare chipped out of the plaster with a blunt instrument. Barry took a few minutes to answer the door, opened it with a grunt of welcome and then vanished again. The house was sparsely furnished, as though by squatters. At one end of the large sitting-room was a small wooden stage crowded with *objets* – a grotesque Edward Lear figure of a Mermaid with dinner-plate ears, carved heads and busts, and a small bronze hare. All over the walls were scrawled drawings of life-sized women; around the fireplace the drawings gave way to a jumble of scribbled utterances – nonsense poems whose absurdity made an ungraspable kind of sense.

In the garden were three more hares. Two of them formed part of a rusty iron sculpture, sinuous figures facing each other solemnly like Egyptian priests. (It's called 'Humourless Omen'.) The third was a larger piece in the same rusting metal, this time in the 'leaping' pose. And there was a fourth inside in his studio, a wax model eventually to be cast in bronze.

You could see the change in Barry's garden. The almonds' whiteness had gone, like melting snow, and given way to the vivid green of their early leaves and the felt-covered pods of young nuts. By March, as if to compensate for the loss of the almond-blossom, there are other trees in flower – peach, apricot, pomegranate, cherry and apple – and the orchards become a whole cosmetic-counter of shades of pink, purple and ivory white. On the hillsides there are wild irises and daffodils with a fragrance long since bred out of the domestic variety, big white daisies called margaritas and pink *cistus albidus* with a simple shape like a child's drawing. In the woods behind the vineyard I found a bee orchid, its dark flower fringed with deep gold velvet.

Spring in the Mediterranean is a voluptuous, fast-paced season with none of the stealth and subtlety of springs further north. This is not the damp, slow, gentle time it is in England, when it is as though nature is waking up with a hangover. In Ibiza it hits you right between the eyes in mid-March with the full complement of seasonal accessories, all-present-and-correct: lambs, warm breezes, baby-blue sky, birdsong. On a backroad I saw a hoopoe, just landed from Africa, with a show-stopping black-and-orange headdress.

All this is not to say that, come April, there won't be a few days of merciless rainfall that has farmers smiling and owners of old *fincas* rushing for plastic buckets to catch the drips from their old roofs. In town, this is the time when Raybanned multitudes reappear from their winter haunts in Paris and Munich and peck each other on both cheeks outside the Cafeteria Montesol. In Santa Gertrudis the talk was of the latest scheme to part tourists from their money. Renée Cohen was organizing a mud-wrestling troupe – the Ibiza All-Stars, recruited from local gyms – to perform in the discos. At around the same time Erika, from the Tyrol via South Kensington, was holding court in the Bar Costa to tell the world about her fleet of rickshaws, then as for the preceding five or six summers, poised to revolutionize transport on Ibiza as soon as Richard Branson, Anita Roddick or some other green-minded millionaire could be persuaded to part with the sponsorship money.

On 20 March, the vernal equinox, there was an old-fashioned Ibiza party in a farmhouse near San Miguel. Seven hundred people, Balearic Beat from an immense sound-system, and every known drug. Fernando was ecstatic. 'What a fiesta, baby! There was *everyone* from Ibiza, like old times. It was paying to enter, but a free bar. I go home at three of the morning. For me, is the best party of this year.'

For anyone who stayed any longer than Fernando it was less fun. Earlier in the evening Erika had seen a group of suspiciously smart young men, strangers in Santa Gertrudis, walk into a bar and wish everyone good evening. 'I was gonna go to the party but at that moment I just knew – I guess my good angel told me it was a bad idea,' she said.

At 4 a.m. the farmhouse was surrounded by police who turned off the music and turned on the lights, searched everyone and took names and addresses. Meanwhile the cars lining the country roads outside were removed with a crane. The drugs haul was impressive.

The morning after the bust the rumours were flying. Cynics were saying it was a typical *razzia de primavera*, a spring raid, a piece of social spring-cleaning intended to sweep the island clean of undesirables before the tourists arrived in May and June. It was even whispered that the police had not only known about the party beforehand but had actually set up the whole thing in the knowledge that every drug-taking freak for miles round would be drawn into their trap like moths to a flame.

Certainly there were more police around than usual – the blue-and-white uniformed local variety, not the fearsome Guardia Civil who only deal with the glamorous end of Ibicenco crime and are consequently resented by the down-trodden Policia Local – and everybody remarked how much more active they seemed. Santa Gertrudis had a taste of this unaccustomed efficiency one Monday morning when two fresh-faced Policia Local were seen strutting around the village giving parking-tickets to all the cars parked on the wrong side of the street. Carlos Sansegundo, a sculptor who has his studio above the Bar Costa, was sitting outside the bar when it happened. 'Well,' he said, pulling on his first beer of the week, 'they get all these extra police in at this time of year. I suppose they have to find something for them to do.'

All over the island, not only in the police station, spring is the signal for a general sprucing-up in time for summer. Mattresses hang out of upper windows; tractors rearrange the fields into clean-cut cocoa-coloured rows. One day in March one of the local papers reported that the folklore group of San Juan had decided to restore the old village well, the Pou de Labritja, and to revive the ancient *ballada* traditionally danced round the well every 5 August. There was even a campaign to refresh the beaches with £¼m-worth of new sand. There was a scrubbing and a polishing and a painting and a fixing. It is the time of year when houses are tradition-ally brightened up with a lick of *cal*, the lime-based paint that maintains Ibiza's fame as 'the white island'. At one time the *cal* came from ovens in the countryside, usually in the woods within reach of the copious fuel their operation required. Last year there was but one working *horno de cal* left, in San Mateo, and now even that has packed up. ('In the end people couldn't be bothered. It was a big pain,' said the girl behind the counter at the village shop.) Now most of the island's *cal* comes from *fuera* – outside – via a warehouse on the road to San Antonio, where José Rafael Bonet Juan purveys the stuff to owners of Ibiza's *casas de campo* as his father and grand-father did before him. Ibiza's traditional houses were white-washed inside and out. The amount of whiteness used reflected not only the sunlight but the economic status of the owner, because *cal* cost money. In poorer households whitewash is still reserved for the roof and a small area around each window, those being the places most in need of its effect, while the chic-er kind of *casa* is positively drenched with it.

José Bonet sells 30,000 kilos of *cal* every year and says that April and May are by far the strongest months. You need roughly thirty kilos to do a whole house inside and out, but not many people can still be bothered. 'There's more paint sold these days than *cal*, much more. It's because with paint you don't have to do it every year. But I prefer *cal*. It lets the wall breathe, and the other advantages are that it's a disinfectant and keeps off mosquitoes.' Doesn't it smell when you're painting it on? 'No way! It's *paint* that gives off gases and poisons people. No, to me the smell of *cal* is the best smell there is.'

Some people think there is more to *cal* than meets the eye. It is said that only women may do the whitewashing and that, *cal* being unfriendly to evil spirits as well as mosquitoes, it once formed part of a semi-religious ritual that took place in Holy Week.

José Rafael Bonet Juan is cynical about such things. The religious significance he thinks is due to the fact that houses might have been touched up a bit on special occasions such as village *festes patronals*, which are all on saints' days. 'And the only reason women do it is because women end up doing all the housework, anyway, don't they?'

In tourist San Antonio, battered by successive storms of bad publicity for its lager-louts and poor amenities, what was needed was not so much a new coat of paint as a full repair-job. 'We've had a reputation for yobbos and aggro on a large scale,' admitted Francisco Linares of the town's Patronato de Turismo, 'and we've got to stop the scandals. What's more 1991 was a bad season. The *temporada* only lasted for two months. People were scared by it. But the summer of 1992 will be better than last year, and the best for two years.'

Outside Señor Linares' office the town looked like a bad day in Beirut. The entire promenade had been dug up leaving pedestrians to pick their way among the rubble, traffic was clogging up a hastily arranged one-way system and the air was thick with noise. Where the previous summer tourists had slurped on over-priced ice-creams in pavement cafés, workmen now sat on grey breeze-blocks with their *bocadillos*.

'As you see, at the moment we are doing a lot of *reformas*,' explained Señor Linares, warming to his theme. 'There will be gardens, fountains, even a "cybernetic fountain" that moves up and down to the rhythm of the music.' That was Phase One. In Phase Two: 'There will be a whole load of little gardens – in fact the whole town will look like a garden. We are widening streets and pedestrianizing them. We are building a covered sports centre, a velodrome, a swimming pool.'

It certainly seemed that something was afoot. The harbour road had been moved a full ten metres nearer the sea, extending the area of garden/fountain/promenade in which tourists would eventually be able to disport themselves. On a grass verge there was now a row of young trees which would turn the road into a shady avenue if the trees ever escaped being snapped in half by vandals. Another innovation was a huge white egg-shaped object incorporating a model ship suspended in a hole at its centre – a piece of municipal sculpture.

Until the late 1950s Sant Antoni de Portmany was a fishing village with little more to it than a fine old church, a scattering of houses along the beach and a perfect untouched sickle-shaped bay stretching out to the west which now pullulates with hotels, apartments, souvenir shops and restaurants serving Full English Breakfasts. An 1868 engraving I saw in an antique shop shows the local priest walking to work on a dirt track that leads past one other house before reaching the church. There is not another living thing in the picture apart from a scrawny dog, or is it a sheep, nosing quietly about at the edge of the path. As recently as 1955 San

Antonio was, according to one long-term resident of Ibiza, 'an absolutely knock-out village'. It is now either an absolutely knock-out cheap 'n' cheerful holiday resort or a mess, depending on your point of view.

Quite apart from all the physical improvements it is making, San Antonio is also making adjustments to its idea of the desirable customer. At the moment roughly half their tourists come from the UK. Much as the town is grateful to the British, it appears to want fewer of them. 'It was a mistake to dedicate so much of our effort to the British market,' said Señor Linares.

They want people with more money. The average expenditure, or 'spend' in marketing terminology, by a San An package tourist on a two-week holiday is scandalously little. They also want more elderly people, because 'Third Age tourism', as it's charmingly known in Spanish, is one of the few types that happens equally in the low season and in the high. As I walked to the car I saw a group of Third Agers picking their way through the potholes, pulling their coats tightly about them against the wind.

Above all, they don't want any more louts. As anyone who read a British newspaper in the summer of 1989 will know, San Antonio gained an unfortunate reputation as a place where a certain type of British male (one who enjoys the occasional small glass of sherry) liked to come for his holidays. The UK press was crammed with stories of drunk and disorderly Brits roaming the streets at 4 a.m. and puking in fountains, beating up Germans and terrorizing old ladies who had made the mistake of walking home through the wild West End. There were some horrid acts of violence. A British tourist once bit the ear off a local policeman. Jesus Moreno Gutierrez was pushed off his motorbike and died as his skull cracked on the pavement. The six British tourists involved were never charged. 'It was an accident, really,' said Antonio Marí Tur, the mayor, desperate not to scare off any more sensible tourists.

At that time an evening stroll around the West End was

an unpleasant experience. Brian Newman, an island celeb who presents his own English-language radio programme and owns Newman's Bar-Bistro in Santa Eulalia, recalls: 'Quite frankly it was frightening. There was just this sea, that's the only way I can describe it, a sea of Union-Jack shorts and tattoos and bottles flying around . . . That whole time was particularly horrific because I was managing a discotheque at the time, the San Francisco club in San Antonio.' The town's wounds were partly self-inflicted. 'The tourist reps got backhanders for taking them round from bar to bar, having a drink in every bar, doing the Conga from place to place – you can imagine it, can't you? The barmen were wallies for paying the reps and the reps were wallies for accepting it. The day Club 18–30 went bust I was delighted.'

All that has changed now, claims the upbeat Señor Linares, adopting the party line that involves furiously downplaying any suggestion of nuisance. Compared to two years ago, last summer there was 'hardly any trouble'. Still, San An wasn't taking any chances. There would be ten more local policemen on duty this year – thirty-three men in all, not counting the twenty Guardia Civil who swagger into town every summer – plus a very un-Mediterranean municipal law about not drinking in the streets.

Some people think it's all too little, too late and taking too long. Nobody wants cheap all-in package tours any more, they say, and if they did they wouldn't come to a place where you can't see the sea from your high-rise hotel for a forest of other high-rise hotels. 'San Antonio has panicked,' said Brian Newman. 'In my view all they're doing is putting gold-plated hinges on the door after the horse has well and truly bolted.'

Most English-speaking people in Ibiza would respect Mr Newman's opinions even if they didn't agree with him. A good number of the 1458 legalized British expatriates (plus an unknown number of the illegal ones and thousands of English-language students) listen to his show on Radio Popular 89.1FM every night of the week from nine to ten. It consists of an amiable mixture of music from the Hollies to House, ads for businesses like the Mandarin Chinese Restaurant in Es Canar ('Mandy is your host, and guarantees your tastebuds a real treat'), the occasional news-bulletin, and the minimum of jolly DJ banter, all apart from the music delivered in Britain's soft Mancunian twang.

Brian Newman likes a joke. On April Fool's Day he told a good one which neatly illustrates something of his listeners' propensities. As the final news item that evening he informed a stunned English community that as from 1 January 1993 the Spanish licensing laws would be changed in keeping with the British system. Alcohol would not be sold after 11 p.m. and, worst of all, optics, those Puritan devices which ensure that not more or less than a ¼ gill of liquor is ever dispensed in one go, would be replacing the Spanish non-system where the amount you get depends on the generosity of the barman. The switchboard was jammed with worried English dipsos. What would they do on a Saturday night? What was Spain coming to when you couldn't get a decent drink without ordering a triple? There would be an epidemic of drinking at home. And what about the tourist trade? It was a calamity. One woman, a bar-owner from Port d'es Torrent, told him, 'Well that's it, we're selling up and moving back.'

Brian wouldn't sell up and move back for the world. He came on a holiday twenty-six years ago, came again four or five times and then decided to stay. 'I love this place. When I came here I just thought, my God, there's this other world! It became an obsession. There's this *pull* to Ibiza, there's this inward force, and it can be a good force or a bad force depending on how you deal with it, but it's irresistible.'

Brian's own family live in Cheshire. 'The last time I went back there I felt like a foreigner. My brother took me out to a pub. It was very strange. My brother said to me, "What's wrong with you, are you not enjoying it?" The pub was absolutely jam-packed with people but there was hardly any noise. I said, "Yeah, it's OK, but there must be one hundred and seventy people in here and they're all whispery. There's no *feeling*.'' He said, "What do you want them to do, get up on the tables and do a flamenco dance?'' I don't know, to me they just exist; I live.'

That spring I lived in a small room in a cottage at the top of the long wooded slope that carries you down from the village houses of San Rafael to the towers of San Antonio.

The first time I saw the house, hidden in a glade of pine trees fringed with overgrown terraces, I'd been to visit Monica's daughter, Christine, who had just moved into it from Brixton with her two baby sons. We drank two bottles of cheap red wine, and the next morning when I tried to drive away I reversed the Mini into the soft red soil of her neighbour's vegetable patch, partially destroying a recently planted crop of broad beans. I was stuck.

Christine suggested we ask next door at the Big House. So we tiptoed up to the big wooden gates, past a coop of chickens and through a wondrous garden planted with flower-beds and rockeries and flowering shrubs. Stone paths led between the borders, past little ponds and fig trees and a fountain. One wall of the house was a riot of clematis.

I knocked on the door and a tall white-haired man wearing new black jeans and a Navy sweater came out and was fraffly, fraffly nice. 'Oh no, what a simply *dreadful* drag,' he said. He had a manner that combined affability with authority, like a prep school headmaster. And he was more English than morning tea.

Everyone in Ibiza, simply everyone, knows Robert Hornby-Smith and his graceful wife Isabel. More than the pillars of the English community, they are its corner-stone.

Their garden-parties are as legendary as their garden. They are as close to the aristocracy as you can get on an island where the niceties of social class have been muddied by money and glamour.

In the context of Ibiza the Hornby-Smiths are both unique and typical. Unique, because no one else has their patrician charm, wealth and restrained English taste all at once. Typical, because like all the other thousands of immigrants on the island they came here to escape from forces which, they felt, were preventing them becoming the people they wanted to be. More precisely, as Isabel related in her clear fluting voice, 'We wanted very much to escape from the restricting social life in England, where everybody does the same and thinks the same. Here, you know, we have friends of all sorts – and a few jailbirds thrown in for good measure.'

Different nationalities come to Ibiza for different reasons. The Germans came because it was cheap and inefficient enough for them to believe they were living the simple life. The Italians, because it was a bit like Sardinia or Capri but you wouldn't have to spend a fortune on body-guards. The Spanish only came in the 1970s when it was fashionable: before that they went to San Sebastian and Marbella and now they're all off to Mallorca to see the King.

The English came on a package tour, liked it and stayed. Ibiza, like England, has a small-scale, manmade landscape, and the social cosiness of islands. 'We wanted a holiday quickly, we were sick of the grey of England. It was forty-five pounds, wasn't it Robert? Forty-five pounds, and that included the fare and a fortnight's stay. We were in a frightfully scruffy hotel in San Antonio. We used to get lost on our motorbikes and end up down some little track somewhere. We would ask the way to Santa Eulalia and people wouldn't know, because they'd never been there.'

The vast majority of the English expats in Ibiza are retired and came here to do nothing, which provided you have the money is not only perilously easy but culturally acceptable. The Hornby-Smiths are retired too – they used to have a farm in Essex until the A12 went through it – but they have bucked the trend of alcoholic sloth and poured all their energy into Projects, mostly of a more-or-less ecological bent. Prince Charles would approve of the H-Ss who have bluish blood and greenish politics. Their entire *finca* is organically run: household waste is recycled where possible into garden compost, oranges and lemons are unsprayed, unwaxed, un-everything and the chickens are not fed on each other. A little shop on the estate sells their organic oranges, avocados, potatoes and eggs at untreated prices. Robert makes a more-or-less organic wine which is one of the better local efforts.

The couple are both zealous members of the island's branch of Friends of the Earth, which they wish had more local members. 'You don't really get that close to the Ibic-encos. I suppose it's the language, but one can't really know them socially.' They have lived here for seventeen years. 'What happened was,' said Robert, 'we met an Englishman who dabbled in property, and he found us this land, which was terraced but terribly overgrown. At that time land in this area was five pesetas a square metre [it is now 600–750 ptas/m²]. Another fellow was buying land at Portinatx at one peseta a square metre and his lawyer said, "Don't buy it, it's too expensive."'

'Our land was absolutely the poorest,' continued Isabel, 'but we had this idea that one could turn it into rich soil. We had to clear the land, but it was never a chore, it was absolutely the greatest pleasure. And everything, now, grows so wonderfully. Will you come and look at my *clematis amandiae*?'

Christine and I followed her through the garden and up some steps to a terrace from where the white flowers tumbled down to the ground in a gentle wave, as though someone had hung up a rich white eiderdown to dry there in the spring sunshine. The air was full of a sweet, clean fragrance. Isabel stood raptly, looking with a smile of delight over her sumptuous garden. To our left she pointed out her Judas Tree, an outrageous mass of purple flowers. Somewhere in the woods behind the house we could hear a cuckoo.

Isabel turned her face towards the sun and shut her eyes

for a moment. She seemed in a kind of ecstasy. 'Isn't it all *simply* divine?' she murmured.

One of the definitive descriptions of spring in the Mediterranean comes up in the *Song of Songs*. It mentions green figs and vines with 'tender grapes' that 'give a good smell'. Without wishing to accuse the Old Testament of inaccuracy, I used to wonder why there were green figs galore in Ibiza in April but no tender grapes. Perhaps vines in Palestine are more precocious. In my vineyard at Javier's house there were buds of pinkish fluff, turning orange and then a feeble green as the buds unfurled into new leaves, and a few weeks later there were clusters of minute flowers, each cluster the size of your little fingertip, which would eventually become bunches of grapes, but to talk about 'tender grapes' would be stretching the point.

Many of the *parras* I had planted were already dead; victims of a double holocaust of rabbits and a stampede of horses which had escaped from a farm over the hill and cantered through the vineyard ripping up everything in their path. And the weeds were bounding up again in forbidding clumps. *Practical Viticulture*, impractical as ever, gave no clues about either rabbits, horses or weeds, and Rudolf Steiner's biodynamic handbook was too busy waxing mystical about 'The Cultivated Plant and the Cosmic Environment' to concern itself with such banalities. Once again, local wisdom might have to be tapped.

I moved into the Hornby-Smiths' cottage as spring came to the fruit trees in its little garden. It was a peaceful place with an untroubled view of sea and greenery, but life made a sweet racket all around. Christine's children romped and screamed, and beyond a partition our Andalucian neighbours staged theatrical rows.

The big white house down the *camino* towards San Antonio belonged to the singer Lulu. In the old days she used to bring the BeeGees, but hadn't been back for years. Perhaps she'd been too busy sorting out her somewhat faded career. I used to sneak into her garden for morning swims, until one day she suddenly turned up with an entourage. There was a week of loud pool parties. Christine and I would tiptoe down the drive and eavesdrop for hours, crouching down with our ears at the fence.

I found a new walk along the old road that crept through the forest towards the hamlet of Buscastell. The track, for that's all it was, eventually emerged from the wood on to a slightly better *camino* which ran along a wall. Between this wall and the last pine trees of the forest was a large vineyard, planted on a slope on poor earth but apparently well-kept and recently worked over with a mechanical cultivator. Unlike mine it was free of weeds and grass.

Further along the road was a dirty white *casa payesa* which must have belonged at one time to a more prosperous branch of the family than were currently in charge of it, since it had a *casa alta* (literally 'high house'), a second storey tacked on to the flat low form of the first. In the farmyard three partridges clucked quietly in their cages. Under the arch sat Vicente Serra, an old boy with a tough white beard who was whiling away the morning with a glass of wine and a cigarette. Vicente had lived on the farm all his life. His wife died some years ago leaving him five sons, two of whom still lived at home. None of his offspring has anything to do with tourism, which is remarkable when you consider the carrots of good pay and long holidays, for waiters or drivers or security guards, that have been dangling in front of them for most of their lives just a few miles down the hill in San Antonio. 'No way! They work the land like I've always done. I don't like what goes on in Sant Antoni. All those lost people wherever you look.'

One of the sons, Vicente Serra Bonet, came out to talk to me too. He looked almost as old as his father. I told them about my vineyard and the apparent similarities between theirs and mine. Both were planted on a slope by a pine forest in hard soil that combined the two basic Ibiza types, red and white. They also suffered from the attentions of rabbits, but the Serras weren't taking the rodent menace seriously. 'Yes, they'll eat a few leaves but *no pasa nada*, nothing'll happen,' said Vicente senior. What if they ate all the leaves all the time, as they seemed to have been doing in Santa Gertrudis? 'Well, that could be more serious. Perhaps your rabbits are hungrier than ours.'

The Costas' vines were six years old, sturdy and beginning to acquire the classic knarled look. The vines' rootstocks are 'the ones that come from outside', i.e. American, and resistant to the dreaded vine louse *phylloxera*. Red and white, Antonio didn't remember the varieties. I should replant the dead ones in the winter. Now would be too late. What should I be doing now? 'Not much. You could put down a little bit of horse manure. And I advise you to take out the grass. Pull it all out, it takes away water from the vines.'

Antonio retreated into the gloomy kitchen and returned with a plastic Fanta bottle and a glass. It was last year's wine, bright purple and still drinkable, clean-flavoured and tasty, though with the bitter rasp of *vino payés*. 'This wine isn't very strong,' said the younger Vicente apologetically, but I thought it was all the better for that. The Costas make it, not in old and oozy wooden barrels like most Ibicenco winemakers but in a tank made out of breeze blocks and cement, which may explain why their wine tastes more like normal wine 'from outside' and less like *vino payés* usually does at six months old, a virulent combination of malt vinegar, Ribena and cold stewed teabags.

Robert Hornby-Smith's wine, made a few hundred metres away, is a different drink again. His vines are Monastrell, a Catalan red, which makes a good table-wine, and an unidentified white which goes into one of the very few white wines made on the island. The latter is as fresh and crisp as a new apple and absolutely un-authentic.

Quite a few of the things which would be standard wine-making practice in an Ibicenco farmhouse are ignored at Château Hornby-Smith. Robert prunes his vines in February and leaves two buds on each branch, just as Toni does. But he avoids filtering the wine through herbs and says sternly that he thinks the Ibicencos 'leave it on the skins for far too long'. He is referring to the fermentation period when the grape-skins can be left in with the juice, bringing extra flavour and tannin to the evolving wine. Makers of proper *vino payés* tend to lump it all together for a week at least. He separates the juice from the stalks and pips and skins after four days.

The biggest difference between his wine and country wine is in the way it is treated once the fermentation is finished. If you order a glass or bottle of *vino payés* at a country *tienda* it's likely the owners will simply have gone into a backroom and filled up the glass or bottle from a barrel. Every time they take some out another blast of air gets into the barrel, so that as the level of wine goes down it oxidizes, all the more so because it contains no sulphur dioxide, a preservative, as commercially produced wine does. So Robert bottles his whole production as soon as possible and opens the bottles as and when he needs them. As a result he has vintages going back to 1984 which are perfectly delicious. A *vino payés* from 1984 would be unthinkable as well as undrinkable.

At a roadside restaurant in San Rafael I met a man who used to run a bar. His was no ordinary bar: it was the most famous, the longest-lived, the most fashionable foreigners' bar in all

Ibiza. In the old days, if you were an artist or a writer, which nearly all the expatriates were, the only place that mattered was Sandy's in Santa Eulalia. There you could collect your mail and phone home while Sandy – 'ruthless, but wonderful' – according to an habitué of the time, mixed the Bloody Mary of your dreams.

There was a parade of celebrity visitors: Elmyr de Hory, whose fake Modiglianis scandalized Europe; Clifford Irving, the fake biographer and biographer of fakes; Nigel Davenport, Diana Rigg and a clutch of London's younger thespians; Nina van Pallandt, the airily beautiful Danish singer who occasionally played the bar with her husband Frederick. When Laurence Olivier – 'darling Larry' – came in 1965 it merely confirmed what the regulars already knew. Sandy's Bar was one of the most glamorous places in Europe.

Sandy Pratt ran his bar for twenty-five years, and enjoyed nearly all of it. 'It was like having a cocktail party in the morning and a cocktail party in the evening. The fifties and sixties were a wonderful period. The war was over and there was this great feeling of relief and goodwill.' The story of the bar is surrounded with a rose-coloured glow. 'When I first sailed here in 1955 there were a handful of foreigners,' says Sandy, who is Irish, from County Meath, but speaks with a quick, soft, well-bred English accent. 'Scandals were everywhere – but they were very naive scandals. Oh yes, there were lots of affairs. The Ibicencos took it all in their stride, in fact they joined in. Nobody had any money. If you had two hundred pesetas you were rich.

'Ibiza was every Northerner's idea of what the Mediterranean should look like. It was a *coup de foudre*. There were two paved roads and very little electric light, *very* little electric light. It was an Alice in Wonderland world . . .' There was an old bus which ran between Santa Eulalia and Ibiza, taking about an hour. 'It was a museum piece, painted this wonderful shade of blue.' As the bus was ambling along you would see jerseys hanging in the trees which had been found and left there to be reclaimed.

In those days Ibiza was a smaller, more ingenuous place. Since then it has grown, like Alice, and lost its innocence. Once ADC to the Governor of Gibraltar John Scott, left his basket on the beach with all his money in it. Later that day the discovery of the basket was announced on Radio Ibiza – then the island's only radio station. Policing was an amateur affair, as well it might be, because there was hardly any crime. In Santa Eulalia the police station was virtually opposite Sandy's Bar. 'Whenever they needed me they would run over and say "Sandy, will you do some translating?" One night there was a French boy who was off his head on drugs. I said, "I don't think it would be a good idea to put him in jail. Why don't you just send him back to France?" And they did.'

It was the drugs that eventually ruined the bar, as some might say they ruined the island. 'When the drugs thing came in I realized I couldn't control it. I remember the first time I noticed it. There were a group of people sitting out in the garden, which was very pretty, and they were passing round a joint. And I said, "Don't do it again"; but of course they did . . .'

So Sandy gave up the bar and took up gardening. He is now Ibiza's most high-powered horticulturist. The rich and famous clamour for a garden by Sandy Pratt, and his work is featured in *Casa Vogue* and all the Spanish house-and-garden glossies. Roman Polanski, who lived on Ibiza for many years and still has a house near the golf course, wanted a garden and called for Sandy. So did John Thompson, the English businessman who is rumoured to be the richest foreigner on Ibiza. So did Luciano Paglia, who owns a Japanese car concession in Italy, and his fellow Italians the Gazzellonis in San Carlos, whose bewilderingly beautiful Ibicenco house has an open-air schoolroom for their children and, inside, one of the greatest collections of African art in the world. 'There is a lot of status attached to a beautiful garden,' says Sandy.

High above the fertile plain of Santa Eulalia, Sandy's own

house and garden are reached by a tortuous *camino* which deters faint-hearted drivers and takes months off the lives of cars. The garden spills out from the doorway of a little white house with china-blue stripes around the windows and on to a broad terrace that buzzes with the fragrance of freesia and jasmine. Here on the terrace Sandy entertains afternoon guests over perfectly brewed tea and cake, getting up now and then to check up on the progress of the rockery or to snip at an errant frond of *Buddleia alternifolia*.

I sat down at a wooden table stained blue with paint and weathered by a couple of winters. You could tell it was finally spring because the light seemed softer, less hard-edged and brittle, and the air carried a scent of buds and early flowers. To the table Sandy brought olives, thin slices of peppery *salcichón*, a Spanish salami, and glasses of cold beer. The large grey-bearded man opposite me was an Italian who ran an antiques business. He knew the Gazzellonis and the Paglias, and we talked about another exceptionally rich Italian neo-Ibicenco who had just died leaving a tenth of his estate to the victims of international terrorism. But he was so expansively, complicatedly rich that nobody had managed to calculate the amount of his total wealth, let alone a tenth of it.

Susie Elliot turned up late. She and Denholm had been in London and had got back last night. She had forgotten about this lunch-party and when Sandy called to check she was on her way she said Denholm was exhausted and she'd 'just got her mouth around a glass' of Veuve Clicquot. Sandy pursed his lips and said in mock-exasperation, 'That makes a change, dear'. Susie is a former actress from Massachusetts who married Denholm after she saw him in a Broadway play called 'Write Me a Murder'. Being a terrific friend of Sandy's, she took over his bar two owners after Sandy himself.

While we ate Sandy regaled us with witticisms. 'What makes a good barman?' he asked rhetorically, before continuing: 'The ability to hold three conversations at once and to make people think that not for one *second* are they being ignored.'

When the bar was in its heyday he lived in an apartment in Santa Eulalia. Then this little cottage came up. It had no water or electricity and an appalling *camino*, but he glimpsed its possibilities and bought it. The telephone took three years, £1000 and a pay-off to a grumbling neighbour to install, and even then friends said he was lucky. The house is, as Jane Austen described her own work, light, and bright, and sparkling. The impression is of cleanliness, order and faultless taste. The tiny windows in the old white-washed walls are framed with a thick stripe of clear blue. There is a fig tree, a medlar and an ancient vine, and flowers bloom in professional profusion.

Inside, Satie murmured on the CD. At other times of day and in other moods, it might have been Mozart or Sarah Vaughan. On the shelves and walls of the short 'long room' were the proofs of Sandy's reputation as a nurturer of neo-Ibicenco creative talent. The only artist whose work I recognized was Manolo Mompó, who had died a few months earlier. Sandy was sure he would soon be deluged with requests to borrow the painting for this or that commemorative exhibition. 'Well, I shan't let them have it.'

I let my glance wander sideways over a shelf-long library of books by long- or short-term residents of the island. In one old paperback, a piece of swinging-sixties pulp called *The Dolly-Dolly Spy*, all girls in hot-pants and men in white flares chasing them on mopeds, the author had scrawled in pencil: 'Sandy. Let me hasten to add that the Ibiza sequence is entirely fictional.'

At the far end of the row I found the autobiography of Janet Frame, and curled up on Sandy's sofa to look through its own Ibiza sequence. Frame had travelled to Europe to escape from the psychic prisons of fifties New Zealand and her own mental illness. 'I felt at peace within my own mind, as if I were on an unearthly shore,' she wrote of her carefree new life at number six, Calle Ignacio Riquer, Ibiza town.

Janet lost her heart to the island and her virginity to an American painter called Bernard. Together they 'called on other Americans, many of them exiles from the McCarthy regime – the film director turned painter who had built himself a villa in Ibiza and who conducted us through his personal gallery of the American Civil War where each of the portraits of the Generals were portraits of himself. We attended recitals of music and poetry at the French Institute. We wined and dined with Edwin's and Bernard's friends, mostly Americans, with the men and women living with their chosen partners in the sensuous sensual kind of luxury enjoyed by the lotus eaters.

'In my afternoon walks or cycling I marvelled at the way the clear perimeter of the island unfolded before my eyes. I wrote ecstatic letters to Frank Sargeson. Ibiza, I said, was all they claimed it would be and all I dreamed. I felt it contained within me and when I had explored the beaches and the salt mountains I cycled past the fields of clay where the clay surface opened its red vein, at the pottery works, and leaving my bicycle, I walked to the wooded interior of the island, to a mass of light-green pine forest where, Catalina and Francesca warned me, the bandits and wild men roamed . . .'

Most villages are famous for something, even if it's only the Hierbas they make in the *tienda* or the after-dinner-mint prettiness of the local church. San Rafael has garnered a modest fame from its church, whose homemade-rococo façade has launched a thousand tourism campaigns, but its real cultural strength is pottery. Strung out at the end of the village, before the road tips round on to the San Antonio highway, are three workshops producing a range of stuff from simple, stout terracotta ware – ashtrays, candle-holders, wide, shallow *cazuelas* for cooking – to fully-fledged signed artworks that would be happier dignified with the term 'ceramics' than lumped in with all the other humble rust-red pottery. Such is the fame of San Rafael as a centre of pot-production that a road-sign now welcomes you to a 'Pottery Village' or 'Dorf des Keramiker'. As from Spring 1991 San Rafael can describe itself as a Zone of Artisanal Protection under the aegis of the regional government – though in practice this means little more to the artisans themselves than that they now have a nice big shiny new road-sign at either end of their village.

When I first noticed San Rafael's profusion of potters I imagined they might be there for some exciting recondite reason, like the quality of the water or the seam of special clay with high tensile strength and vibrant colour that the potters might have discovered nearby in the well-watered valley of Buscastell. Some say it is because the potters are all South-American (that much is true) and San Rafael reminded them of a South-American village, low dusty indifferent buildings dumped casually along the main street. The truth is that they're there because of the Englishman Bernard Leach, whose writings are the Bible of all self-respecting ceramicists. In one of his books Leach discusses the importance of setting up your workshop close to centres of communication and roads. With that in mind the potters pored over a map of Ibiza and saw that this medium-sized village was ideally placed – midway between San Antonio and Ibiza town, the island's two main commercial centres, but sufficiently far from either and from the busy main road to be good for quiet, concentrated work.

Immigrants from South America, in the opinion of Emilio dell'Agnolo of Ibiza's Latin American Centre, 'create fewer problems of integration than the Moroccans' and for the most part can't complain about their treatment by the State. His view wouldn't be shared by the hundreds of South Americans in Ibiza who arrived after 15 May 1991 – the Spanish government's cut-off point for non-EEC immigrants – and who exist in a shadowy world of cash-in-hand jobs, remote *fincas* in the countryside and perpetual terror of being pulled over by the police and asked to produce their papers.

But for Carlos Icardi, one of the three San Rafael potters,

life is good. He got out of Uruguay in 1977, propelled by the
country's repressive politics, stumbling economy and antedi-
luvian morality. 'I left there because I was young, and the
young people were more clever.' Before he left he had taught
manualidades, making things, to children. Ibiza, Ibiza. He had
heard the name, thought it sounded strange, looked for it
on the map and hadn't been able to find it. Mallorca yes,
Ibiza no. Then he read something in the paper that made
him sit up: 'It was a news item that blew my mind because
over there in South America there's a very retrograde morality. The news was that in Ibiza there were Amazons going
around on motorbikes with no clothes on! And the local
authorities were taking steps to combat these Amazons.
Nudes on motorbikes in the street! Wow! Let's get over there!
'When we arrived here in seventy-something there was a
wave of South American people. They brought their understanding of different materials, like ceramics, jewellery and
things like that, which are now part of Ibicenco craftsman-
ship.' At first there were five of them, all Argentinians and
Uruguayans (two of them have since dropped out, leaving
'Es Moli', 'Can Kinoto', and Icardi). They bought a wheel
and fiddled with it one after another, learning from each
other's efforts while clutching their Bernard Leach. It was a
heady, chaotic time. 'There were other people who tried to
do what we did, at a more organized level, and it didn't
work out. They all fought over it. In our case it all happened
in a rather natural way.'

Their creative progress on the island followed a familiar
Ibiza paradigm of mutual enrichment: grateful for their new-
found freedom, they paid back the debt by re-establishing a
tradition which had barely existed when they arrived. 'Here
in Ibiza there isn't a kind of "popular ceramics" like you can
see in Mallorca or anywhere on the peninsula. You can't say,
ah, this little bottle is typical. Here, what there was, was
alfareria (earthenware). The advantage of that, for people like
us who settled here, was that there was no opposition in the
sense of someone saying, "No, this is Ibicenco, so you've

got to do it *this* way." It was a freedom that the place had, and people knew how to make good use of it.'

Icardi's teacher, and until he died in February 1992 the guiding light of Ibiza's craftsmen and women, was a man thought by many who encountered him to be a genius.

Joan Daifa was born into a family of *payeses* in Jesus in 1907, and his roots remained deep in the Ibicenco countryside and culture. As a child he looked after the livestock on the family farm. He never went to school. At seven he had his first contact with clay in a house in Ibiza town, where the Credito Balear bank is now, which had a pottery making storage urns for oil or wine, bricks, pitchers, and tiles. At twelve he was diverted from his eventual career by a job as guide to a blind man who sold lottery tickets in the street. His weekly wage was 2 pesetas. Finally he joined the master *alfarero* Antonio Arabi 'Rafal', working alongside him for forty-four years.

Carlos Icardi knew and loved Daifa as man and maker. 'I came into contact with him when he was making pieces and I was decorating them for him. I was just getting into ceramics, and a friendship developed between us. He was fascinated by the colours, because he didn't know about them, he didn't know about glazes either, because he was an *alfarero*. Anyway, he started trying things out.'

Both Carlos Icardi and, posthumously, Daifa, were showing at the annual Easter craft show in Vara de Rey. Daifa's stall was at the front of the show in the place of honour next to the information desk. A small selection of his work had been borrowed from private collectors and his family. Nearly everything was of the same sun-faded ochre – Altamira red, the colour of Old Europe. There were pots, large and small, some unadorned, others with the whimsical, apparently spur-of-the-moment addition of fantastical beaks and limbs. There were primitive statues with jug-shaped bodies and strange grinning sharp-toothed faces such as a child might make. Some of these had thin arms stuck rigidly to their sides, and eyes like saucers. A large leering male figure had spindly hands clamped around a spindly cock. Halfway between function and depiction, the figures had the same grotesque, unsettling quality as the Carthaginian figures in the archaeological museum. There was a rawness that you could interpret as crudity; by the same token there was a vibrant, almost Picassoesque energy.

A few steps across the square were a couple of Ibiza's hundreds of jewellers. Isabel Echavarri and Claudio Graziani make elegant, sinuous, VISA-friendly pieces for the neck, wrist and fingers, in a style touched with the merest suggestion of sixties. Like most people at first they sold in the markets. 'We were just playing,' said Isabel. Then a woman bought a necklace and put it in the window of her shop. It was silver, but everyone thought it was platinum. From then on they have been reading, looking, learning. 'We visit museums, learn about chemistry and alchemy – it's an endless road.' They came to the island in 1973. 'Ibiza is connected with our spirituality. It's also an ideal place for human beings, because it's a province but at the same time it's Europe in miniature.'

Half of everything on show in the Vara de Rey was leather, worked into bags and belts and jackets. Leather played a major role in the fragile economy of the early hippies. It was easy to beg or buy the raw materials, cow- or goatskin, and didn't require any great capital investment; the basic techniques of leather-working could be learned in a few days; and inspiration came naturally from Morocco, India and North America, where many of the leather-workers had travelled.

In the success of leather-working as a primitive industry were the seeds of its own failure, because real industries began to offer the same kind of items at a lower price and quality to a clientele that was insensitive to the differences. Soon the market became saturated with the same shapes and textures, the same bags and belts and jackets, in a thousand market-stalls all over Europe. Leather became a hippie cliché, like joss-sticks and dope-boxes.

Jeronimo came from Argentina fifteen years ago and was quick to tell me he has his papers thoroughly in order. He makes slender copper candlesticks and candelabra, artfully tarnished and reasonably priced, and shared a stall at the fair with Genevieve Binst, whose strange faces and busts moulded out of coloured leather are at least a variation on the thirty-year-old theme.

Jeronimo plied his trade in the markets like everyone else, and reflects wistfully on those fat, fruitful years and the lean years that followed them. In the seventies it wasn't unusual for a stallholder at Las Dalias or Es Canar to make 70–80,000 ptas (£420–£480) a day, so that by the end of the summer anyone who had even the remotest *nous* about selling could be rich. You could rent a house for 5–10,000 ptas a month, and food prices were risible. Saving was naturally out – that was something only capitalist breadheads got into – so people blew the lot on wintering in the East. 'It was cheaper to go to India than stay here,' said Jeronimo. 'And the weather was better.'

The man on the next stall, a thin person with bright dark eyes and straggly black hair, agreed. He and his wife used to travel most winters before the chill winds of recession and sensibleness began to blow through Ibiza's craft sector. Now he paid 50,000 ptas rent, there was the electricity bill to think of, and for the first time ever he was 'getting into tax and all'. Somehow it just seemed a better idea to stay home with the kids than trip off again around the world. Someone they knew had just bought a TV . . . 'For sure it's different times, but the truth is we lived very very well before.'

I'd often seen Yaron at the markets, where he sold oneiric musical instruments. He is Israeli-born and gets his influences 'from life'.

Yaron lived on a hill near San Rafael with his wife, an Italian belly-dancer who performs at parties and happenings, on the occasions when they still happen. I went up to see them in their white *finca* on a strange day when a blast of pre-summer heat had filled up the valley with dense sticky mist. 'I am old,' announced their neighbour who had hobbled up to examine my Mini, 'and I've never seen a time like this in all my life.'

The evidence of Yaron and Roberta's respective occupations was all around. In the orchard in front of the arched *porxet*, among the wild gladioli, was a Moroccan tent shaped like a merry-go-round with graceful swags leading up to a central pole, where Roberta sometimes dances on hot summer nights. Under the arches hung a wind-chime – to all intents and purposes Yaron is the sole purveyor of wind-chimes to all Ibiza, which is a better business situation than it sounds, since Ibiza is quite *gone* with the wind-chime – and, more mysteriously, a community of gourds of various sizes, drying on strings in quiet organic clusters. Like all good hippies he used to play the drums, and made a few following the Ibicenco tradition, out of the hollowed-out trunk of a freshly cut pine tree. But the first instruments he produced seriously were wind-chimes, which were easy to make and popular because they required no effort to play. The very first one was made from random lengths of aluminium chair-leg. 'You can make them from any old material; empty Butane bottles, iron, bronze, old bottles.' The business moved up a gear when somebody asked him for a particular Indian *raga* and somebody else wanted a chord on the Neapolitan Sixth. But man cannot live by wind-chimes alone. 'To live from this was already a miracle – you cannot put your future in something like that.' So he diversified, into the brilliant and beautiful objects that have made his name: maracas and marimbas and calimbas and other objects that defy description as well as nomenclature.

And then he discovered gourds. All the time we talked in the kitchen of his *finca* he was scraping away at a small dry shell which made an echoing woody sound under the knife. The drying process had left faint patches of grey, green and orange, the traces of lichens and a long damp winter, which had to be removed from its stone-coloured surface. It would either end up as a box etched with patterns and with a star-shaped lid like a Hallowe'en pumpkin, or as some kind of musical object, Yaron couldn't say what – it all depended on his whim.

He rolled a joint, lit it, and puffed away as he worked. Like Carlos Icardi with his proto-traditional pottery, creatively speaking Yaron is giving back to Ibiza more than he takes, particularly when it comes to gourds. At one time they were cultivated and used, with typical Ibicenco resourcefulness, by people in the countryside. At the *matanza* a large bulbous gourd might be used for water. Yaron knew a man who carried around his *vino payés* in one wherever he went. ('He was a drunk one!') And with a long-necked type with a big belly the Ibicencos would catch swarms of bees, tempting them in with lemon and honey at the neck end. Most of the gourd species grown on the island have sadly disappeared owing to cross-pollination and general lack of interest. Clearly the virtues of gourds as storage vessels have been eclipsed by the plastic bottle. 'I have always liked them. When I started there was one old man here who kept bees – he had some of them, and he gave me the seeds. I've made a Bedouin lyre, an African harp and a calimba, but you can make an infinity of instruments according to the gourd. Ibicencos don't make musical instruments out of them. But they will do! In a few years when I've been making them, you will see, maybe it will catch on.'

This gourd thing was getting perilously, wonderfully close to an obsession. 'You know it's like a virus – when it enters it's there.' Yaron is now looking for irrigated land (his own *finca* is too high and dry) on which to do his gourd experiments, to plant the seeds he's begged and borrowed. Only when you're truly committed, you see, can you begin to understand the fabulous riches of the genus *Cucurbita lagenaria*. There are Finger Gourds and Spoon Gourds, Ladle and Scoop Gourds, Big Bell Gourds and Dipper Gourds. The Dipper was one Yaron had new seeds for and planned to plant that autumn.

He had even joined the American Gourd Society, an

organization which takes gourd-fancying to the outer limits. The Society's annual Journal, which I found on Yaron's sofa, is a vade-mecum for eccentrics. There were suggestions for organizing your own Gourd Theme Party. There were tips for making hats from Gourds, and photographs of Gourd Art. There were serious articles on subjects like 'The Value of Gourds to Science'. And, at the front of the book, there was this touching little poem. I read it out aloud and we both laughed – but unlike mine Yaron's laughter was un-tinged with mockery.

> If I must choose, the bottle gourd comes first.
> Rejoicing in its history, I scan
> Its symbolism, place in magic art,
> Tradition, and great usefulness to man.
> *My Choice* by Eddie W. Wilson

Easter in Ibiza is a time of anxious excitement, less over the resurrection of Christ than the resurrection of the tourist industry. Predictions are made by anyone in a position to make them, only to be followed by counter-predictions and allegations of bad faith. In April the councillor of tourism, Jaume Cladera, announced to a group of businessmen that the following season would see an average rise of 5 per cent in all the main tourist markets. Also the Holy Week holidays, when the engines of Ibiza's tourist industry grind into action, would be better than last year's because they were happening in April, not March. Another bigwig, the socialist deputy Antoni Costa, went further, predicting a rise of 8 per cent in the numbers of British and German visitors to Ibiza and Formentera and an 'excellent' season in general. The industry itself wasn't quite so sure. The local hoteliers' association, whose members had filled only between 50 and 60 per cent of their beds for the summer, were sceptical of all the official optimism. Their president Gonzago Miragall claimed that this would 'not be a spectacular year for tourism'. Holy Week, moreover, would be 'fairly weak'.

The travel agents thought that was wrong too. Holy Week would be great. 'Everything's been full up since a month ago,' said one. 'For instance, coming from Barcelona to Ibiza on the 13th, 14th and 15th is virtually impossible, the boats are full up too and there are no car places left.' But they agreed with Miragall about the summer. 'We don't think people have made up their minds where to go for their holidays. There are a lot of enquiries about coming to the Pitiusas, but nobody's deciding. They'll see if Expo '92 offers anything interesting or is just a bore, then they'll decide whether to go there or spend the summer lying in the sun.'

As well as these secular controversies Easter also excited strong religious passions, but typically of Ibiza some of these had little to do with Christianity. Perhaps it was due to the general rise in temperature or a kind of cultural bolstering-up before the tourist hordes arrived to sack and pillage, but a mild epidemic of Tanit-fever seemed to be creeping across the island. (Tanit, you will recall, was the Carthaginian goddess of love, death, fertility, and everything.) In recent years Tanit has lent her name to a travel agent, a street in Ibiza town and a block of flats in San Antonio which is so ugly I am surprised the great goddess has not personally demolished it as an offence to her Queenliness. She is almost as popular as the Virgin Mary. One day in Holy Week this announcement appeared in the personal columns of the local press:

SUPPLICATION to Tanit. Queen of the rain, queen of the sun, queen of the heavens, queen of the stars, queen of the seas, queen of the earth. Blessed be the great goddess, she who has no beginning nor end.

When it was known that the bust of her which is the principal glory of the Museu Puig d'es Molins was to be whisked off to Seville, there to form one of the main attractions of the Balearic Pavilion, there was a full-page feature in the paper debating the rights and wrongs of her 'translation'.

Most of those who gave an opinion thought Tanit's trip to Seville was a good idea so long as everything possible was done to ensure the sculpture's safety. But a few were violently opposed to it. 'Something happens to her then what do we do?' said a worried Isabel Vich, 18. Some might say there was no point in worrying about a mere image of Tanit, a mere artificial likeness, when the goddess herself is alive and well and living above a Chinese restaurant in Figueretes.

Renée Cohen was just a nice Jewish girl from Philadelphia until one fine day in 1961. Not having been on the island long, she was walking along the street when Isidoro Macabich, the famously dull historian, stopped her and revealed her true identity. 'He said I was the reincarnation of the goddess Tanit. He told me, "You just *are* her". I didn't believe him at first, and in fact it's only in the last few years that I've truly begun to realize my powers as a goddess.' She believes her divine vocation means that she can and must 'save' Ibiza. 'That's why I'm here. I left for good five years ago and now I'm back to save this place and make sure it stays magical.'

Renée isn't in any doubt about what she has to save the island *from*. There are too many ugly inappropriate new buildings, too many unscrupulous capitalists cashing in on the island, too many bus-loads of tourists. There are too many Catalanists imposing their alien culture on the place (she is a little bit confused about this one). 'Oh yeah, and there are too many fuckin' gypsies.'

They gave her number in 'The Artist', a rubbishy ex-pat broadsheet peppered with in-jokes and misprints. The article described her recent activities in America, which included giving New Age consultations to movie-stars in the back of a limousine. It also mentioned her notorious Snake Dance which set Ibiza a-quiver in the sixties. I rang her and asked her what she was into these days. She reeled them off like a Brooklyn shop-assistant: 'Well, honey, this year I'm doing numerology, past-life regression therapy, and Tarot.' I said I was from England and she said she liked our attitude to witches, choosing to ignore our fondness for burning them in large numbers. 'Yeah, in the States they really like, flipped out if I said I was into witchcraft. But in England it was great, people would say, "What do you do?" and I'd say "I'm a witch," and they'd say, "Oh, that's interesting, I'm a wizard."'

We arranged to meet that day and go to Es Vedrà, the mountainous islet off the coast which is Ibiza's equivalent of Ayers Rock. She was taking a 'sun-bath' on the terrace when I hooted the horn outside her place. Later she almost apologized for the location: 'It's not very glitzy, not very suitable for someone like me, but it's where I used to live thirty years ago and it's got a great vibe.' I got out of the car and looked up. All I could see was the peeling blue paint of the 'terrace' (a balcony looking out over the road) and a Chinese wind-chime hanging outside, chiming.

In a minute or two she came round the corner. She looked a lot more glamorous than the time I'd seen her in her Madame Arcati outfit in the Christmas market in Las Dalias. This time she had red leather boots and a red jersey dress, and between them black shimmery leggings. Big decolletage, big peroxide hair, Yoko Ono glasses with a red plastic trim, clanky jewellery ('it's made out of a toilet chain I bought at the hardware store. Isn't it fabulous?'), heavy eye make-up, and a sly smile turning up the corners of her lip-glossed mouth. We went to Cala d'Hort, a small bay with a restaurant where you can sit and watch the sun go down over Es Vedrà as you eat your *paella*. We arranged a table outside, or rather Renée ordered the waiters to arrange one, and she sat me down facing the rock, which thrusts itself craggily out of the water like a rough-and-ready natural Pyramid.

Ibiza was sacred to Tanit, Es Vedrà is the spiritual centre of Ibiza, and Tanit is Renée; therefore, Es Vedrà is sacred to Renée. QED. She calls it 'my home'. 'Can't you just feel its power?' she asked me. I wasn't sure, but it certainly was a mesmerizing sight, an immense shadow against the late-afternoon sky as it faded slowly from blue to pale orange. I got up to order more *all-i-oli* and olives, and when I came back Renée was holding up her hands in front of her, her eyes shut, as though recharging spiritual batteries.

A group of Spanish people sauntered past, wondering where to put their table, and briefly made the mistake of standing between Renée and the rock. She flew at them. 'It's a magic place, it's a powerful place, and you happen to be standing between it and me. Get out of the way.' They were taken aback and didn't move immediately. She then said, loudly and commandingly, 'You are standing directly in front of my eyes.' Finally they moved off in a state of mild shock, and she turned to me with incredulity in her face and said, 'Jesus, what assholes!'

Whether you can feel its power or not, Es Vedrà has charisma. A true rock star, it is popularly supposed to have appeared on celluloid as 'Bali Hai' in *South Pacific*.

In 1855 the Carmelite friar Francisco Palau, an ultra-conservative prelate who was exiled from his native Catalunya and sent to Ibiza, spent a week meditating in a cave on the rock with nothing more to eat or drink than the rainwater that dripped from the roof of the cave. Palau's first day on Es Vedrà was spent in prayer and meditation. On the second day he began to experience a series of visions, of escalating intensity, which he describes in his book *My Relations with the Church*. 'The day passed and the night came. The sea was at peace, the air very soft, the sky somewhat overcast by dense black clouds, a crescent moon [the symbol of Tanit] . . . The moonlight was very dim. And I saw in front of me, coming from afar, a shadow whose distant countenance I could not perceive; and it was coming closer to me. As it drew nearer I could make out what it was. The figure came alone, and was as white as the moonlight itself; and the figure represented a girl of 16 years, all white, all lovely, all amiable. At the moment she arrived the heavens opened and in the radiant sunlight I saw who it was that I had before me . . . I was aggrieved that I couldn't see her with the clarity I wished: a veil covered her face, but was transparent . . . She was silent and so was I, but a dumb voice was speaking and possessed words . . .'

Clearly this is not some hallucination brought on by lack of food and sleep but an authentic example of contact with extraterrestrials. The 'dumb voice' that Palau describes is plainly a nineteenth-century manner of describing what we would call telepathy.

What the hermit saw would have been an OVNI, a Spanish UFO. Since his visions there have been hundreds of sightings on Ibiza, a number of them in the Es Vedrà area. Lights in the sky, flying cigars, strange hovering metallic objects that singed the tree-tops before vanishing soundlessly into space (this last, in San Rafael in 1976, was witnessed among others by a sub-official of the army and a school-teacher) – so many sightings have been recorded that more than one commentator has come to the logical conclusion that there must be a submarine base, handily located in the waters between Ibiza and Mallorca, from which OVNIs are being sent out on regular missions to terrorize and fascinate the Ibicenco population.

Back at the restaurant, a yellowing cutting from *La Prensa*, 1976, was produced from a brown envelope. It showed a much younger Renée ('I always did have a fabulous body') garlanded with snakes for the famous Snake Dance. The waiter brought a bottle of wine and Renée forced him to look at the cutting too. 'You see, I'm the reincarnation of the goddess Tanit and this' – she flung her hand out towards Es Vedrà in a gesture that made her loo-chain necklace clank – 'is my home'. She added, 'I always get loads of press stuff wherever I go, because I'm such an international and exciting kind of personality.

'I'm famous for my parties at Pacha. In fact I invented parties in nightclubs. The people from Studio 54 came down from New York to see what I was doing, but they didn't offer me a job, oh no, they just ripped off all my ideas. I gave so many parties I can't remember which was my favourite, but one of the best was my Hollywood party. We had a red carpet and I interviewed everyone that came in on a video screen, just like a movie premiere, and we had girls swinging naked on trapezes and another girl done up as Goldfinger, naked and covered with gold. We brought these huge movie lights from Barcelona and at the end all the lights went down and they wheeled in an enormous cake, and I burst out the top with a bottle of champagne in each hand, spraying everybody . . . Oh, it was faabulous, honey. People – were – just – amazed. They were, like [she opened her eyes and mouth wide in an expression of shock]. It was just Total Glamour.'

But that was in her carefree salad days, when she said 'dammit, Tanit'. These days she is all too aware of her heavenly duties. How does it feel, I wondered, to be a goddess? 'Well, it's a terrific responsibility, for sure. There's just so much work to do to save this island. I haven't been back for long so I haven't been able to do much yet. But I will.' She took another swig of wine and gave a long, long sigh that became a throaty chuckle. 'Oh yes, I will.'

Summer

The *temporada* begins with apricots and coaches. Both come in quietly, in the first two weeks of June, get themselves noticed in the third week and by the start of the fourth have taken their place in the phenomenology of summer.

The apricot is the first fruit of the season. In the garden at Christine's house, while the trumpet-like hibiscus flowers fanfared an ever more vulgar coral red, I'd been watching the apricot tree in the garden as it drank in the warmth of the lengthening afternoons. Ever since the end of May I'd tried the fruit almost every day. At first it was as sour and crunchy as crabapples; then it took on the bitter-sweet tang and yielding flesh of greengage. Now, with the first pale tourists on the streets, the apricots were suddenly gloriously ripe and as fat as small peaches. They were the colour of Tequila Sunrise, or a Hare Krishna robe.

The situation was suddenly urgent: how to make use of this fabulous resource before the fruit fell off the tree in a week or two and the lizards got all the benefit? Christine and I set to making purées, syrups, jams and pies. We even tried drying them on the roof, but the birds and ants got there before the sun. Elsewhere on the island a Belgian cook made a perfect classic *tarte aux abricots*, which Sandy served at Sunday tea.

The first tourists arrived at the end of May, with the returning birds. On my way home from a day's weeding in the vineyard I spied two of them in their unmistakable plumage: shorts too short, legs and arms pasty and porridge-white, bags and cameras clutched tightly to the body. These early birds wore a look of vague embarrassment, like the party-guests that arrived too early.

The coaches are another sure sign of summer. They appear from nowhere and multiply with sinister speed, all bearing mysterious numbers on their windscreens – M21, E4, F36 – so that their passengers will be able to identify them as they step out of the airport into the car park in the squinting sun. (The logistics of transporting tourists from their various flights from Birmingham, Stansted, Glasgow or Gatwick, in the correct coach, to the correct resort and hotel, are of a similar order of complexity as the arrangements for reuniting Indian businessmen with their home-cooked lunch.) They arrive at the more easily accessible beauty-spots and their cream-complexioned contents spill out, feed and move on, like Serengeti herds.

A sunny Friday afternoon in Santa Gertrudis, and it felt like a Saturday. There were not one but two coach parties loose in the village, swarming into the Bar Costa, swivelling their video cameras like anti-tank guns on to the waiters, the yapping dogs and the church tower. The ethnic art gallery Origins had shut its doors in self-imposed curfew for the duration of the invasion and a clutch of mild-looking English people in shorts were peering with menacing curiosity through its barricaded windows. Meanwhile in the Restaurante Santa Gertrudis, that Stygian village-hall of a place where two or three old *payeses* are usually glued to the bar with a drip-feed of Hierbas Ibicencas, there was an extraordinarily ritzy French wedding party going on. Women in Lacroix dresses and hats and men in Armani suits were sipping glasses of white wine while their designer children played with the mongrels in the street. Later I saw the invitation on someone's mantelpiece. Everything about it – the thickness of the card, the swirly script, the tortuous syntax – said 'snobisme'.

There was no doubt about it, the village was booming – and not everyone was pleased. Theo from the auctioneers' was heard to mutter about Ibiza's ceaseless pace of change and what a very good and restful time he had just had in the Cotswolds. Claudia looked out of her office window to where a bulldozer stood in an orchard ruining her peerless view of Ibiza town and Formentera and said wistfully, 'They're killing all the trees. It's getting to be like the Amazon.' Carlos Sansegundo, the sculptor, had already decided you would have to be a masochist to enjoy the bourgeois nightmare that Santa Gertrudis was in the process of becoming.

The most visible index of any boom is the building. It had not escaped the notice of the gossips in the Bar Costa – because large signs had sprung up on the outskirts of the village telling the whole world the glad tidings – that the old village centre was about to be hemmed in by two new *urbanizaciones*, one on the San Mateo side and the other, which it came as no surprise to discover had Matutes money behind it, sprouting like a cyst on the turn-off from the San Miguel road. As time went on the two projects seemed to be vying with each other in the sheer amount of ugliness they could bring forth. By June the Matutes party had hacked great red scars out of the gentle green landscape. These scars would eventually be cauterized with asphalt and become the approach roads from the village to the *urbanización*. On the other side the first house in 'Sa Nova Gertrudis' (the new Gertrudis) was rising in a havoc of grey breeze-blocks behind a corrugated-iron fence.

When it came to public relations 'Sa Nova Gertrudis' definitely had the edge. The French company behind the development had set up a sales office in the main square, and although it was hardly ever manned at least you could peer through the window at a model of squeaky-clean luxury homes in neat rows interrupted with the blue stains of pools. The catalogue they gave out, when it wasn't spouting architectural cant about 'natural growth', respect and integration, was flying off into realms of embarrassing New Age hyperbole that would surely fool only the most gullible of prospective purchasers. 'The entire site will be integrated in its topographical and tangential reality with the ancient village of Santa Gertrudis', wrote the architect, ' . . . with the desire and hope that among the sap of replanted olive trees and the fallen branches of trees that have been replaced or removed, there may be born, grow and evolve a new kind of animated beings, firmly rooted in respectful coexistence, humanity and mutual affection, in the most universal feeling of life, as a final cause and effect of everything created and existing.'

By mid-June the summer was juddering into life, like a car that's been in the garage all winter. The tourist season had begun, but with worrying sluggishness. Those few hotels that had plucked up courage to open their doors were little more than half full, the streets were empty at night and barmen were yawning all over town. There was nothing for the tourist industry to do but wring its hands and wait.

The season arrived more punctually in the countryside. By day the sky took on a hot blue and seemed to share its heat and colour with the sea. There was a glassy clarity to the air which everybody noticed, casting their eyes to the horizon where the white and green of Formentera were sandwiched in two clear strips between the blue intensity of sea and sky.

There were more and more flowers, big blowsy garden-flowers barging past the shyer meadow-flowers left over from late spring. Cascades of bougainvillea covered the walls of expensively restored *casas payesas* and geraniums in surprising shades of blood-red and pink and bruised blue reached plague proportions in their gardens. Sandy had stopped watering the monstrous geranium-bush clambering up his garden wall – 'it's too big already', he said firmly – but it refused to die. Pink oleanders crowded the roadsides. In the fields, some of them Cider-with-Rosie gold with the first corn-crop, red and purple poppies were a new substitute for the meniscus of yellow *oxalis* that had covered the *campo* throughout the winter. Fallow fields were a purple haze of thyme-flowers.

The evening stretched out deliciously, like a cat in the sun. In the winter it had been cramped and huddled and you wanted to eat early and sleep soon afterwards. But the Spanish, who are peculiarly sensitive to changes of heat and light, allow their mealtimes to slide around the day according to what feels most comfortable. Before I knew it I was eating at midnight and sleeping at two.

At Javier's house the orchards buzzed with heat and insect sounds: wood-wasps, clouds of flies and giant crickets that clattered through the air if disturbed. By night there was a sudden plague of small but vicious mosquitoes that seemed to have evolved out of the mosquito's one and only design fault, the tell-tale whine that warns you of its approach. Fortunately there were also geckos. They appeared with innocent eyes, stuck motionless with suction-pad feet in the corners of rooms, where they feasted discreetly on mosquitoes that would otherwise have feasted discreetly on me.

The vines, which I hoped by now would be waist-high and laden with grapes, were only as tall as my arm from elbow to fingertip and engulfed in a scrum of weeds. I was overjoyed to find a few tight bunches of tiny, waxy grapes, but that was the only good news. The leaves that had sprouted on most of the plants were a paler, sicklier green than my neighbour's vines in San Rafael, which were as bushy and verdant as vines in picture-books. Among the Tempranillo variety, down in the bottom two rows, the death toll was depressing. I examined each *parra* in turn: twenty-seven were clearly alive and sprouting dark green, wrinkled leaves; forty were dry sticks, showing no signs of life at all; ten were missing, presumed dead; and there were nine 'don't knows'. Further up the slope where I'd planted Garnacha there was a better ratio of quick to dead. Seventy-three vines were alive, thirty-one were dead, four missing and six dubious.

I met Toni for crisis talks at the El Paso. We decided there were three possible reasons for the vineyard's general state of ill health. One, it was high season, if not for tourists, then for rabbits, who would be emerging with their new families from holes in the scrubland below the vineyard to nibble the tender shoots of the first two or three rows. Two, the root-stocks we had chosen for the Tempranillo might have been the wrong ones for the soil, or indeed Tempranillo might have been the wrong variety altogether. Grape varieties are happier in some parts of the world than in others. That would be the fault of Señor Lorente in Xativa. Three, though there had been plenty of rain during the spring, the weeds might have taken all the water – this would explain the leaves' insipid colour. That would be my fault for not weeding thoroughly enough.

Only one of these possible problems could easily be remedied. Señor Tur Planells and his pack of *podencos ibicencos* from next door were making valiant efforts with the rodent menace, but more hi-tech methods of extermination were out of the question. A fence would be ugly, cost too much and the rabbits would undoubtedly find a way round, or under, it. Poison was tempting, but unpardonable in a project whose credentials up to now had been impeccably organic. As for the root-stocks and the variety, it was too late to do anything. But the weeds could be pulled up, which at least might allow the roots some room to breathe and drink in any remaining moisture in the soil.

I hired a hand-held motorized cultivator, a powerful little beast like a lawnmower crossed with a tank which roared and grunted as it churned up the weed-choked ground. I started in the morning, and by the end of the afternoon I was half-dead with sweat and sunburn but the vineyard looked healthier than it had done for months. In celebration I plucked a bunch of bullet-like unripe grapes and sucked on their juice. They were as sour as sloes.

Though I'd taken windswept walks along the sand and eaten chilly picnics around driftwood fires and even occasionally gone for exhilarating cold swims at Portitxol and Cala Aubarca, since last October 'the beach' in the sense of a set of activities performed in a bathing-costume had only existed in the abstract. Now it had an objective existence again, and Fernando and I began to spend our days on the longest, sandiest, sexiest, most beach-like beach in the whole of Ibiza.

South of Ibiza town, the resort of Playa d'en Bossa and the village of San Francisco is the island's only large area of flat uninhabited land. Much of this land was gobbled up by the resort encroaching from the North and the international airport when it opened in 1967, but the landscape that remains has managed to keep its eerie, otherworldly beauty. These are the Salinas, the salt-flats which from the time of the Carthaginians until around 1950 constituted Ibiza's economic *raison d'être*. A narrow, horribly pitted tarmac road meanders among fields of stagnant water as calm as mirrors, each framed at the edges with a crust of white. They could almost be paddy fields apart from the absence of stooping people in oriental straw hats. There is a faintly rotten sea-smell. After a while the road crosses a wooden ramp and passes a couple of huts and an old windmill, and suddenly you are by the sea. There is a car park, a kiosk selling the *Sun* and after-sun, and a path following the edge of the salt-flats before it winds into the dunes.

Es Cavallet was made an official nudist beach in 1978 after decades of anti-nudist vigilance by the Guardia Civil. Nowadays a mild kind of sexual apartheid operates among Es Cavallet's naked visitors. At either end of a half-kilometre stretch of beach are two *chiringuitos* (beach bars with roofs of brush and bamboo). As in the Calle de la Virgen, the far end is gay and the near end is not. Otherwise there is not much difference between them. Both *chiringuitos* serve beer and *bocadillos* to similarly bronzed and bouncing bodies. Perhaps at the gay end the music is cooler and the bodies even more scrupulously well-presented. And there is one other crucial difference. If you take the path that leads away from the gay *chiringuito* into the dunes you enter a maze of sandy paths among a forest of old, twisted pines. This area, between the Salinas and the sea, is a refuge for rare plants and migrating birds, and in the winter nature has the place all to itself. In summer there is competition. On every corner a semi-clad body watches and waits, wearing the macho scowl that is thought to be correct for the serious sexual shopper. Every pine grove is a-rustle with activity. On hot nights the sound of the waves is mingled with grunts and groans, like an all-male version of the legend of the Mermaids.

At three o'clock on a Sunday afternoon in June the atmosphere at Es Cavallet was so laidback it was barely alive. The music was the mellowest imaginable New Age Folk, all echoing harps and wispy Celtic voices, wafting over a sea of glistening skin. It was the afternoon after the night before. Most people, said Fernando, had been at Anfora, the gay disco in a cave in the old town, till it shut at 6 a.m. and quite a number would probably have gone on to Space, which wasn't gay but by that time in the morning nobody much cared. The routine for many of Ibiza's hardcore nightbirds, gay or straight, was to tip out of the discos into the morning sun, have breakfast, hit the beach and sleep all day, go back to the hotel in the evening and mellow out until midnight, crawl round a few of the bars in Sa Penya and prepare to repeat the whole process again.

A yacht called the Monte Carlo Jo was anchored out there in the denim-blue water. On deck was an Ibiza scene: a girl in a silver-lamé bikini was doing her t'ai chi while her male companion, in black swimming trunks of the type known as 'skimpy', did press-ups. Later they both disappeared from view apart from two legs, one of either sex, moving very slowly from the horizontal to the vertical in time with the music. On another boat, cryptically named 'Qué–Why?' after the famous lubricant, there was a playful, sunstruck orgy of caresses and laughter. The sea around the boats was dotted with a flotilla of Li-Lo's, each bearing a recumbent body. Fernando said this was a new type of cruising peculiar to Es Cavallet: to be thus becalmed and naked on a Li-Lo meant you were an object of attention for swimmers in the clear warm water.

We bumped into Tim, an advertising salesman from north London on holiday for a week. Tim had a moustache, a perfectly even tan that he'd been working on all week and hair cropped GI-short in the gay fashion of that summer. He had been going out dancing at Anfora and Amnesia, doing E and coke on alternate nights. Last night had been an E-night. 'What with the clubs, the drugs and the beach, there just aren't enough hours left in the day for sex,' he moaned.

I left Tim and Fernando rolling a joint and went for a walk in the woods. Beyond the dunes there was no sea breeze but it was cool and peaceful under the pines. Inland the salt-flats glistened like a mirage. That week a flock of flamingos had stopped off in the Salinas on their way from the Camargue to Africa: I saw a pair of them take flight and flap awkwardly across the water, their strawberry-ice-cream pink briefly bright against a miniature mountain range of piles of salt.

Whether the sun-seekers and sex-fiends are aware of it is doubtful, but behind this bewitching landscape lie several chapters of Ibiza's past and a few crucial paragraphs of its future. After the Catalan conquest in 1235 the salt-flats were jointly owned by William Montgri, King James of Aragon and the other conquerors, who also shared the profits from this, the richest of the island's resources. But in 1267 they handed over all the rights of extraction to the Ibicenco people, reserving only their ownership of the land. During the darkest years of the next five centuries it was the salt-trade that saved Ibiza's dismal economy. Ibiza in the sixteenth century was the Mediterranean's major purveyor of salt, and the income from the Salinas paid the ransom for Ibicencos captured at sea by pirates. For centuries, the arrival of ships from the Spanish peninsula, the North Sea and Baltic ports was an important point of contact with the outside world.

The eighteenth and nineteenth centuries saw the Ibicencos progressively removed from their direct economic relationship with the salt-flats. After the War of Spanish Succession they were confiscated by the Castilian conquerors as the island's punishment for siding with the archduke Charles of Austria during the War. And in 1871 they were sold by the State to a private company for the immense sum of 1,160,000 pesetas.

The Ibicencos continued to work the salt-flats, but from now on it was pure exploitation. There were no machines – Spain had no Industrial Revolution – and mules couldn't be used because the salt ate into their hooves. The water evaporated over the summer, leaving around 100,000 tonnes of salt spread over 400 hectares which had to be dug out with axes and carried in baskets (usually on the head) to a primitive railway which took it to the miniature port of La Canal. Old photos show the bizarre whiteness of a Siberian winter as far as the horizon, when in fact salt-extraction normally took place in the crucifying heat of late summer. The deadline was the first rains at the end of September. The work was back-breaking and, cruelly, workers were paid by weight, not by hours. *Antes* it was often younger sons who had done badly in the inheritance stakes and who, for example, needed money to get married, who took the jobs. Often a young engaged man would have to work for two successive seasons in order to save enough.

With the economic tidal-wave of tourism largely wiping out the importance of the salt-industry, the salt-flats came to take on a different kind of value. The so-called 'Fight for the Salinas' pitted ecological interests against nakedly commercial ones and became the most significant episode in the political life of the island since the beginning of tourism. According to Ibiza's most vociferous ecological group the Grupo de Estudios de la Naturaleza (GEN) the 'fight' was nothing less than a Manichaean confrontation between 'ambition and life'.

The surprise was that it hadn't happened before. By the late seventies most of the coast of Ibiza had already been built on and the most beautiful bays (Cala Tarida, Cala Llonga, Cala Corral, Cala de Sant Vicent, Cala Vedella, Es Canar, to say nothing of the bay of San Antonio) were ruined, but the tourist industry was still hungry for coastal land. In the 1972 Provincial Plan for the Balearic Islands the salt-flats of Ibiza were described as 'urbanizable', and five years later the first proposals were made for a large-scale development of the area. A company, Ibifor SA, was set up to promote and sell the *urbanizaciones* to be created on the former salt-flats of Ibiza and Formentera (Ibiza's sister island has a Salinas of its own).

This time the development was strangled at birth by the Provincial Town-Planning Commission after it had been denounced by Ibiza's influential College of Architects and there had been demonstrations in which the front page of the *Diario de Ibiza* described Ibicencos and Formenterenses 'waking up as a people'.

More than ten years later the alarm-bells sounded again. Beside the salt-flats is a large area of almost virgin land which includes the hills of Puig des Falcò and Puig des Corb Marì. These hills were now threatened by two new urbanization plans involving 617 dwellings. The demonstrations started again and on 11 May 1990 a 'Save the Salinas' campaign was officially inaugurated at the offices of the GEN. Throughout the campaign, the GEN distinguished itself by fearless investigation and clever use of publicity. On 16 June six campaigners locked themselves in the Cathedral. Banners, posters, stickers and graffiti – some of the latter still visible – all carried the same message: 'Salvem ses Salines'. One of the first actions the GEN carried out was to present leaflets to the quartet of powerful figures behind the development

– Antonio Mari Calbet, president of the Consell Insular; Gabriel Cañellas, president of the Balearic Government; José Serra Escandell, mayor of San José; and the tycoon Abel Matutes Juan – denouncing them as guilty of conniving in the destruction of Ibiza's most precious natural resource. The extent of the involvement of these four was only discovered as the GEN continued to dig. It was revealed that Gabriel Cañellas and his wife, who owns a large chunk of the land in question, stood to benefit directly if the zone was built on. Most of the other owners of Salinas land were, according to one member of the GEN, 'if not politicians, then friends of politicians'.

The ecologists' idea was to push for the Salinas to be included in a catalogue of areas to be protected under the Balearic Law of Natural Spaces. Abel Matutes called this proposal 'an initiative that is clearly Communist and totalitarian in style'. On 25 May his brother Mariano Matutes, president of Ibiza's governing Partido Popular, announced that he too disapproved of any protection for the Salinas. After all, he said, the two *urbanizaciones* planned for the area were no more than 'dos manchitas' – 'two little stains'.

At the time of the controversy a new book about the rich wildlife of the Salinas written by two young biologists, Daniel Fernandez and Jaume Estarellas, showed that the area destined to be built on was also a habitat for several plant and bird species that were listed in the national Catalogue of Threatened Species. This gave the GEN another weapon. Together with the Ibiza branch of Friends of the Earth they reported the development to the European Commission as an infringement of the European law on protected species. Shortly afterwards Friends of the Earth issued the following press release. It was the first time that anybody had made the connection, at any rate in such forceful terms, between environmental contamination – which was what the Salinas development amounted to – and the escalating crisis in the tourist industry.

'Ibifor . . . claims to be building a tourist complex. In

addition to the negative impact that this will have on a habitat of great natural value, it does not seem that it will do anything to improve the crisis affecting Balearic tourism. The crisis has its origins, precisely, in the "excess of offer", its low quality, and in the irresponsible destruction of an environment of indubitable natural and aesthetic value.'

The 'Save the Salinas' movement believed it was making headway when the haggling started. First the Partido Popular offered to reduce the surface available for building. Then the mayor of San José suggested that instead of the original 617, only 80 'chalets' would be built. 'There will be no hotels, no *urbanizaciones*, nothing comparable with a tourist development,' he assured. The campaigners were determined to reject all compromises to the safety of the Salinas – they were plans 'of urbanization, not of protection' as José Ramón Balanzat of the GEN saw it – but things seemed to be going their way. Until they saw the first draft of the Natural Spaces law, and were horrified to see that somehow the politicians and moneymen had contrived to have the Salinas excluded from the catalogue.

In fact it was a temporary setback. On 30 January 1991 the Balearic Government in Palma de Mallorca voted by thirty votes to twenty-nine to have the Salinas included in the final draft of the Law of Natural Spaces (LEN). The salt-flats and surrounding countryside were awarded the status of Area Natural de Especial Interés (ANEI) which affords the highest protection under the Law. As it stands no one may build a house on an ANEI unless he owns more than 200,000m^2 of land in the area. Since nobody owns that much in the Salinas the Law effectively put a halt to all construction.

And yet, and yet. Neil Rock, the voluble Yorkshireman who does most of the big-time campaigning work for Friends of the Earth Ibiza, was not a happy man. He reminded me that the President of the Consell Insular, the island's local government, had recently called the LEN immoral and said he couldn't call on the citizens to uphold it. More ominously still, the day after the LEN was passed Gabriel Cañellas had announced that if his party won the forthcoming provincial election he would change the law. The following May the Partido Popular did indeed win the election . . .

The clearest way to understand what this island has been through in the last two generations is to look at old photographs and compare them with the sometimes unappetizing reality of Ibiza now. In a 1930s picture taken looking down from the Church at Santa Eulalia, northwards along the coast, three figures – a young woman with a clay pitcher under her left arm, a man in a straw hat and a boy in braces – gaze down the hill, like the camera, at a compact, low, white village of perhaps one or two streets in the midst of lush countryside.

The coastline is surprising to modern eyes. Fields simply fizzle out into beach, without interruption from trees, fences, buildings or roads. The promontory of Punta Arabí, at the edge of the wide bay of Santa Eulalia, is completely untouched, as is the rest of the coast which stretches away as far as the lens can see. A contemporary version of the same view is hardly recognizable as the same place. The town seems to have sprawled down to the sea in a graceless rush, like a lager lout on his first day at the beach. The small hill of Punta Arabí pokes forlornly out of a forest of hotels; the horizon is speckled with the white froth of development.

On the beaches the changes have been even more dramatic, given that *antes* they were frequented only by fishermen, who built their stone huts into the rocks. Non-fishing Ibicencos seldom went to the beach. I once met an old lady in Santa Inés who has never been in her life. Before it became one of the big names in Spanish package tourism Playa d'en

Bossa was a fabulous, lonely arc of sand where the Birdie Song was something you might have heard from the branches of a fig tree. Lady Aitken, mother of MP Johnathan and actress Maria, remembers walks at Es Canar, along the coast from Santa Eulalia, where she could ramble dreamily for hours, weaving among dunes and pinewoods, and not see a single soul.

There's a theory, not a very likely theory but a romantic one, that some of the tribe who were expelled from Canaan by the Israelites and ended up in Ibiza might have chosen the name Es Cana, with or without the 'r', in remembrance of their homeland. Even though Es Canar now crawls with coaches and heaves with hotels, in the deep pinewoods behind the coast you can still find a quietness tinged with the melancholy of exile.

In the early sixties it was still virgin land, except that there were half a dozen houses in the area which all belonged to fishermen and farmers. The Boom came along marginally later than in other Ibicenco resorts, but by 1966/1967 the land was changing hands, fishermen and farmers were getting rich and the hotels were going up like a row of skittles along the coast. When it happened, it happened fast. In early 1967 the road linking the new resort to Santa Eulalia was still not passable by coach. There was frustration among the business-men: how could the foreigners be persuaded to hand over their foreign currency to all the sparkling new hotels, bars, shops and restaurants of Es Canar if there was no physical means of depositing them in said hotels, bars, shops, etc.? Later the same year a series of adverts announced an 'extra-ordinary offer'. For 225 pesetas per square metre the pur-chaser received 10,000 square metres of flat land in Es Canar. The price included water-supply and beach. What more could a property-developer want? The land had originally been agricultural but was obviously far more suitable for 'hotels, residences, apartments or chalets. Great Investment! Unique Opportunity!'

In 1992 Es Canar was described by Thomson's, the

biggest foreign tour-operator on the island, as a 'popular modern resort' which has 'lost none of its essential beauty and character'. It is unlikely that anyone who knew the place thirty years ago would agree with that statement, but as a tourist resort there is nothing wrong with Es Canar. There is a little harbour and a miniature promenade, the water is shallow and sparkling, and people enjoy themselves.

The morning of 1 July found me in Ibiza airport, waiting for a flight from Glasgow. Of the 300 passengers on CKT253 a good coachful were heading for Es Canar. They streamed out into the Arrivals Hall, to be met by a crowd of jolly Thomson's reps in yellow suits who looked them up on their lists and sent them off to the coach-park.

'Lang? Yes, you're in the Ibiza Mar, that's coach F. Kirkpatrick? You'll be staying in the Tanit Park, and that's coach . . . J. Straight up to the end of the terminal, out of the door and you'll find the coaches just in front of you.' This lot were Scottishly polite and well-turned-out, and there wasn't a hint of rowdiness. You only get the lager-louts and hooligans on the English flights, said one of the reps.

Before the flight touched down there had been a few hitches in the dizzyingly complex arrangements for getting people from the airport to their correct resort and bed. With five minutes to go the head rep, Lisa Cosgrove, who was doubled up with gastro-enteritis but could still manage the dazzling smile of welcome that is the holiday-rep's stock-in-trade, called the others over and they clustered around her with their Thomson clipboards. 'Anybody for the Glasgow? Listen, there's some changes. With the Glasgow people, on Coach B there's now an El Cortijo extra . . . and then, where are we, on Coach F there's now 7 extra Marina Palace, 7 extras, and they're Square Deal, so you'll get the names off the Square Deal list . . . and then there's Ibiza Mar, three for the Ibiza Mar, and it's now Coach G, which is actually coach 79.' It was all rather confusing, but the reps all nodded their heads and practised their welcoming smiles at each other.

While flight CKT253 made its way to the coaches I spoke

to Linda Black, a boisterous lass from Liverpool. It was her second year as a Thomson rep. Last year she'd been in Ibiza and had such a good time she asked to be sent here again. In the winter she'd been 'doing Benidorm'. 'I was on "Young at Heart". Package deals for the over-fifty-fives are really big now, especially in Benidorm. The entertainments are the main thing. They go on Mystery Tours, then they get Beetle Drives, Whist Drives, Old Time Dancing, Bingo, you name it. Dancin' the night away. The reps have to go on training courses to learn the Quickstep and how to call Bingo. You see the same old people month after month – "Hello there, Mrs Collins, are you having a lovely holiday?" "Ooh, yes thank you, dear." They love it to death.'

I was off to look at the Hotel Panorama in Es Canar, where Linda had been stationed the previous summer. 'It's a Thomson Sun hotel, so it's the best, kind of à la carte. You'll get very high standards. Probably one of the best hotels on the island. The thing with the Panorama is the entertainments, y'see. They lay on special things for the Thomson Sun people. You get yer Karaoke, Sun-Stretch, TV Gala Shownight, all that. So there you go, you've chosen well.'

It looked OK in the catalogue. 'The Panorama enjoys a picturesque harbourfront setting, close to the beach,' reads the caption under a picture of a large, white, four-square building in Mediterranean Modernist style with windows looking out across the masts of a few white fishing-boats. Another picture on the opposite page zooms in on a massive pool, not so much kidney-shaped as stomach-shaped, with a palm-roofed tropical bar on an island in the middle. The Panorama is a 'Thomson Sun Highlight' so it gets two whole enthusiastic pages documenting its food (burgers and sandwiches at the poolside snack bar and pizzas 'for a special treat'), entertainment ('at night the hotel really comes alive') and round-the-clock service from the ever-eager Thomson team. With all this and more on offer it would clearly be impossible not to have an 'unforgettable' holiday.

The Es Canar people were in coach G. Among them were the Weirs, who'd been up all night to catch the flight at seven. 'We're from the centre of Glasgow – not from the schemes.' They had only been to Mallorca before but found it 'a wee bit dry', so they thought they'd try Ibiza where the landscape might be greener. Apart from that they imagined Ibiza might be 'more or less the same as Majorca. I expect they have all the dialects here . . . er, Catalonian, Majorcan, and Ibicencan too,' said the knowledgeable Mr Weir. His wife said she liked the sound of Es Canar: 'Es Canna, Es Canna,' she practised. 'It's a wee bit Scots, don't you think?'

The day they arrived the weather was going through a bad patch, an unseasonal spell of drizzling humid greyness. The Glaswegians, who had come from blue skies and high-summer temperatures in Scotland, peered out of the coach window in fatalistic amusement, as if they knew all along it would happen to *them*.

We were pulling out on to the main road to Ibiza when Lisa launched into her in-coach speech. 'Welcome to the *sunny* island of Ibiza,' she began, pausing to see the effect of her irony. But her audience had gone strangely quiet; we were travel-tired, perhaps, or simply caught up in the awe of being abroad. 'As you can see we're just having a little bit of an interval in the beautiful weather we've been having. But hopefully it's going to pick up very shortly and you're going to have a lovely time here on the island of Ibiza.' Lisa spoke as if she had a permanent smile on her face, which she almost did, and put her emphasis in odd places, like an air-hostess. We were going to have a lovely time here on the island *of* Ibiza.

We rolled past Playa d'en Bossa and its very very pretty, very very beautiful beaches and the 'little resort' of Figueretes, where Lisa told the coach (correctly) that Figueretes used to be a fig plantation but is now a very very built-up area, and (bizarrely) that the resort acts as a dormitory town for the entire Ibicenco population in the winter months when the island has 'closed down'.

Round the string of roundabouts on the way to Santa Eulalia, and all eyes were trained on the citadel of Dalt Vila. 'That's the Old Town up there,' commentated Lisa, 'and it's actually got a sixteenth-century cathedral on the top, that's a sixteenth-century cathedral, well worth a visit *during* your stay. Hopefully you'll get the chance to come down here to Ibiza town, that's something to take your cameras to. Also a chance for you to have a little walk down the cobbled streets and see the typical Ibicencan people hanging out their washing across the street and the ladies in their black traditional costume. That's during the daytime. During the evening it's just that little bit different, you can have a look, *in* Ibiza town, for all the weird and wonderful people we have here, and that's Ibiza town at night.'

The roads were so empty we got through Santa Eulalia and down to Es Canar in record time, with the result that when we arrived at the Panorama some of the rooms weren't ready and the travel-weary Scots had to wait with their bags in the foyer. Soon the grumbling started. 'We were up fae five o'clock this morning – I mean it's a long time, that,' protested Mrs Donaldson whose husband had just flaked out beside her on a squidgy leather armchair. 'He had a bit of a sleep last night, but I couldn't get off, I was so terrified of missing the flight.' Suddenly Mr Donaldson perked up and said, 'I've just lost three stone and had half me stomach oot wi' cancer. And now they're making me wait for a room. It gets worse and worse every year.' I think he meant life in general.

Next morning at ten we were all invited to the Welcome Party. This is a package-tour event which in the hands of Britain's biggest tour-operator has become an institution. Lisa had called it 'a chance for you to find out everything that's going on during your stay, and to have a little bit of a drink with us to celebrate your holiday, so that's the Welcome Party'. Slowly the guests drifted into the ballroom/bar, an interior designer's nightmare of marble-cladded pillars, plush low puke-coloured chairs and smoked glass coffee-tables, to the sound of loud disco music. The dress code was holiday-wear, shorts, shirts, trainers and cameras, plus jumpers. Outside it was still grey and grumpy. 'Mam, I wanna take my top off,' moaned a child. 'When the sun comes out, love, not now, it's too cold.'

Drinks were served in little brown glasses which my neighbour frowned at as he took his off the tray. Derek Rodgers was a sensible-looking man with slick black hair in a bowl-cut and polyester shorts revealing legs so pale they couldn't have seen the light since his last holiday, which was in Menorca. The reason for his low opinion of the small brown glasses was that at home in Hightown near Liverpool he runs his own business distributing glassware and bar-equipment, and thus might be called an expert. 'He's always checking up on the way they do things abroad,' explained his wife Mavis.

The Rodgers first came to Ibiza seven years ago. It was Mavis's first overseas trip. 'I would never go abroad, because I'd always heard the bad things about it. You get mugged, you get stabbed, and all the rest of it.' Derek: 'She imagined Ibiza as, like, ten miles of sand and nothing else, and twenty million people crammin' on like sardines.' Mavis: 'It never appealed to me, so it was more like I was forced into coming.' Added to which Mavis gets travel-sick on any flight longer than two hours, so holiday-wise they thought they'd better stick to Spain. They could have tried Italy, but Derek had been to Lido di Jesolo and didn't like it. 'Italy's too flat and crowded, and the sea's not so nice as Spain.'

From the moment the sun came out on the beach at Portinatx Mavis was converted to abroad. The next year they went to Tenerife and hated it, but they knew part of the reason for that was the nagging memory of Ibiza. 'So we booked up for Ibiza last year with one of the companies that went bust, and we ended up going to Menorca. So then we had to come to Ibiza to allay the ghost.'

The Rodgers are more adventurous than the average package holidaymaker, especially considering they have two

kids, Amanda and Mike, who share the low boredom thres-
hold common to ten- and eleven-year-olds. When they were
last here the family hired a car for a few days and had a look
round the island, taking in the hippie market, Ibiza town at
night, and 'all the little villages'. Tour-operators normally lay
on all sorts of excursions but they wouldn't be going on them
unless it was something really special, like the time they went
to a Medieval Evening in the 'medieval' castle in Tenerife and
watched knights jousting while they ate.

If they don't have the car they'll wander round the shops
and have a coffee or some lunch – 'We tend to stick to what
we know. Not chips and burgers, but salads, chicken, that
sort of thing. Spanish food? Mavis goes for the *lasagne* and
the *bolognese*. Not the *paella* though, we wouldn't trust it – I
don't think it's safe, especially with the kids.' The Thomson
team of six or seven girl reps, all wearing the Thomson
uniform and callisthenic smile, were assembling on a small
podium at the side of the bar. They were so bubbly they
were in danger of exploding. The disco tape came off and
they did a little floor show complete with chorus-line dance
steps and a lip-synched song about 'Thomson Fun'. Then
they stepped forward one by one and said their piece. First
Natasha from Norfolk gathered up the kids, trawling through
the audience for the recalcitrant ones and prising them off
Mum, and led them off to the Big T Club. Next Wendy from
Essex filled us in on the 'Island Panorama', the popular coach
excursion which enables package tourists to see just that little
bit more of Ibiza than they would if they were stuck away
in their resorts. It seemed to me that anyone going on this
trip, if they weren't put off by the price of 3200 pesetas
(around £20, which however included lunch) would come
away with at least a nodding acquaintance with life beyond
the package. Wendy even took time to tell us about one of
Ibiza's chief glories, Hierbas Ibicencas, which is made by
macerating local herbs in alcohol and has been the cause of
many an evil holiday hangover. 'There is a myth about Hierbas', she said, 'which is that it makes all the men more virile

and all the women more beautiful. As you can see from our very own Lisa – she's never tried it.' At this Lisa got up and gave Wendy a theatrical slap, and the audience, previously glum, broke into laughter like the sun coming out from behind a cloud. They were moving into holiday mode.

For those who might have been-there-done-that with the Island Panorama there was Simply Ibiza, a more sophisticated trip which aimed, with apparently unconscious irony, to take its tourist coach-parties to places 'untouched by tourism'. Lunch would be thrown in at the 'typical Ibicencan village of Santa Gertrudis'. Simply Ibiza, in fact, was the very reason Theo and Harold shut up shop at lunchtime twice a week. Whatever else might happen on these people's holidays they could not possibly be bored, especially at night when, as the catalogue had claimed, the Panorama really did come alive. There was Karaoke on Monday, TV Gameshow Night on Wednesday, Flamenco on Sunday, and on Tuesday a Gala Shownight with 'top acts flown in from the UK'. If you didn't feel like staying in, there would be coaches leaving once a week for the Hillbilly Hoedown or the slightly more raucous Bronco Barbecue where you can be thrown off a mechanical bucking bronco before tucking into 'your own meats, lashings of salads and potatoes' washed down with (an ominous detail, this) 'unlimited wine from barrels set around the gardens'.

Ibiza's cosmopolitanism sometimes verges on the surreal. In a week of package-holiday nights at the Panorama you could, if you had the stamina, take a dizzying journey from Japan (karaoke) to the south of Spain (flamenco) to the Wild West for the Hillbilly Hoedown, and wind up in New Zealand for a Maori-style barbecue at the house of two expatriate Kiwis called Rose and Art. To complete the cultural mélange, when you had sipped your Bali Hai cocktail at Rose and Art's and finished your meal of 'steaming succulent pork or lamb' followed by lemon meringue pie you would be serenaded with sounds of the sixties and seventies by Sean – 'from Ireland'. Practically the only Ibicenco element of your evening would have been the lemons in the pie, which Rose and Art grow in their own orchard.

When the Welcome Party came to a close the sun was out and there was a rush for towels and sun-cream. I went to see the manager, an urbane man called José Antonio Geli who like 60 per cent of his staff wasn't from Ibiza. (He was from Gerona. They were mostly Andalucians.) José Antonio told me that the hotel was built by an Englishman called Adrian Hayes in 1966 and how, years later, it passed to some Italians who moved the pool from the front to the back and added the Pizzeria but otherwise kept Hayes' sell-'em-cheap package philosophy intact. In 1984 it was bought by Med Playa, who had seven other hotels on the island, and in 1991 it was dumped by Med Playa and taken over by a Mallorca-based company, who were moving into the Ibicenco market. Most of the hotels in Es Canar are 'two star' and there are no four stars, so the Panorama must be one of the best in the resort – though probably not, as the girl in the airport had claimed, one of the best on the island. José Antonio modestly thought that in its category in its own way his hotel had reached 'quite a high standard'.

He was married to a local girl and lived here all the year round, accustomed to the swingeing fluctuations of the *temporada*. The hotel opens officially at the beginning of May and shuts at the end of October. 'One, five, thirty-one, ten'; José Antonio recites it like a mantra. When the last guest left his work wouldn't be quite over, because there'd be staff salaries and suppliers' bills to pay, the accounts to be done and budgets fixed for the coming year, so in fact he is normally at his desk till December. Then he has a long, well-deserved holiday. 'In the winter it's my turn to be a guest, like all the people who stay here in the summer.'

The Panorama is unlike most hotels in the world, and like virtually all hotels in Mediterranean holiday-resorts, in that its guests arrive under the aegis of a tour-operator. There are eight of them in various European countries working to fill the Panorama, but none of them works harder than the

British company Thomson. Thomson buys sixty places in the hotel over the whole season for its 'Sun' programme, which is a very useful slice of the Panorama's business. Some hotels are 100 per cent devoted to Thomson. This is all very well, but if there is a bad year in the UK market and Thomson does less well, as happened in 1991 and 1992, the hotel feels it painfully.

Look at the island as a whole and you'll find the same problem of overdependence writ large. Mass tourism is Ibiza's life-blood. More than 70 per cent of the active population earns their living from it directly or indirectly, and there can hardly be a single Ibicenco soul, neo or not, who hasn't been affected by it in some way, even if they were once stuck behind a crawling tour-bus on the road to San Antonio. Anything that happens in the tourist industry — whether there is a blip in the market, or tourists are spending fewer pesetas than usual, or someone has bitten off a policeman's ear, or there were 12.7 more Danes in Ibiza last summer than the summer before – gets on to the front pages of the two local papers before you can say *paella* and chips.

In the review of the year published by *La Prensa* at the close of 1991, the tourism story was in third place after the local elections (in which the conservative Partido Popular swept aside the left-wing PSOE as they had done every year since democracy) and the new Law of Natural Spaces. The headline of the story announces snappily that 'A Timid *Recuperación* of Tourism Allows us to Glimpse the End of the Crisis'.

The good news in *La Prensa* was that the market increased last season by an estimated 0.3 per cent on the previous year. The bad news was that The Crisis was still around. For the previous two seasons at least the C-word had been on everyone's lips, up there with Abel Matutes, hippie parties, the drug problem and the current performance of Barcelona Football Club as a major topic of bar and dinner-party conversation. But it was hard to judge how much of a crisis this really was. There was no sign of British-style grim-facedness and belt-tightening: the streets were as full as they always had been of smartly dressed young women, and two cars per family was still the rule rather than the exception. But financial embarrassment is easy to hide. As a society, perhaps, Ibiza has felt the shock at a deeper level. For thirty years the island got richer and richer, like a gambler on a winning streak. There was no reason to imagine that life would ever be difficult again. And now it is.

In 1936 the *Diario de Ibiza* was the island's only newspaper. It was a charming hodge-podge of small-town gossip and 'news-stories' about the almond harvest in the *campo* and Don Antonio Tur Torres losing his wallet in the Paseo Vara de Rey. On 21 July, two days after the War broke out in the rest of the country, the paper's main story was about tree-planting in the town, followed by a small-ad for a grocer's shop: 'For Seville olives and onions in vinegar, visit Colmado Planells.' Further down the page was a paragraph noting the disappearance of a bicycle. The *Diario's* leader assured its readers there was no cause for alarm: 'In our city, as in the rest of the island, there is complete calm. Various patrols of volunteers and Civil Guard are keeping watch. Work is going on completely as normal.' But hidden away in a corner was the ominous phase 'Visado por la Censura Militar': 'surveyed by military censors.'

At this point Ibiza was under right-wing rule. Elliot Paul, whose 1937 book *Life and Death of a Spanish Town* describes the Civil War as experienced by the village of Santa Eulalia, wrote that in 1934 there was a 'fascist' Sergeant in charge in the town who would only give out hunting licences to those who were known to be Right. (Paul himself is known to have been Left.) On 14 July there had been a demonstration of armed 'fascist' volunteers in Ibiza town and on the 20th Comandante Mestre, military commander of the castle in Ibiza, proclaimed martial law and imposed a 10.30 p.m. curfew. Mariano Llobet remembers that members of the left-wing Popular Front were arrested but that no one was killed.

None of this had been reported by the *Diario*, but in the coming weeks it began to be clear even to its most credulous readers that the island's 'complete calm' presaged a storm. One day it reported that the mail-boat from Alicante had failed to arrive. Another day, the merchant Don José Costa Torres was detained for having hidden a number of bags of sugar. Evidently this was because supplies of basic, imported ingredients such as sugar and coffee had run out and there were no more steamers from Republican-run Valencia and Barcelona. More serious was the petrol shortage which meant that powered fishing boats couldn't go out and buses couldn't run.

On 5 August, again according to Elliot Paul, Republican pamphlets were circulating with the headline 'Hoy tomaremos Ibiza', 'Today we will take Ibiza'. Next day the town was bombed. Only half-a-dozen bombs fell and no one was hurt, but the shock to the island was great. Two days later, Republican troops arrived by boat from Barcelona and Valencia. And on 11 August the *Diario de Ibiza* suddenly described itself at the top of the front page as the 'mouthpiece of the Popular Front' and was full of references to 'anti-fascism', the 'new revolutionary order' and 'the heroic Catalan and Valencian comrades under the command of Captain Bayo who have freed the island from rebel military power'.

A week later the Reds were fully in control, supplies were coming in from Barcelona and Mestre had been arrested. And the *Diario's* rhetoric had grown preposterous. 'Long Live the Republic! Death to Fascism! Spain, Europe, all the civilized nations . . . whose citizens come to honour us with their visit . . . will be able to pass on to their countries the pleasing impression that Ibiza is the only place on earth in the world where the spirit of generosity and liberalism triumphs so effortlessly.'

'The spirit of generosity and liberalism' did not apply to Right-wing fugitives in the countryside, who were warned they would be 'very severely punished' if they did not surrender. Many opponents of the Republicans thought it prudent to flee the island altogether. At 9 in the morning on 9 August, four people including the mayor and municipal judge of Santa Eulalia had boarded a boat at Cala Corral. There was no petrol for the motor, so they went by sail. It wasn't known where they went or what had happened to them. On 12 September (a Saturday), barely five weeks after the Republicans took over, it was all change again. This time the bombs that fell on Ibiza were Franco's. They started at three in the afternoon, just as the town was coming out for its leisurely afternoon walk. One fell on the Café Mar y Sol, one on the petrol store, one in Calle Castelar, one near the Old Market in front of what is now the jeweller's Casa Viñets, and one on the Fonda Can Sires, a small family hotel, killing everyone inside.

What happened next was possibly the greatest single tragedy in the island's history. Older Ibicencos still look back in anger. Republican troops, trapped on the island in a state of great psychological stress, took all the Nationalist prisoners up to the castle and massacred them with guns and hand-grenades. You could hear the gunfire all over town. Thereafter the Reds got out of the island in whatever way they could. After the killings Ibiza town was deserted, stunned and silent. There were perhaps a dozen people left; all the rest had fled to the countryside. 'Ibiza was left alone and wounded with nobody in charge; somewhat destroyed, and morally devastated', remembers one witness. Surviving issues of the *Diario* come to a sudden halt on the 13th – just one day after it had changed its name to 'Workers' Solidarity' and published a feature quoting Stalin on the contradictions of Capitalism. From the six months after the Francoist invasion not a single issue remains in the official archives.

But the *Diario* of March 29 1937, the first after the long gap, tells us all too clearly what had happened in between:

'A FATHERLAND: SPAIN
A LEADER: FRANCO

Over the ruins of Marxism, with the generous blood of those who are now fighting without rest, will flourish your Spring. We must revive an intense love for Spain, the most glorious nation on earth.'

The island was occupied by Spanish Nationalist and Italian troops. It was a mirror-image of the previous régime. Now there were vicious reprisals against 'Reds' just as there had been a few weeks ago against 'fascists'. A former prisoner in a concentration camp for 'Reds' in Formentera remembers 'shootings at sunset' and weeks of terrible hunger. According to a recent book about the German artist Raoul Hausmann – one of the small number of foreigners who had settled in Ibiza during the early thirties – the mayor of San José, Llorenc Carbonell, who had been appointed by the Republicans, was persecuted and killed by the Nationalists. The communist leader Antoni Ribas escaped to the mainland but was captured and interned in a concentration camp in the South of France. Hausmann himself owned that rare thing, a radio, moreover he was known to have Leftist sympathies, and was immediately accused of collusion with the enemy. Foreign citizens were repatriated in two boats, one French and one German.

Compared to the way the Civil War went in other parts of the country Ibiza's experience of it was brief and relatively painless. But its impact on Ibicenco society and on individual lives was as great as anywhere, perhaps greater given the social tranquillity that had reigned here almost uninterrupted since the pirate invasions in the seventeenth century. The full history of the war in Ibiza has never been written, probably because the deep wounds it caused have still not properly healed. The historian Ernest Prats, who wrote the twenty-nine-part history (in Catalan) of Ibiza and Formentera that came out every Saturday with the *Diario de Ibiza*, refused to write about it even though the newspaper wanted a history up to the present day, saying it would be 'too dangerous'. All we have to go on is oral history, clouded as it is with prejudice and bitterness. One of the reasons Ibiza has voted solidly for the right-wing Partido Popular ever since the new dawn of democracy in 1978 (Formentera, oddly, is more in line with the rest of Spain in preferring the socialist PSOE party) lies in the memory of Republican outrages during the five brief weeks of their control in 1936. Javier's great-grandfather was killed by the 'Reds'; not surprisingly his granddaughter, Javier's mother, talks about them now with barely-concealed indignation. She was a child at the time and remembers being evacuated from the town to the family's summer house in San Antonio. She was ill with angina. When the bombings started they spent the night along with other women and children in the Cave of Saint Agnes, in the countryside above the town.

The War divided families against each other and themselves, nursing enmities that sometimes erupted into violence. Pedro Planell's family come from Santa Gertrudis – 'in Fruitera, where most of the water was'. A feud developed between Pedro's grandfather, a Republican, and the owner of the next-door *finca* who was a Nationalist. One day his grandfather was cutting wood some distance from the house when the neighbour came up behind him with an Ibicenco knife, the type used to slit the pig's throat at *matanzas*. 'Every young man in those days had his pistol and his knife. The guy stabbed my grandfather in the back and the knife cut through to the front, that much, up to there. So he turned back with his axe and killed the guy. He'd been walking about 3km, then they had to put the horse onto the wagon to go and get the doctor. They put towels round him and he stayed like that for about eight hours. In the end he was judged and condemned to 30 years of prison for killing a Nationalist.'

In the country, some of the most vivid memories are of the soldiers that went from house to house taking anything of value. Mostly they came in search of food. An old woman who has lived all her life in the village of San Rafael told me: 'If you had food you stored it where nobody could steal it from you. Around here there were sheep, there were chickens, people did eat, even if sometimes there was only carob and figs . . . you got what you could. In the city there was nothing. And yet people got round it because a lot of them had relations in the country. And the relations, like us, we picked wheat, we picked beans, we picked everything they needed and gave it to the family.' Not only did country people hide their food, they also grew it in secret. Toni's mother knew people who milled flour at night from corn grown in remote fields. Once the soldiers had satisfied their hunger they looked for jewellery. In any household that possessed it the collection of long gold chains, necklaces and a richly decorated cross that made up the *emprendada* was a precious family heirloom. Many of them were stolen, sold and melted down. Catalina Juan Ribas' grandfather had one *emprendada* and another incomplete set – 'he was keeping them for his daughters, and his wife and her sisters. When the people came in from that war, the one in '36, they went round all the houses asking, and they took everything away from him. My grandfather gave it all away. The ones who were a bit cleverer had it all hidden under the earth and said "There's nothing here".'

The journalist Joan Lluis Ferrer began his report on the state of Ibiza's ecology with a graphic illustration of the island's pace of change in the last 30 years. If you could compress the whole of Ibiza's history in the space of one hour, he wrote, the Carthaginians would have arrived in the first five minutes and the Moors ten minutes later. The Catalan invasion happened at half-past, and at quarter-to the Corsairs took to their *xabecs*. Four minutes to the hour and Ibiza saw its first feeble glimmer of electric light. With thirty seconds to go the island's first hotel was built. And in the last second of the hour there has sprung to life a monstrous industry capable of handling 100,000 tourists at any one time in 700 hotels and 3000 bars and restaurants.

At the start of the sixties Ibiza had not advanced much further into the modern world than it had at the end of the thirties. It was still predominantly an agricultural society. Even in 1965 when the tourist boom was well under way 45 per cent of the active population still worked on the land, nearly all of them on their own individual farms or allotments. *Antes* the only industry of any importance was salt – in the late summer harvest of 1950 the salt-flats produced 75,000 tons which it took the entire available workforce of the *campo* to collect. In the distant past there had been a small-scale export of apricot pulp to Edwardian England, but as a 1908 study of the island remarked drily, the main defect of this as a business was that it could only exist for a single month each year – the month the apricots were in season.

In 1960 the island's hotels put up just over 30,000 visitors. This was not mass tourism, but a trickle of adventurous bourgeois travellers, like Laurie Lee who came 'to finish a book, because I write on wine, and it's cheaper. You got there by a slow boat, full of beatniks and Germans . . . I had no notion what to expect, I knew nothing about Ibiza, and the young gentlemen from Palma in their blue dacron suits had coughed when I asked them about it. "Very rough and brutish", they said, "very backward. No cars and no society".'

But even then Ibiza was changing. Lee was disappointed to discover that the 'bone-white temples' he had glimpsed from the boat were in fact early holiday bungalows.

Compared to the South of Spain Lee knew and loved, it was already rich. 'So now to Ibiza . . . something resembling a miracle has happened', he wrote in *I Can't Stay Long*. 'Without labour or seed, floating harvests of wealth now fall on this sterile island . . . Only a few years ago its people were dying in the street, now everyone is plump and busy. How this could have happened, how long it may last, are things too uneasy to ask.'

The dying in the street bit was hyperbolic, but it illustrates the pace of change. During the first half of the sixties the number of visitors per year more than tripled to 102,538, and in 1967 (the year of the International Airport) the graph goes haywire. By 1973 the annual total had rocketed to more than half a million and has stayed there ever since, with minor excursions into the 400,000s in times of 'crisis' and the 600,000s in times of *recuperación*.

In the space of a few years, *antes* suddenly turned into *ahora*. The Franco regime had realized that tourism offered a possible cure for Spain's economic anaemia. The country needed foreign money to fuel the planned recovery. As it happened the fuel came from three sources: foreign loans; money earned by Spanish workers abroad (in 1973 there were half a million of them in Germany alone); and money spent by foreign tourists in Spain. Franco set up a Ministry of Tourism which had Tourist Offices in every major European capital. There were special credit arrangements for hoteliers and financial advantages for foreign investors. It shows how committed the government was to tourism that it encouraged the proliferation of charter flights – crucial to the development of the package tour – which in some cases existed in direct competition with the state airline Iberia. Life for the tourist was made easier by simpler visa and customs formalities and the newly-devalued peseta. The effects of this economic shot in the arm were dramatic. During 1966 more than 17 million visitors spent 74,743 million pesetas (then $1,246,710,000) in Spain. Sums like this helped the Spanish economy grow faster during the sixties than any other in the world except for the Japanese – though from a low base. In 1960 there were only nine cars for every 1000 citizens; in 1970 there were seventy. Over the same period the Spanish TV audience grew from 1 per cent of the population to 90 per cent.

Ibiza felt these material benefits as much as anywhere. But with them came profound social and cultural changes that nobody could have predicted. Tourism threw Ibiza's agriculture into crisis, mainly because it offered Ibicencos an alternative they had never had before. A job as a waiter or a chambermaid paid more and felt less like hard work than digging potatoes or picking almonds. There began an inexorable draining away of the workforce from the countryside towards the city and the tourist towns of San Antonio and Santa Eulalia.

The tourist boom was accompanied by another parallel and related boom in the construction industry. More has been built in Ibiza in the last twenty-five years than in the whole of the rest of the island's history – much of it of abysmal quality. In 1965, mid-boom, Ibiza was 'importing' 2,500 tonnes of cement from the mainland every month. Spain's average consumption of cement at that time was 250 kilos per head per year; Ibiza's was 650.

All the new hotels, restaurants and bars needed people to build and staff them, and there was not enough labour on the island to do it all. This brought about the next great social change. 'Guest workers' in their thousands came from impoverished Andalucia and Murcia and later from Argentina and Uruguay, reversing the century-old trend of Ibicenco emigration to Latin America. Ibicenco hoteliers were so desperate for staff in the Gold Rush years of the sixties that they turned to waiter-hunting. They would take a trip to some dust-blown Andalucian town in the Sierra de Jaén, sit down with the mayor in the town square and announce: 'We need thirty waiters.' As long as they had legs and arms, the joke went, nobody cared about their waiting skills.

On August 12 1967 the *Diario* published an interview

with a twenty-one-year-old from Cuenca who was working as a builder in San Antonio. 'Do you earn enough to live?' he was asked. 'Of course! Every month I send home 500 ptas [now £3] to help them. We are eight brothers and sisters and five of us are still very small.' The boy had a girlfriend. Was he going to bring her to Ibiza? 'Definitely. I want her to see this, to know what it is to live well. She hasn't seen the sea yet, and doesn't know about tourists in bikinis and all that. I've told her about it, I go home for Christmas, but there's no way of making her believe it.'

Twenty-five years later the tide of immigration, swelled by smaller waves from South America, the Maghreb, Germany and Britain, has culminated in one inescapable fact. Because 63 per cent of the resident population is *forastero* – to say nothing of the millions of holidaymakers who swarm along the coast every summer – the 'real' Ibicencos, heirs of the Carthaginians, Moors and Catalans, are now outnumbered on their own island.

As well as finding themselves with a minority culture the Ibicencos must now decide how, or whether, to revive a dying one. And as they are discovering, there is nothing more difficult. Yes, there are folk-dances in every village square and Catalan is taught in schools and there are now several bodies (notably the Institute of Ibicenco Studies and the island government's Council of Culture) doing noble work preserving traditional cultural manifestations in a more or less artificial way, but time is running out for many of the rarer things. So much is vanishing so quickly that, like species in the Amazon rainforest, it is hardly known about before it becomes extinct.

Ethnologist Kirk Huffman, based in Ibiza but busy in the South Pacific and at academic conferences worldwide, has made a kind of hobby noting customs, songs, people, beliefs that are the last of their kind. A woman he knows is the last practitioner of a kind of magic healing whose roots go back far beyond Christianity. A handful of Ibicencos, he says, can still use the whistling language with which a message could be passed from one side of the island to the other in half an hour. Only another handful can still sing the rude *porfedi* songs with their weird ululations. Kirk is most fond of the last of the pig-smugglers. This needs explanation. In Formentera the pigs are big-boned and skinny, but are sold *by pig*, whereas in Ibiza they are smaller but sold *by weight*. Therefore it made sense to smuggle the pigs over from Formentera, fatten them up and sell them for *matanzas*.

To listen to Kirk talk about these things is to follow a depressing litany of disappearance. 'We desperately need an ethnographical museum,' he pleads. 'There is the most incredible wealth of stuff that in ten years' time will all have gone when the generation who came to maturity just before the Civil War dies out.'

In an antique-filled flat in the modern part of town lives a friend of Kirk's who is a member of what is, in a way, another rare and disappearing species: the *haute bourgeoisie* of the old town. *Antes* Javier Ferrari Planell's family had a grand three-storey house in the Plaza de la Constitución, the old market-square. It still stands, balconied and shuttered and painted a rich red, opposite the miniature Greek temple of the market. In the Civil War a bomb fell nearby while people were sheltering behind the big wooden door of the house. Under several layers of brown paint the shrapnel marks are still visible, like a metaphor for the War itself and its persistence in Ibicenco memory.

I visited Javier in his family's new apartment and we drank whisky and talked about the changes. From the terrace was a view of characterless off-white modern blocks in the post-boom style. Before all this was here, said Javier, there were orchards and farms and a few low whitewashed buildings – a carob-pod wholesaler and another place where carob was distilled into a bitter-sweet liqueur called *palo*, and two little *tiendas* at the end of Vara de Rey called Ca'n Cabrit and Ca'n Funoy which both sold sacks of lentils, rope and camping gas. Where his block of flats is now there was a *casa payesa*.

'When I look back now I realize that something was changing, but at the time I didn't. I suppose I really began to realize twelve or fifteen years ago what kind of life my parents and my grandparents had lived. There had always been changes, but now everything was speeding up.'

The Pereyra is a pink-and-white colonial-style building which opened its doors as a theatre in 1898 and thereafter became a bar/theatre/boxing ring/political meeting-place. Now the theatre is unused and the foyer is a jazz bar. 'It was the social soul of the island. Country people used to come down to market with their carts on Saturdays. In those days it took longer to get to Vila from San Carlos than it does to fly from Madrid to Los Angeles. They came down with their merchandise, did the market, then there were private rooms in Pereyra where they could have a shower and change. The women stayed in the apartments alongside while the men played cards. The white walls were stained yellow with years of cigar-smoke. When people ran out of money they bet their horse or their cart.'

Javier took another pull on his whisky and we sat in silence for a minute, wondering what it means to lose a way of life for ever. A police car screamed by in the street below, where thirty years ago a woman in a long black skirt might have sat in her porch weaving esparto-grass in the evening sun.

'The crisis' can be explained in four words: the Brits aren't coming. British tourism has always been Ibiza's daily bread, supplying more than half of its visitors in 1989. But in 1990 there were 20 per cent less of them. That was because of mortgage rates, interest rates, the weakness of sterling against the peseta, and a rash of news stories presenting Ibiza as cheap and nasty and full of vomiting hooligans. Then the Gulf War broke out, just at the time when people in Britain were poring over holiday catalogues in front of the fire. Suddenly it didn't seem like such a good idea to travel anywhere at all, and Ibiza was practically next door to one of Iraq's biggest allies. Another drop in the figures.

But there were longer-term reasons too. The poor infra-structure, the shoddy accommodation, the high prices; not least, competition from Tunisia, Turkey and Florida. Newly eco-sensitive customers were tired of the endless building work, the despoiling of the countryside, and families were being frightened off by the swinging sex-and-drugs image that had worked so well as a lure for groovy seventies youth. After thirty foolproof years the magic finally seemed to be wearing off.

As for the future, there are two theories. Some, like the English DJ Brian Newman, and Ian Cowper, head of the Ibiza outpost of the Thomson empire, think the crisis is a short, sharp shock that has brought the Ibicencos to their senses. In this view, if the island can keep the Law of Natural Spaces, clamp down on drugs and spruce up its hotel rooms (as it now must under the Balearic government's new Law of Modernization, which is so strict that it will do away with 3,000 beds in San Antonio alone) it can go on milking the cheapo package-holiday formula for ever.

Others think Ibiza is facing seven or more extremely lean years. In July people on the street were starting to mutter that in spite of all the blithely optimistic predictions last spring the 1992 *temporada* might actually turn out to be worse than 1991's. You could see their point. Those hotels that had bothered to open were only 60 per cent full. You could still find a parking-spot in Vara de Rey with relative ease, and the Calle de la Virgen was dead. Obviously people had been distracted by the Expo, the Olympics and cultural Madrid. But the question was, would they come later in the year or would poor Ibiza be forgotten completely? As the summer went on there were more tense, nervous headaches. Francesco Alberti, president of an influential group of Balearic businessmen, said he thought the crisis might go on for years. He brushed off as 'simplistic' the idea that all it needed were two good seasons and everything would turn out fine. 'We mustn't forget there's a crisis, and it's going to be hard to get out of it.'

For the time being, there is plenty of life left in the package tour and all its works. There were no signs of crisis at the Hillbilly Hoedown, unless it was the kind brought on by an explosive mixture of alcohol, sunburn and singing-along. I went along with Christine. The ticket said 7.25 p.m. – northern Europeans eat early. We arrived at ten and the horse-shoe and lassooing contests were over, the 'Moonshine' had all been drunk and the Western-style ribs 'n' beans had gone, but the unlimited sangria was flowing freely.

The Hoedown takes place at The Hoe Down Barbecue in Santa Gertrudis, where Toni's mother had her first experience of foreigners. It's a cross between a restaurant and a concentration camp. The coaches approach the site up a *camino* leading off the main road, unload their charges and park in rows outside the Barbecue. The grounds are surrounded by a high wall and forbidding wooden stockade gates. It is a moot point whether these are to keep gate-crashing locals out or the Hoedowners in. Either way, once inside there is no escape. They are hustled through the horse-shoe throwing, lassooing, 'moonshine outside the Sheriff's office', etc. etc., then into an immense refectory where they are sat down at ranks of tables and given to eat and drink before being ushered out into a special arena in the garden for the 'foot-stomping music'.

There must have been five hundred people in there when we arrived, and the industrial-sized kitchen at the back was working at full stretch. There was an overpowering smell of school dinners. Christine and I commandeered a jug of unlimited sangria and wandered around (the benches were all taken), open-mouthed at the scale of the operation. It was *Metropolis* meets Butlins, a factory of fun.

As the plates were being cleared – a major undertaking in itself – a small band took the stage and struck up with 'Take me home, country roads', whereupon the whole place erupted in a bibulous, sweaty-faced roar. We made our excuses and crossed the road to the El Paso.

Ibiza has had its best fun and earned its fame as a haunt of the rich and/or famous. The middle classes and upper classes have largely stayed away, probably because there was none of the High Culture they were used to getting from Tuscany, and because they had heard the *working classes* came here.

Probably the first member of what might now be called the jet-set, as well as the first drop-out, to visit Ibiza was the Archduke of Austria, Luis Salvador of Hapsburg-Lorena. Born in the Pitti Palace in Florence in 1847, son of Leopold II, the last Grand Duke of Tuscany, he spent his early years in the suffocating gentility of the court of Vienna, embarking on a new life as a travel-writer and layabout in his late teens. He based himself in a *finca* in Mallorca, La Estaca, where he fell in love with the peasant girl Catalina Homar (whom he later introduced to the Empress Elizabeth of Austria. The two got on famously – 'as if they had known each other all their lives', said the Archduke) but is known to have made at least two journeys to Ibiza, one in 1867 and the other twenty years later. He spent the summer of his first visit tramping the island's country roads on the back of a mule, and a year later his four-volume work on the Balearic Islands, including his own engravings of picturesque scenes, was published in Leipzig with a dedication to the Emperor Franz Josef I.

The Archduke was an energetic and appreciative tourist and a sensitive writer whose only fault was a tendency towards pedantry. His is some of the best and completest coverage Ibiza has ever had. The visitor to the Pitiusas 'is received with the highest cordiality no matter what the hour, and regaled feelingly and unreservedly with all that these good people possess, which is rather scanty.' He noted that of 21,808 inhabitants there were just 2–3,000 Castilian speakers and that only 1000 people could read and write. On the other hand he found the ports of Ibiza and San Antonio 'truly lovely', and went into raptures over the 'magical mirror of the dark blue sea, which merely by its transparency allows us to see things close by as distant, in a piece of perpetual trickery that fools even the most accustomed gaze. The charm emanating from the sea is indescribable, as is the temptation, at times almost irresistible, to make oneself one with it, stupefied by its magic.'

Powerful and influential figures have always been drawn here as if by invisible threads. Franco came on an official visit in 1955 and Charles de Gaulle came on holiday. Colin Powell, the big-cheese American general, stays with friends here. There have been aristocrats, too – mostly of the Euro type, flitting through on yachts and snapped by paparazzi in the KU – but few of them have given Ibiza so much of their time and affection as the Archduke Luis Salvador. A notable exception must be Smilja Mihailovich, aka The Princess, possibly the most famous female on the island and certainly the most glamorous. Smilja is an international socialite, a businesswoman, and a journalist whose Saturday column in the *Diario de Ibiza* is a *Jennifer's Diary* of *delightful* events and *enchanting* people who are usually rich, famous or both. When I wanted a glimpse of Glam Ibiza it was towards The Princess that I naturally directed my steps.

Ringing the doorbell of her house beside the golf course in the chi-chi *urbanización* of Roca Llisa – just down the road from her friend Roman Polanski – I felt a twinge of nerves. The Princess is known for her tendency not to suffer fools gladly.

She lives right next to the first hole, which is lucky because she is mad on golf, and had just been to Palma to play a game with Seve Ballesteros. A water-filled bunker glimmered in the midday sun. The house was small, luxurious and smelt of a rich old lady – perfumes, pills and powders and an absence of draughts – which is what The Princess is, although she looks two decades younger than her seventy-four years. I could see her through the glass front door, miraculously svelte, adjusting her tight Prince of Wales check trousers, Chanel blazer and lots and lots of make-up. The *Hello!* people had just been. The house was crowded with photographs of her in orbit with a galaxy of celebrity friends. Smilja with Mick Jagger ('Ah, Mick, I love him'); Smilja with Placido Domingo ('Ah, Placido, a darling'); Meryl Streep with someone else; Queen Sofia in a dress with a deep décolletage ('she has had so many pictures taken and she says this is the one she likes the best'). Everywhere her own happy face, framed by a white-blonde perm, with a red-lipsticked smile that jumped out of the picture.

She was born and grew up in Belgrade, a city-girl who now has no time for capitals. 'I never hanker after Charlie Chaplin's city lights, never, never, never. I go to Hollywood for the Oscars, I go to Cannes for the cinema festivals, I go to Tokyo, I go to Rome . . . but when I really want a holiday I go to Formentera. It is the last human luxury, positively the last. The sea, the transparency of it, the beach, the way the people live . . .', she rhapsodized.

The second phase of her life was lived in Paris with her husband, a Yugoslav diplomat. But in 1961 she got the yen to travel. 'A friend of mine, Louise Valmorin, you know, the famous novelist, told me about Ibiza. I'd never heard of it. But I was in Paris and I was so fed up with all the receptions and everything. I took a house through the *Herald Tribune* and took the boat from Barcelona. It was a First Class cabin, but I couldn't sleep because there were pigs underneath [I don't think she meant tourists] and I couldn't use the bathroom because no water came out of the tap. I arrived and took a dreadful taxi, very dirty, to the house, where I waited for ten hours for the owner to come. At last he arrived, a peasant, but a very *beautiful* peasant, and I nearly threw my bags at him. I was wearing a Chanel suit and white gloves and I'd been sitting on my Hermès bags for hours. Then I invited him for lunch and we became friends. There was an old olive tree where I used to put candles when I had my parties. It was virtually on the beach – I almost had my toes in the water. The house was furnished with white wood, so very primitive, but quite, quite beautiful. I fell in love with Ibiza like you fall in love with a lover.'

From these bohemian beginnings she has catapulted herself to the very summit of Ibiza society. Julio Iglesias, an ardent Ibizaphile who had dropped in to the island for a few days in June to 'recharge his batteries', was pictured in her column canoodling playfully with her in the most exclusive restaurant on the island, Las Dos Lunas. 'Felipe Gonzalez,' she told me, 'is one of the sexiest politicians I know.' Her very best friend, however, whose photograph stands alone on an occasional table beside her bedroom door, is dear, dear Roman. Polanski now comes very rarely to his flat-topped white modern Ibiza house and does so mainly to recover from a punishing workload. But Smilja naturally sees him whenever he shows up, and has even taken to appearing in his films.

On the wall of Smilja's sitting-room hangs a Modigliani painting, a portrait of one of the artist's favourite thin-necked young girls, which glows with the rich orange light of an authentic masterpiece. It is signed 'Elmyr'. Modigliani, Smilja told me, was a speciality of the master faker Elmyr de Hory, who lived and died on the island and was of course another of her dear friends.

Old Ibiza hands become misty-eyed and smile at the mention of Elmyr, as if to say, 'We shall not look upon his like again, which for the world's sake is probably just as well.' His life was a picaresque novel. Born into an haute-bourgeois family in Budapest, his early adventures took him to Paris, where he studied under Léger; back to Hungary and a spell in a concentration camp in Transylvania; and back to Paris, with a handful of diamonds hidden in the lining of his coat. His first fake was a small drawing in Picasso's Grecian style. That was the modest beginning of a prodigious output of works by 'Dufy', 'Degas', 'Derain', 'Modigliani', 'Matisse' and others which by 1969 had made a total of $60 million on the international art market. Many were so convincing they received affidavits or *expertises* from the artists' widows. His most amazing coup was a written statement by the Dutch Fauve painter Kees van Dongen that van Dongen himself had painted one of Elmyr's fakes. The artist looked at the painting, chuckled lewdly and said, yes, he remembered the model well.

The great tragedy of Elmyr de Hory's life was that he saw so little of the financial fruit of his efforts, which was increasingly collected and enjoyed by his seedy middle-man Fernand Legros and Legros' 'travelling companion and personal secretary' Réal Lessard. But for a while at least Elmyr was rich, and while he moved around the world, hopping from Paris to Madrid to Brazil to America, he never moved outside the most dazzling social circles. In New York he was friends with Anita Loos and Lana Turner, and Marilyn Monroe was a guest at one of his many parties. Zsa Zsa Gabor, whom he had known in Budapest, commissioned him to paint a ¾ length nude portrait of her holding a strategically positioned guitar. 'She complained that one of the tits was too much in the centre,' he said later.

Everyone was taken in; or at least, everyone who mattered. In Japan, Legros and Lessard sold a 'Derain' oil, a 'Dufy' gouache and a 'Modigliani' drawing to the National Museum of Western Art. André Malraux, then French Minister of Culture, happened to be in Tokyo at the time and was asked his opinion of the new acquisitions. The prices the Japanese had paid were not unreasonable, said Malraux, where masterpieces such as these were concerned.

When Elmyr came to Ibiza he was fifty-five and the island was in full swing. He had a house – 'La Falaise' – built by the German-American artist Erwin Broner, incorporating a secret room which the maid was forbidden to clean – this would be his work-room. Nobody knew about his fakery: he once told a friend on Ibiza, 'If I was ever depressed enough to tell you my secret, you'd be as shocked as if I told you I was Martin Boormann.'

Together with the entire demi-monde of Ibiza he hung out at La Tierra, and gave goulash parties at La Falaise. As described in *Fake!*, the de Hory story written by another neo-Ibicenco of the time, Clifford Irving, he emerges as a figure for whom 'flamboyant' would be an understatement. 'His hair was dyed an apparently ageless jet black, he sported a monocle on a gold chain, all his sweaters were of cashmere, and . . . he came to wear a wristwatch from Cartier and drive a red Corvette Sting Ray convertible . . . He spoke five languages, all fluently, none perfectly.' Nearly everybody loved him. For the Princess Smilja Mihailovich, he was 'an ugly little Hungarian Jew; but with *charm*!, with *charisma*! There was some kind of rebellion in him, because, you see, he couldn't wait to be famous. He needed the money for his boys. Oh yes, he was always surrounded by the most beautiful boys. They would always get the latest Cartier watch, the latest Cadillac car. He was always in love, which is the most *perfect* state to be in. He was absolutely *delicious* to know.' An enemy quoted in *Fake!* calls him 'a snob and a parasite'. The Swiss painter Edith Sommer-Irving, ex-wife of Clifford and a close friend of Elmyr's, says of him mischievously: 'He was fun. Until he got famous – then he got a little boring.'

His fame, or rather notoriety, came when the Texas oil millionaire Algur Hurtle Meadows discovered that the forty-four paintings by Dufy, Degas, Vlaminck, Modigliani, Picasso and Derain that he had been sold by Fernand Legros were not what they seemed. Inevitably the trail led back to Elmyr. He was never arrested as Legros and Lessard were, though he did spend an agreeable two months in Ibiza jail under a curious collection of charges, one of them homo-sexuality. When Ibiza found out the whole truth about him he basked in celebrity – which for him, like love, was the perfect state to be in. He had acquired a steady boyfriend, appropriately named Mark Forgey. The only two clouds on the horizon were Fernand Legros, who had found Elmyr's diary and set about hounding and victimizing everyone he found in it (including Sandy Pratt and Ursula Andress's Italian boyfriend); and the French authorities, who were pressing for his extradition. This last was his greatest terror, to the extent that he told friends that if he was forced to leave Ibiza permanently he would kill himself and leave everything he had to Mark. By 1976, looking stressed-out and ill, he was telling Sandy Pratt that he had good grounds for fearing this was the year the French would get their way. Finally on 11 December of that year he committed suicide by washing down a handful of pills with alcohol. The irony was that soon afterwards Algur Hurtle Meadows, his main pursuant in the courts, also died and everyone lost interest in the whole affair.

When Orson Welles came to Ibiza to shoot his film about Elmyr *F for Fake* he is supposed to have said at a press conference, 'I came to Ibiza in search of a forger and I find myself surrounded by them on all sides.' The island is a place of fakes, fantasies, shifting identities and flexible realities. It was Clifford Irving who sold a false biography of Howard Hughes to his publishers in New York for $1m, and his wife Edith who dressed up as 'Helga Hughes' and paid the money into a Zurich bank. Edith, who got two years in a Swiss prison for her part in the affair, now says it was all an imaginative prank, cooked up to provide a sensational how-we-pulled-it-off story that Cliff could then sell legitimately. 'It never occurred to us that we wouldn't pay the money back. Out of the $1m there was perhaps $100,000 missing, and the book contract would have covered that. It all got too heavy.'

Perhaps it is something to do with its receptivity to pretence and disguise that the island has always attracted actors and actresses by the score. The great thespian centre was always Santa Eulalia, more particularly Sandy's Bar, where they would congregate and talk theatre. At various times in the sixties and seventies you could have walked into Jimmy's in the evening and seen Laurence Olivier and Joan Plowright, who rented a house in the then-chic, now-dowdy urbanization 'Siesta'; John Mills, who stayed at the Hotel Fenicia in Santa Eulalia; Nigel Davenport; Diana Rigg; Denholm Elliot; Maria Aitken; more recently Rupert Everett, whom Maria brought with her after their double triumph in Noel Coward's *The Vortex*. The lighter side was represented by Terry-Thomas, Leslie Phillips and the great Sid James. The latter came in September 1965, after the shooting of 'Carry On Cowboy'.

Most of the above merely rented houses, but a few became proper neo-Ibicencos who actually settled down and bought. Diana Rigg had a grand house outside the village. During one of her absences in London, the house became a drug-infested hippie commune. The occupants sold everything in the house – tables, chairs, pictures, mattresses, even a quantity of empty gas-bottles. When a friend of Diana's saw the house after they had been turfed out it was completely bare. The maid had had to burn the sheets. Diana left the island and has not been back.

Terry-Thomas bought a house – at Denholm Elliott's suggestion – at the head of a deep valley looking down to the sea at Cala Boix near San Carlos. Ibiza people remember him as charming, quite as outrageously English as any of his I-say-old-chap caricature roles in films like *Those Magnificent Men in their Flying Machines*, and almost reckless in his generosity even to people he hardly knew. Yet his recently published autobiography, *Terry-Thomas Tells Tales*, reveals another side. He once described Ibiza as, 'a dreadfully smelly place full of contrived people', and seems in other ways to have been out of synch with the liberal, laissez-faire rhythm of the island. He had a thing about gate-crashers. 'My idea of throwing a party was that it should be exclusive. I soon learned that in Ibiza people wouldn't accept that. There were many who would make it their business to find out "Where is tonight's party?" and just arrive . . . On one occasion a black man I had never seen before loomed out of the darkness and said "Where's the bar?" I said, "Over there." And he went straight off to a twenty-foot drop. I never found out whether he survived.'

Terry-Thomas died in 1991, which left only one major thesp on the island, Denholm Elliott. In the last years of his life Denholm became Ibiza's version of Michael Jackson – holed up in his house in Santa Eulalia, very occasionally glimpsed shopping in the market looking pale and haggard in dark glasses, and frequently absent from the island on mysterious trips to London. Then, in September 1992, he died of AIDS.

Hollywood has not been so much in evidence except at the trashier summer-season end of things. Errol Flynn came through on his yacht 'Zaca' in the fifties. Donald Sutherland came to star in a dreadful movie called *The Trouble with Spies*, in which most neo-Ibicencos of the time seem to have had walk-on parts. Apart from Welles' *F for Fake* and Barbet Schroeder's *More* there are hardly any other Ibiza-based movies of quality – with the honourable exception of a 1960 short by Peter Finch, star of *Sunday Bloody Sunday*, *The Day*, which used local Ibicenco actors in a touching drama of pre-touristic life.

Goldie Hawn cavorted at Benirrás and spent a fortune in Pedro Planell's leather-shop, meanwhile on the nudist beach in Formentera Brigitte Nielsen was showing off her new, improved breasts. Some years later Brigitte's ex-husband Sylvester Stallone came on holiday – 'for the marvellous girls in Ibiza', he told a TV interviewer. Perhaps Sly was referring to Raquel Welch and Brigitte Bardot, who'd appeared at various points in the summer of 1975 – though not at the same time. Bardot was here for the opening of a new restaurant in Dalt Vila. Asked about the island, she said the thing that surprised her most was 'the cosmopolitan atmosphere it breathes, and the variety of people here and the way they dress, without age-limits. To tell the truth I live in the same atmosphere all the year round, but I didn't expect to find it so well-developed on this island!'

When famous people take their holidays in Ibiza they have two choices of accommodation: they can either rent discreet *casas payesas* fitted up with every known convenience, or they can stay in the kind of hotel which is used to catering to their capricious and expensive tastes. Such a hotel is Pike's, a converted farmhouse reached by a Swiss-cheese *camino* out of San Antonio. Bradley, son of the flamboyant Australian owner Tony Pike, told me: 'The kind of musicians and business people we get have particular natures that divert them from going to normal five-star hotels.'

What they get for their money at Pike's is a dining room with designer-crumbling walls and fashionably un-matching furniture, a squishy TV den crammed with cushions, not many bedrooms, and the feeling of being a guest in someone's home. A very rich person's home. The house used to be called Ca'n Pep Toniet. It was a ruin when Tony Pike bought it more than ten years ago, because that was the only thing he could afford at that point. He had left England when he was seventeen; got married at nineteen; been divorced; been sailing on a Caribbean yacht when it sank; met a girl on the life-raft and proposed to her on the spot.

Bradley was mellowing out in his apartment within the grounds of the hotel when I met him. The warm night had set the crickets whistling for the first time that summer. Guests, none of whom were recognizably Famous, drifted through the back-lit garden to the pool bar where they can sit sipping cocktails up to their waists in the water. Bradley gave me a shot of vodka in a heavy glass and explained how he met Monique, who was in the shower at the time. 'A lot of the guests just like to lie around, so we take them to Formentera. You're sitting there with your toes in the sand, and all these nimble young lovelies are nipping along the beach. That's how I found *her*.' He gestured with his arm in the direction of the bathroom. 'Actually we were on the yacht. I noticed this bunch of girls and mentioned them to my father, and he said "Go on then, invite them on board for a drink".'

Monique, a wide-eyed Nordic blonde, emerged from the shower with a towel round her and gave her side of the story. 'I am living here now since last summer, but I used to come here every year. I got to know the island pretty well, so when I heard the name "Pike" I just thought: Danger.'

As well she might. Tony Pike is well-known for bestowing his favours generously on the female sex, most famously in the case of Grace Jones, who is so well known around the hotel that everybody calls her Beverley. 'That's her middle name. She's Beverley during the day, but when she gets dressed up she's Grace. She's a great woman, very strong. She's got her head screwed on.'

Pike's has put up a fair number of stars in its time. George Michael and Andrew Ridgeley, the components of Wham! and both Ibizaphiles, stayed there during the video filming of their tackily brilliant disco hit 'Club Tropicana'. George still uses Ibiza as a hideaway/base for his concert dates in Spain. Julio Iglesias once hired out the whole of Pike's for a month before his arrival on the island, during which time the hotel had to stay empty in readiness. Boy George had his birthday party in the KU.

That was all in the eighties, but Ibiza's magnetic attraction for pop's aristocracy had begun a good deal earlier. While we were talking Bradley jumped up and rummaged through his records for an old boxed set he had picked up somewhere and forgotten to play. 'In a Land of Clear Colours' is that quintessentially seventies item, a 'concept album', and includes a book with rambling prose-poems courtesy of American sci-fi writer Robert Sheckley, a figure on the sixties/seventies Santa Eulalia scene. 'In a Land . . .' was an all-Ibiza production, recorded locally in 1974 with collaboration from songwriter Peter Sinfield, artist Jean Willi and avant-garde producer, Brian Eno, whom the team managed to persuade to produce three minutes of music which they stretched over a whole album.

The list of musicians and singers who have played or stayed in Ibiza or Formentera is a fairly amazing one. Bradley told me about Pink Floyd, holed up in a Formentera *finca* one summer in the sixties where they produced the soundtrack to their tripped-out movie *More*. (An old Dutch hippie who lived in the 'Floyd *finca*' some years after them remembers it was a grand house and had stables for seven horses.) Bob Marley played the bull-ring. Tina Turner bought up most of the leather outfits in the Calle de la Virgen. Frank Zappa, Joni Mitchell, the Bee Gees, Sting, Cher, Robert Plant, Bob Geldof, Divine and Nico, singer with the Velvet Underground, all passed through. And all of them left alive apart from Nico, who fell off her bike and died outside a bank in Ibiza town.

Times have changed and Ibiza is evidently no longer the star-spotters' paradise it once was. Pike's' clientele reflects this: the flash glamour has gone with the passing of shoulder-pads and coke spoons. 'The big gamblers are always the biggest partiers, and they've spent all their money,' said Bradley. 'Also the KU not opening has put the island back a lot. People *came* to Ibiza because of that place. They used to have concerts there. Once they had Spandau Ballet, Kid Creole and the Coconuts, James Brown and Talk Talk, all in one season.'

Exactly why celebrities are drawn here is a difficult question to answer. It may have something to do with the spread-out topography, which enables them to hide away from groupies, the press, and curious non-celebrities. Then there has always been a tight network of celebrity-friendly restaurants and clubs which they can flit among in anonymous jeeps. What swings it, perhaps, is that so many other celebrities have trod the ground before them.

Visible rich-and-famous activity is at a low level in the 1990s because Ibiza has dropped off the jet-set itinerary, also thanks to the new discretion that impels showbiz people to stay at home with their kids rather than go out to nightclubs, snort cocaine and get their picture in the papers. Practically the only surviving pop star is the slightly shop-soiled figure of German singer Nina Hagen, whose photo-wedding to a teenage punk on the beach at Benirràs is a subject of gossip. On the Santa Eulalia scene the occasional glimpse can still be had of Roger Taylor, of the group Queen. His friend and fellow Queen member Freddie Mercury was a massive fan of Ibiza who enjoyed a mutual love-affair with the island. He and Montserrat Caballé first performed their Olympic hymn to Barcelona, not in Barcelona but in Ibiza. In the last year of his life Freddie planned to buy himself a mansion here, large and luxurious enough to satisfy his love of the flamboyant and over-the-top but, for reasons which were only fully understood when it was revealed that he had died of AIDS, the plan never came to fruition. He spent his last summer staying at Roger Taylor's house, where he went from the bed to the pool and back again. He told no one he was here, least of all the Press, and the only reason the normally omniscient Sandy Pratt knew he was there was that Roger's maid had told him so.

It's in July and August, the central months of the *temporada*, that Ibiza finally transforms itself into the luridly fashionable, sun-worshipping, bar-crawling, disco-dancing, drug-taking, tourist-trapping holiday-island that a thousand dreams and prejudices are made of.

The hotter it became the closer the island came to Africa, as though it were drifting South on a summer wind. In August Ibiza town smelt like Morocco: simmering garbage, dust and baking roof-tiles. The country *looked* like Morocco, everything sizzling and throbbing with desert heat. Colours lost their vigour – the red earth had faded into a dull crust of suburban beige, and plant life took on a parched and weary look. My vineyard was worryingly dry and yellow even though the grapes were swelling with juice, but Toni forbade me to water the plants: a dose of drought would be character-forming for their roots. Flower activity was at an all-year low. Only the palms seemed at home with these temperatures: they fanned themselves gently with sleek green fronds. The day was a long *crescendo* and *diminuendo*, peaking in four hours of *fortissimo* afternoon heat that made even the lizards head for the shade. In the resorts people struggled bravely on, eating lunch at one and dinner at eight and lying on the beach in between, but everyone else found their routine uncontrollably altered. The afternoon was off limits until seven. Lunch might be at three or four, in the cool of a shuttered room, and dinner was pushed closer to midnight than North Europeans and Americans would have thought possible.

A lot of what is good about the Ibicenco summer happens after dark. Ibiza's nightlife may not be as big and brash or as numerous as New York's, or as exhaustingly young and trendy as London's, or as vice-ridden as Amsterdam's or Valencia's, but anyone who has sampled it will tell you it has a special quality that you won't find in any other corner of the nocturnal world.

To savour this quality – an amazing, carefree convergence of glamour, hippie togetherness and unbridled hedonism – you need to be in the right place at the right time. You would be unlikely to experience it, for example, in the streets of San Antonio. San An is the Blackpool of Ibiza: cheerfully vulgar, unashamedly unglamorous. When Fernando and I went out one night in the West End, as the town's teeming bar-and-club district is known, the first bar we visited had a dozen people sitting on the beer-sticky floor in a line doing the notorious Rowing Dance to a deafening soundtrack of seventies disco. Out on the streets there were crowds of kids, girls perching on the flower-tubs, boys standing in rollicking groups around them, and everybody drinking, smoking and shrieking above the racket. Perhaps because there was a blue-jacketed Policia Nacional on every corner, the atmosphere seemed boisterously good-natured, not aggressive and threatening as it was supposed to have been in summers past when residents lived in fear of pot-bellied British bootboys.

Yet San An by night is still not for the faint-hearted or people who have a problem with bad taste. At one o'clock in the morning in the Bar Simple, where we stopped for our second rum and Coke, there was a group of twenty-something Englishmen in red-faced, raucous mood. They had taken off their clothes, which were thrown in a pile in the corner, and wrapped their T-shirts round their groins like nappies. They were playing some kind of endurance game which involved ingesting a mixture of crème de menthe, Tia Maria and San Miguel beer. The resulting brown, soupy mess was passed round in a brandy-balloon. 'They do this every night,' said the barman, who had a tired look. 'Last night it was Hierbas Ibicencas, red wine and sherry.' Next to us at the bar were a mother and daughter from Sheffield. The mother was fat, the daughter thin and malnourished-looking, and both were dressed up for a night on the town. The girl wore false scarlet nails which kept coming unstuck. One of them fell in her drink and she had to fish it out with a toothpick. 'Eh Mum, have you got that glue? If one of these things falls off one more time I'm gonna go bonkers. Now listen to me, Mum, we've got half an hour drinking time left, then we're off down the Star for some serious boogieing, right? So get that drink down you.' Her mother nodded meekly.

Away from the wild West End the town was more peaceful. The only action seemed to be at the Milk Bar, away from the sea-front off the Plaza de España. Here there was no nappy-wearing or drinking of revolting cocktails. The walls were draped with lengths of milk-white material which any-where else in San Antonio would be asking to be re-decorated with diced carrots. The clientèle was mostly London clubbers in London clubwear. Some of them had been coming to Ibiza every summer for five years, ever since the double birth of Acid House and 'Balearic Beat' gave Britain its biggest youth-cultural happening since Punk. One of them, Rachael d'Souza, was wearing a black zip-up jacket by Michiko Koshino. 'Eighty-five quid in the sale. Funny, in the old days when I first started coming here you never would have worn black, and label stuff was well out. It was all dungarees and handkerchiefs tied round your head, wasn't it. It was amazing, you could wear what you liked, listen to what music you liked, you could generally be what you liked in life. You should talk to Nicky, he owns this place, he was here in the early days.'

Rachael pointed to a small man with a black Seven Dwarfs haircut who was clunking another House tape into the machine behind the bar. I'd heard a lot about Nicky Holloway. He was one of the English club-owners and DJs, along with Danny Rampling, Paul Oakenfold and others, who brought the Ibiza sound to London in the winter of 1987. But he'd been coming here for years before that. 'I first came on a Flair package holiday and stayed in a hotel in San Antonio which was awful. Cheap one out the paper. In them days I was quite happy with the Star Club and the bars and that. I came every year for three or four years, and slowly but surely started wanting something better, so I started travelling out the town and looking round the island. When your average English tourist kid/clubber comes on holiday he always ends up going to San Antonio the first time, until he realizes the score.'

In 1986 things started getting interesting. At the time Nicky was running a London club night called Special Branch and teamed up with Club 18–30 to organize an Ibiza clubbing holiday. 'We had *murders*. Our kids didn't want to go on their silly trips and donkey rides and the parties they organize, so all the reps hated us 'cos that's how they make their money. One night we'd take over the Star, another night Extasis or Es Paradis. We'd have a look around Ibiza town, but as for the big clubs, we didn't even know they existed. In 1985 I did go to KU a couple of times, but it was too expensive for us. Five quid a drink.'

It was the next year, Nicky says, that everything changed for him and his friends. It all happened for two reasons: they discovered Amnesia, and they discovered Ecstasy. 'There was Paul Oakenfold, me, Danny Rampling and Johnny Walker. We hired a villa for a week in San Antonio. Everybody that year was going to Amnesia, but people in the know had been going the year before and the year before that. I remember everyone out here was talking about Ecstasy, and none of us had ever done it before. I wasn't going to do it, but then the others tried it, and we saw what was happening to them and thought, "Come on then." So we did it the same night, and we all went to Amnesia. And that was it. I mean, it changed my life. You know what it's like, you think you've been born again, don'cha?'

MDMA is Ibiza's drug, just as cocaine is Manhattan's and grass is Jamaica's. A *Sun* headline from 1989, ECSTASY ISLAND!, was true even if the scare-mongering and sheer nonsense contained in the article which followed it were not. Ibiza was the first place in Spain and one of the first in Europe where Ecstasy was first detected and the first seizures were made. The drug already had a small, exclusive following in Britain when the House boom began in 1987, but thereafter it quickly spread through the club and rave scene to become young Britain's favourite party-drug, consumed in pill or capsule form by hundreds of thousands of enthusiasts every weekend.

Nicky is unequivocal: 'To say it wasn't the drug that made it happen would be a lie'. Before 'it' happened music was divided up by rigid barriers: Ecstasy dismantled them. There was black music – that was for dancing to – and there was white music – that was for the hi-fi at home or for punching the air to at rock concerts. Before the summer of 1987 London's Ibiza-inspired DJs were listening to hip hop, 'rare groove' and a little bit of early, non-acidic House. 'Then we went to Amnesia, and it changed our lives. They were playing House music plus, well, I suppose it was really English rock music. Balearic Beat was more of an attitude, meaning that you could play anything. I remember going up to Alfredo [the legendary DJ at Amnesia, now at Pacha] and saying "What the hell's this?" And it would be a band like Nitzer Ebb, from Basildon. We'd never heard of it before. In England there was a black music scene and a white music scene, and if you were into black music you didn't buy white music.' Ibiza had never entertained those musical preconceptions, and if any of its visitors had them they were quickly sorted out, along with any Anglo-Saxon inhibitions, by a dose of MDMA. 'The thing the E scene did was that it made white people be able to get out on to the dance floor and dance, whereas before, the white kids in the disco were at the bar getting pissed while the black boys stole their girlfriends. It completely opened all that up to everybody.'

The English contingent in Amnesia in 1987 was little more than one hundred people, who looked on their new experience as something precious and guarded it jealously. It was a paradigm of tourism: having stumbled on this paradisical scene they didn't want any *more* San An tourists finding out about it, thank you very much. It was their big secret. When they got back to London some of them started up their own clubs, mainly to cater for last summer's hardcore crew. Paul Oakenfold had The Future, Danny and Jenny Rampling had the Shoom, and at first the clientele was limited to people who'd spent the summer in Amnesia. In London at the time the club scene was all about, in Danny Rampling's words, 'Hip hop, and funk, and pretentiousness. Unfriendly attitudes. Flight jackets and black 501s and DMs. Everything really stereotyped. Shoom was definitely a reaction against that. It was the backlash.' Shoom happened in a sweaty gym near London Bridge. 'It was a hot basement, not a large open-air exotic Mediterranean paradise, but it was paradise once you got through the door and down the stairs . . . It jumped very quickly. People caught on to it as something really different that welcomed gay people, straights, fashionable people, hippies, whatever, and people were crying out for that in London.'

In the wider world nobody understood; neither did they understand the cryptic 'XTC' T-shirts some of the Ibiza crowd were wearing. Nicky Holloway played Alfredo's records at his soul nights in London and people were simply dazed and confused. But then i-D magazine ran a four-page piece on the amazing phenomenon of clubs where people wore old plimsolls and faded dungarees decorated with Smiley patches, danced frenziedly without apparent need for alcohol, and said things like 'Are you on one, Matey?' In May 1988 Nicky Holloway opened The Trip at the Astoria Theatre, and a month later there were 2000 people on the Charing Cross Road trying to get in. 'It just snowballed overnight – I've never seen anything like it,' he says.

In 1991 Nicky had the Milk Bar in London and its two Ibiza offshoots, the Milk Bar in San Antonio and a mini-Milk Bar at Pacha. Together with the Café del Mar on the seafront, where hipsters go to watch the sunset, Milk Bar Ibiza is the crème de la crème of San Antonio's otherwise uninteresting nightlife. Like everyone else in that summer of the crisis turística Nicky was moaning about the relative lack of punters. 'Last night it was packed, but the night before was crap. That's how it goes. In recessions, people get discerning. They pick and choose the nights, don't they. Years ago, every night was a Saturday night, and they were all as good as each other.' He looked around his bar with a touch of wistfulness. There were coolly dressed young people on every side, but the atmosphere was strangely muted for a night at the height of the season. 'To be honest with you,' he said in conclusion, lowering his voice as far as possible without being drowned out by the hammering House, 'I don't really think Ibiza is a place that's on the up, I think it's a place that's peaked. And that's coming from someone who loves it here, I mean I really do love it. I just don't think it's the same as it was.'

Late next morning I rolled up at Amnesia, a disco which

a lot of people say is also not the same as it was. Fifteen years ago Amnesia was an old *finca*, set back on a gentle slope behind the San Antonio road, with a working farm and *casa payesa*. (You can still see the troughs from which the animals ate.) It started in a small way, as a place where freaks and artists could congregate for cheap, bohemian nights out. It was exclusive and beautiful: there was a big garden (which is still there) full of palm trees and bougainvillea, and you danced among the walls of the old house. Then it started to grow, as the old houses did, piecemeal, sprouting another bar here, another dancefloor there. When the municipal noise-pollution laws came in in 1990 it grew a glass carapace, elegant as a Kew Gardens greenhouse, in three vast arches over the dancefloor. Despite all the changes, for most of its life Amnesia has been, if not the biggest (that title belonged to the inimitable KU), then the youngest, hippest and most happening disco in Ibiza.

I turned the Mini off the *camino* and into a dusty car park, finding the car a morsel of shade under an old plum tree that had left its ripe fruit in a wide green arc in the dust. The gates at the entrance to the club were shut and a big dog prowled behind them, so I sat on a low white wall under the porch where at night people queue to be scrutinized by doormen. A notice fixed to the wall opposite reminded prospective clubbers that 'ALL INVITATIONS ARE INVALID'. This was a sign of Amnesia's new regime and the Barcelona owners who had recently clamped down – to the disgust of Ibiza's resident liggers – on people getting in without paying.

After a while a sad-looking young guy sloped past with a knapsack on his back and sat on the wall beside me. Carlos, from Asturias in the north of Spain, was looking for a job. He knew the job prospects in Ibiza were dismal this summer, but anything would do. If it came to it and they didn't need barmen, he could be a bus-boy. Collecting empty glasses was actually Carlos's speciality. He even did it at the KU, which is a bit like doing the dishes at Buckingham Palace. The reason he thought he might succeed was that many of the old KU crew had moved over to Amnesia when the KU closed down, and nightclubs have their Old Boy networks just like English public schools. The man he thought he ought to see was Danny Gonzalez – ex-KU, now doorman and second-in-command at Amnesia. Clubs and bars inspire their own myths more than anywhere. Looking back on it now, the KU is wreathed in them. In the popular imagination, KU was a place where more immorality went on than in the lower reaches of Dante's inferno. Stories abound of cocktails laced with mescaline and Ecstasy served in ladlefuls to everyone in the club. Carlos told me he saw nothing like this, that it was all a rumour cooked up by Amnesia to get the Guardia Civil sniffing round its great rival. As for the cruising, nobody denies it. Not for nothing was the club supposedly named after a Caribbean goddess of love. 'You could get anything and anyone you wanted,' I was told by one habitué. 'A black man for a white man, a white woman for a black man, Chinese, African, you name it – and it started at 5000 ptas. Mind you, nothing sleazy actually went on inside. You never once saw anyone making love: staff would come up and gently tell the couple they were going too far.'

The KU sits and sulks on the hillside of San Rafael like a great battleship slowly rusting on a sandbank. It's hard to believe now, but on a good night in the mid eighties this sad-looking shell might have incorporated two or three thousand party-people, among them businessmen, rock stars, hippies, politicians, the odd tourist, the odd nightclub kid from London, and an awful lot of scantily clad girls. In its heyday the KU was nothing less than an immense nocturnal pleasure dome. You could drink at one of seven bars, one of them gay, one of them Brazilian, and dance under the full moon among tropical greenery. If you got hungry there was a fine Basque restaurant patronized by every Euro-celebrity worth their salt. If you felt like cooling off, one of the dancefloors incorporated a pool. There were thirty-five monstrous parties every summer, the best of which was generally agreed to be the Brazilian carnival which had troupes of dancers and musicians flown over specially from Rio. At its best the KU was magical, unforgettable.

Like Amnesia it started small and grew big. Until 1978 it was called Club Rafael and was managed by the Frenchman André Stzeyplitz. Locals and cognoscenti came here for lunch and to sip their afternoon cocktails away from the swarming beach. Then it was bought by three Basques, one of whom was the famous footballer José Antonio Santamaria, recently murdered by ETA terrorists, and swiftly became the most talked about and expensive disco on the island.

The way the Basques ran their club had more than a touch of *folie de grandeur*. By the late eighties the KU sound-system was so powerful that on a still summer night its booming could be heard all over the island, and murdered sleep for anyone in San Rafael. The club's huge lasers could be seen from the mainland and were deemed a danger to night-flying aircraft. Everything had to be the biggest and best, including the owners' bank-balances. They got greedy. They halved the size of the pool in order to squeeze even more punters into the club, and before long people were arriving in coachloads. At the same time the Basques were building up a mini-empire of other KUs in San Sebastian and Tenerife.

And the *KU de grâce* was the roof. In 1989 the exhausted residents of San Rafael had had enough, and it was partly in response to their protests that the local government brought in a law banning open-air discotheques. Amnesia rose to the challenge with a retractable glass structure that meant you could still dance in the morning sun. KU, on the other hand, put up a badly designed four-square roof whose ugliness shocked even the club's most loyal fans. The sense of limitless freedom had gone.

While I'd been talking to Carlos two more cars had drawn up in the Amnesia car park. One belonged to Danny Gonzalez, the man Carlos wanted to see about the job. Out of the other, a battered van with a German number-plate, stepped a girl in grey paint-spattered leggings, sandals and a hippie-market waistcoat. I recognized Sola from the Bar Costa. She had recently shot to fame as the hostess of a wild full-moon party a few weeks back in a *finca* near Santa Gertrudis and she was now consolidating that fame with a spell as designer-in-chief at Amnesia. We went inside the club and sat under a palm tree. Sola rolled a joint and got out her portfolio. There were designs for murals, posters and the Amnesia logo, all in the same vaguely psychedelic sci-fi style. She was pleased with these, but Amnesia's new owner wanted sunsets and palm trees instead.

Sola and Amnesia go way back. She first knew it in 1983. 'Amnesia was the freest place I had ever been in my life. I used to come with my sunglasses and dance while the sun came up. It was like a party in Goa. It was total liberty – beautiful, crazy people, unbelievable freedom. I didn't like the KU, it was too commercial and there were too many ugly people, *family* people. They were the people who went to bed; Amnesia was the people who stayed up!' She got a job as a poster designer: DJ Alfredo told her the themes of the parties and she came up with the posters.

Last year everyone agrees that Amnesia took a tumble. It seemed that the Barcelona people weren't used to the way things worked in Ibiza. They charged everyone on the door. They hired a DJ who played nothing but horrible, soulless techno music. 'They had a hippie party and they didn't play hippie music. They had a reggae party and they didn't play a reggae record. Then they hired the cheapest girls from Barcelona to work behind the bar. There was not enough attention to the people of Ibiza.' Sola thought the future of Ibiza's nightlife lay in private parties like her famous full-moon party. 'They are what the people want. I feel there is so much need to live crazy things that people are prepared to put their energy together and make a party. At my party, there were so many people helping me, not with any expectation to make money. One knew about music, one knew about decoration, one knew about making felafel . . . In Ibiza now there are only people who don't care about money, because if they cared about making money they wouldn't be here!'

More people were arriving, all in search of work. Steve came by on his motorbike. The Recession had put paid to his show in London, and he was thinking again about murals. He and Sola wandered off into the garden and sat by the blue pyramid/fountain that is Amnesia's very own spiritual symbol and marketing gimmick.

Tanit wanted a bar. He was wearing a bright orange metallic space-age flying jacket that crackled as he climbed off his bike. Tanit was tall, black and muscular, and his hair flailed about him in long Rasta plaits embedded with coloured beads. He had called himself Tanit for so long that his real name was lost in the mists of alternative Ibicenco history. All that anybody knew was that he had worked in the KU for years, then opened a bar with an American-Indian theme in the Paseo Maritimo, and now wanted to set up in Amnesia. He and Danny hugged each other – any bar with Tanit behind it is destined for good takings, so Danny was pleased to see him. Later I told Renée about Tanit. She had not heard of him and his name before, and flew into a fury at this outrageous impertinence. 'What an asshole! I'll run him off this island!' she fumed.

The day was on the way up to its summit of gasping, immobilizing heat. Feeling drowsy and dried-out under Amnesia's greenhouse roof I went back to Christine's house, slept all afternoon and most of the evening. Later I ventured out into the warm night, wide-eyed with summer-night adrenalin, to check up on the Calle de la Virgen.

It was the first time I'd been down the Calle for a few weeks, and the difference was startling. High summer had turned it again into its true self – a hilarious sparkling parade of dressed-up Euro-bodies with money in their pockets and toothpaste smiles. The word along the street was that at last, in the first week of August, the tourists were back. The air was drenched with a feeling of delighted relief, like a rainstorm after a crippling drought. Where a fortnight ago the Calle's bar-owners and shopkeepers had been wringing their hands, now they were rubbing them. Perhaps now they'd be able to replenish their woefully depleted winter coffers.

For some there was no occasion for glee, only for frustration. At the gay end, George was complaining. It was all very well that the season had finally picked up, but how was a girl to make enough money for twelve months in just under two? 'Well, I'm not putting up with it much longer. Last year I shut the bar in September and went to stay with my boyfriend in Valencia. People said, "You can't leave now, you're mad!" I said, "You just watch me."'

George's bar is a tiny, tasteful place, mysteriously called Questions. It was called that when he bought it, and since the name was already in the Spartacus Guide, the international gay Baedeker, he decided not to change it. It is pastel-painted and pleasant, but suffers by being surrounded by bigger, brasher bars which have hogged the dwindling gay limelight.

George thought gay Ibiza had had its day. 'You know,' he began, mixing me a quintuple gin and tonic, 'the gay scene here used to be *wonderful* ten years ago. The streets were absolutely *packed*, you couldn't move for men. It was lovely! But it's slowly fallen off year by year.' The island is still one of the Mediterranean's prime gay resorts, along with Mykonos, Sitges, Torremolinos, but George is down on it. 'Gay tourism used to be big business here – even straight Ibicenco couples were getting into it. At the start of the summer all the eccentrics would turn up, the big beautiful transvestites, but they're not coming any more. The one I remember is Manuel. He was a beautiful Brazilian transsexual who did promotional work for Pacha and shows around the place – but classy stuff, not tacky drag. His impression of Grace Jones left people flabbergasted.'

I walked back up the street, past the rows of clones perched on their bar stools outside Teatro, and up a stone staircase into the crumblier, lesser-known part of Sa Penya.

Within a few steps the dressed-up, chattering parade of high-summer Ibiza had given way to scenes such as you could have witnessed at any time since, or before, the Civil War. Old men were playing cards at little tables outside ordinary bars – bars that had no music, no fancy names and a light-bulb hanging over the counter. On a corner I saw a gypsy woman picking mites out of another woman's hair. The mite-picker looked up surprised, assuming I had unwittingly strayed off the tourist track. Hers was the strong, kindly face of a *materfamilias*.

The old town, which has preserved its traditional dignity more successfully than the ex-fishing quarter, has a calmer nightlife than Sa Penya, even if most of it is unaccountably gay. On the corner of two whitewashed streets where old black-clad ladies bring their chairs outside to chat, is the leather club Crisco. On the first floor of this club is a room where black-clad men perform sadomasochistic sexual acts. If the old ladies are aware of this they don't appear to care. Just round the corner from the Church of Santo Domingo, across the road from the ramparts where most of the gay cruising goes on, I found a more decorous bar than Crisco, with tables outside and schmaltzy Sevillanas drifting out over the terrace. I sat at a table, ordered another gin and tonic, and was soon joined by the owner, Daniel, who was tall and Gallicly gracious.

Daniel rejected George's gloomy prognosis of the gay scene. 'There are just as many bars as always: I have Crisco near and the Bronx is my neighbour, then Incognito and Angelo's up by the fish market, JJ's and Teatro and Galeria in the Calle de la Virgen, then there's the Bar Benidorm, Questions, Bobby's . . . For me it's getting better and better every year. There's less trouble up 'ere zan in the Calle de la Virgen, because I don't deal with drugs or prostitution, and my bar it's not a noisy bar. But there's a bit more, how do you say it?, a little bit more class up here in Dalt Vila. I'm a very good friend of all the boys in the Calle de la Virgen, they are all my friends, but as for the bars, well . . . let's just say they're a bit *tatty*.'

A waiter came by and Daniel beckoned him over. 'Listen, *chéri*, did you clean the inside of the glass wiz a napkin before? Because it look very dirty.' He held up the offending glass in front of his employee, who removed it sulkily. 'It's ze little details, you know,' he murmured to me. 'Sometimes I work like a German, I know, but I'm sorry, I want the ashtray *there*, the glass *there*. Like with my barman, every night I have to tell him a hundred times "close the fridge", "clean the floor", "do this", "do that". But it has to be right. Gay people notice details.' The seventies were the liberation years for gay people as the sixties had been for straights. Daniel came to Ibiza in 1973, when the scene was swathed with jewellery and fabulous gowns and surrounded with a dizzying haze of perfume. Clones came later; for the moment, drag was it. In those days there was a flamboyant all-year-round foreign gay population, particularly British, which has now shrunk to a tiny, claustrophobically discreet community of friends. Daniel doesn't know why the others left. 'Maybe they got bored.' But it couldn't have been the repression. Gays on Ibiza have never had that problem, despite the occasional mutterings of the Right. (Abel Matutes once said there were too many of them, leading the kind of life they ought to be 'indulging in back home'.) Daniel points out, however, that there may be a dose of pragmatism in Ibiza's apparent tolerance of homosexuality; after all, gay men spend more money on luxuries, not having to spend it on school fees, they are always nicely turned out, don't get uproariously drunk except on special occasions, and don't generally go out stoning old ladies in the street. With a bit more promotion, 'pink tourism' could be the future.

Just after midnight I walked back down to the Calle de la Virgen. The police were already getting heavy with the fines – George had had to turn off his music and the half-a-dozen drinkers in the bar were about to desert him for somewhere that could afford to pay the 5000ptas price for atmosphere. 'See ya later love,' one of them cried cheerily as he vanished down the steps to the harbour. Halfway up the street I met Fernando, who was looking hollow-faced and pale. I wondered whether he'd fallen back into old habits. He was hoping to end up at Amnesia, which was having one of its foam parties tonight. With him was a girl I recognized from the town, a moon-faced creature who claimed, Fernando told me later, that she had acquired her wax-pale complexion by avoiding the sun for five years. She immediately asked me for money and I gave her some, half-knowing what it was for. Her surname was Riquer Arabí, like the nineteenth-century corsair who famously captured the English ship 'Felicity'. Perhaps she was a descendant.

Fernando led me up a side alley to a bar whose doorway opened shyly at an oblique angle to the street, so that I had never noticed it before. Inside the bar was one large room with a high ceiling and ancient, uneven plaster walls which had been painted an ochre-rich orange with big blue worlds floating in it. This blue was a warm, Southern shade like the painted window-borders on Sandy's little *casa payesa*. On shelves and in niches around the room were strange naïf sculptures, some of them with the same touch of childlike *grotesquerie* I'd seen in Joan Daifa and the Carthaginian maquettes in the Archaeological Museum. The biggest of the sculptures was a roughly modelled papier mâché figure, painted blue with multicoloured blobs. The bar-owner and creator of this object, Joaquín Medina, told us it was based on a story he had written about a siren living on the rock of Es Vedrá.

Another gin and tonic. Joaquín's bar was filling up but he still had a moment to talk. Like Pedro Almodóvar he grew up in La Mancha and left it – La Mancha being the sort of place where all you can do is leave – in the late seventies. After three years of wandering he went home, but, 'I couldn't live there any more. So I came to Ibiza in the autumn of 1982. What did I do first? I breathed, I had a little beer and a little joint, and I thought "Wow! Here I can live."' The feeling of freedom was what persuaded him, and the sky over Ibiza, which was as wide and bright as La Mancha's. Joaquín bought the lease on a little bar in Sa Penya and, out of respect for his roots, called it Pámpana, the *manchego* word for a vine leaf. Later it became Nación Tierra – no relation to the sixties hangout La Tierra – and Joaquín painted it from top to bottom and filled it with fantastical works of art. 'For me the whole room is like a painting.'

I looked at my watch again; it was nearly two o'clock. Back on the Calle the night had moved up another gear. The narrow street had become a long white tunnel of party-people, shouting in a Brussels of languages, swept along by a relentless tide of music. Fernando's friend had disappeared up another alleyway, but another friend had just come by, a girl in a grey cotton boob-tube. They went into a brief huddle under the shrine of the Virgin Mary and Fernando came back with a look of furtive excitement and two neat silver-paper packages in his fist. He slapped one into my palm and whispered in my ear, 'Is good, baby. Is the best. Is from California. We going to have some good time tonight. Oh yeah, baby.' I untwisted the foil a little to see a fat light-brown pill sitting innocently inside. It had been expensive, but there was no way of sampling the true splendour of the Ibicenco night without finding the money, just once, for this most luxurious of substances.

We dropped in on Anfora, a gay disco in a cave. Down-stairs was a dancefloor, upstairs a bar with porn movies flickering pinkly on a TV above the barman's shaved head. In the orgy-room there was a hot, pink darkness. Sense was reduced to touch and sound. Anonymous hands shot out from the sweaty blackness; there were stereo slurpings and moans, comically interspersed with the occasional giggle. A deep German voice said, 'Wo bist du denn?' and an effemi-nate English one replied, music-hall style, 'He's behind you!'

Then on to Pacha, five minutes by Mini along the har-bour. As discos go Pacha is grand and baroquely beautiful. By disco standards it is also old, being poised on the brink of its third decade. It opened in 1973, which may make it the first in the world. In its early years they played reggae and hippie music, and hippies came. Until the KU opened Pacha was the trendiest nightclub in Ibiza, and now the KU has gone it is again, almost as though the sheer ritziness of its rival had cramped its style.

Nineteen summers old, and Pacha still looks exotic, eccentric, extravagant. There are three dancefloors, one at the light-strewn centre of this massive disco and the other two at different levels in outlying areas. The smaller of the dancefloors – which is the only part of Pacha that stays open in the winter for Ibicencos to boogie in – is surrounded by steps where you can lounge in a soft cascade of cushions. In the billiard room the music is gentler and there are pools of light and deep sofas to sink into. There is a restaurant somewhere, although I never managed to find it. And at the top of a staircase above the *Sturm und Drang* of the main dancefloor, hidden away behind a double door, is a place called El Cielo: Heaven. When Fernando and I stumbled in there was a strange party going on, with glamorous Euro-hippies and tinkling New Age music and a luminous punch in a big glass bowl on a pillar like a votive offering. A man with shoulder-length hair, a grizzled face and a crystal on a leather thong round his neck, came up to me and flashed a big, ultra-violet smile. He'd been coming here for six years: 'It's like an itch – you have to come back and scratch it.' He said he was a poet. To prove it, he put his mouth to my ear and whispered: 'If you look beyond that which you see, you will see that which is beyond.'

Back on the dancefloor Alfredo, the DJ, had just followed a clutch of hardcore House tracks with an old Bob Marley record, and people were laughing as they danced to its familiar, chugging rhythm. On a dais under the lights was Vaughan from London, wearing a leopard-skin hat and mirror-shades. He was a professional disco-dancer who came to the island in the summer and wintered in various other European cities – 'I go to Madrid, I go to Stuttgart, a bit o' London, but I still haven't found anywhere better, mate.' Dancing on a dais on the opposite corner of the dancefloor, in Eastern garb, whirling a pink silk scarf around his head, was the man from the full moon party who had read my Tarot at his own little stall in Pacha last year; and on the step below him was a white-bearded man who Fernando said was a sixty-year-old Argentinian, also paid to dance, who spent the winter in St Petersburg, which, of all places to spend the winter struck me as one of the least advisable.

I began to feel a prickling, twitching sensation in my scalp and a ripple of nausea lurching between brain and stomach. I bought myself a glass of water, went outside and sat against a palm tree. The night air was warm and syrupy. I shut my eyes for a few minutes. Next to me two girls were discussing the virtues of Ibiza as compared with another Mediterranean clubber's paradise that was being touted that summer as a rival destination.

'Great night, innit?'

'Yeah, great. So, what d'you reckon generally?'

'S'great. Better than last year.'

'D'you reckon? Better than Rimini?'

'Yeah, Rimini's full of Italians.'

When I opened my eyes the nausea had gone but my head was full of noise and everything seemed vivid and vibrant, as though the world was giving out ten per cent more stimulus than usual. A face grinned at me from across the pathway. I registered the grin before the face and tottered across to join it. Sharon was an American journalist. It was her first night in Ibiza and she just could *naht* believe it. She'd just been sitting in the Calle de la Virgen when a group of angels came past. 'I swear they had six foot wings. Then there was this troupe of blue people, all painted blue from head to foot. The girls were topless with rings through their nipples. I just thought, "This has *gaht* to be some kind of hallucination . . ."'

I rediscovered Fernando at Nicky Holloway's bar at the back of the club. His pupils were even wider and blacker than usual – they seemed to have spilled out like crude oil over his irises – and he wore an expression of dumb bliss.

By now my head was roaring like an express train. Alfredo had moved back from the party favourites to heavy, abstract, three-in-the-morning music loaded with screaming sampled soul voices, sizzling cymbal-sounds and a deluge of artificial handclaps. I was hearing the music as immense slabs of sonic matter whose architectonic structure was suddenly, overwhelmingly, perceptible. We danced like dervishes for two hours. Then Fernando remembered Amnesia. It was 5.15 a.m. and the foam came on at 5.30. If we left now we would make it with five minutes to spare to watch the build-up. So we ran back to the car, breathless and boiling with energy.

Under the greenhouse roof the party was at its height. Pacha might have had its 'Flower Power', its 'Erotic Dreams', its summer-long string of themed nights out, but Amnesia had 'Espuma', its only real party-night and a guaranteed good time. For the rest of the week the place may be echo-ingly empty, but when the foam is on the cash-tills at Amnesia's entrance ring merrily on high.

Amnesia on a foam night is a vast time-machine for transporting 2000 grown-up souls back to gibbering, giggling childhood. It starts out like any ordinary night: goggle-eyed people jack-knifing rhythmically on the dancefloor, com-plaints about the price of drinks, discreet deals out in the garden. When we walked in Sola was sitting at Tanit's new bar. On the barstool next to her was a very small person I thought I recognized. It was the very small person I'd seen run past dressed as a Caliph in the Calle de la Virgen, last year on my first night in town. His name was Olly, an Italian from Barcelona. We shook hands and hugged. His hands were as hot as mine.

Above the dancefloor on a balcony were two giant can-nons pointing out and down. People were glancing at the cannons and screaming 'Yeah!' to the DJ's taunts of 'Do you want Espuma??' The mood was moving from expectation to hysterical excitement. The dancers up on the balcony were climbing on the cannons and pumping up and down on them, legs astride. People clutched one another in antici-pation. Meanwhile the music seemed to grow more and more disco-tacky. 'Do you want Espuma?' the DJ boomed out one more time, and on the roaring affirmative there was a sudden blaze of white light throughout the building, fireworks whizzed and banged and the cannons were turned on to the dancefloor. It was like some kind of religious rite, with Foam replacing Tanit as the deity invoked.

It showered over the crowd in two immense arcs of fat white flakes as big as your hand. In a few seconds it was at ankle level and moving in a sluggish flood, like a glacier, out into the rest of the club where people were already stranded on a desert island of podium and palm tree. When it reached waist-height the dancefloor was a sea of gyrating snowmen. The foam covered people's heads like riding-helmets and their arms with long white woolly sleeves while the snowdrift swelled up to their armpits, quivering and bobbing like the 'Instant Pudding' in Woody Allen's *Sleeper*. One girl had come prepared with swimming-goggles and was plunging into the soapy tide so that she disappeared from view like a swimmer in the surf. The white lights blazed again and it was like a drug-crazed skiing holiday, a snowbound Carnival. Then it went dark, someone held aloft a cigarette-lighter and the neck-high foam and still-falling flakes were weirdly illuminated.

We stayed and danced a while under the palm tree and moved on when the exhilaration palled, dragged away on the rollercoaster of the Ibicenco night. By the time we left the new day was peeping through the roof at Amnesia's delirious dancefloor, but there were still things to do, people to meet, money to be spent. At Space there was still noise and energy when the sun cleared the top of the big hotels in the nearby resort and began pouring down its morning warmth. People were drifting out on to the terrace, finally defeated by the intense grinding techno that was still thundering on mercilessly inside. The mental rush and roar had given way to a gentler glow of gin and joints.

Out here at 9 a.m. the atmosphere was genially groovy. There were RayBans, cups of steaming *café con leche*, and post-Ecstatic smiles. Four drag queens, arriving in triumph from their long night's journey into day – one of them nibbling on a chocolate truffle – were given a generous round of applause. A low-flying plane, coming into land at the airport next door, screamed overhead and there was more applause, as though the clapping and cheering were to welcome this newest batch of party people.

From Playa d'en Bossa we took the ring road, waltzing dazedly round its chain of roundabouts. The roads were clogged with furrow-browed office-workers in SEAT Marbellas, cursing each other and the airport busfuls of tourists for making them late. Beyond Ibiza town the traffic slowed down and thinned out and the long, straight road to San Miguel was as empty as I remembered it from the clear days of January. There was high-season heat in this early sun. Red dust blew up from the fields in tiny tornadoes and dry fringes of wild fennel rustled in the roadsides. We stopped in Santa Gertrudis, where the Bar Costa had just opened, for coffee and *tostadas* gilded with sweet olive oil. None of the foreigners were up, but a few *payeses* were kick-starting their morning with Ducados and brandy. Sitting at the bar was Señor Planells. He coughed out a High Tar greeting.

'How are the *parras*? They looked good when I went past this morning. Yes, I walked through with the dogs and had a look. *Muy buenas*. Soon you can make *vi pagés*. Next year. You bring your grapes to me. I make it for you, like I make my own. Remember, the best in all Ibiza! Next year you will see.'

Up at Sa Rota the forest was quiet. At the back of my head there was still a nightclub whine, like a fly in a jar.

Javier, back from Tenerife for the Ibiza season, was on the stone dais above the field doing his t'ai chi, his movements a solemn ballet of arthritic slowness. The house was taking shape. In six months it might be finished. Javier's odd jobs in the Canaries had left him with money, which he was now happily spending on *cal* for the walls and new canes for the *porxet*. His next major project was a proper bathroom to replace the wooden pallet among the geraniums and the tarnished mirror propped up on a rock beside the cactus patch.

In the orchard below the house the figs were black and swollen. I took the path that led past the tree through the forest to the lower field, where my heartbeat raced at what I saw. Tanit had been at work. In the space of a season the vineyard had grown out of its childish stalky phase and flourished. Except in the lowest rows of Tempranillo, which rabbits and geology had made unhappy, it seemed to me finally a real vineyard, a small ocean of vivid green refreshed by last night's dew, its outer leaves stirred by a minuscule breeze. From every slender branch hung neat bunches of grapes. Since June they had turned a rich purple-black, dusted blue with bloom. I picked a handful and ate them one by one. The skins were tough and bitter and drily tannic, but the flesh inside was sweet and cool.

The day was growing dozy with heat, and I was alone. Fernando had sloped off to bed in his little red cottage. Javier was making breakfast up at the house. I found a patch of soft earth at the field's edge where the pines threw down a fragrant shade, and slept till lunchtime.

BIBLIOGRAPHY

Alarco von Perfall, Claudio. *Cultura y personalidad en Ibiza* (Madrid, 1981)

Barbero Garcia, Adriano. *En la isla del dios Bes* (Madrid, 1984)

Barceló Pons, Bartolomé. *Evolución reciente y estructura actual de la población en las Islas Baleares* (Madrid/Ibiza, 1970)

Braudel, Fernand. *La Méditerranée et le monde méditerranéen à l'époque de Philippe II* (Paris, 1949)

Calendario de Agricultura Biológico-Dinámica (Editorial Rudolf Steiner, 1991)

Carr, Raymond. *Modern Spain 1875–1980* (Oxford, 1980)

Castellò Guasch, Joan. *Bon Profit: el libro de la cocina ibicenca* (Ibiza, 1991)

Dades Balears (Palma, 1989)

Fay, Stephen, et al. *Hoax* (London, 1973)

Ferrer Clapès, Michel. *Sta. Eulalia del Rio: Historia Gráfica de un pasado reciente* (Ibiza, 1992)

Frame, Janet. *An Angel at my Table* (London, 1987)

Gaviria, M, et al. *Turismo de Playa en España* (Madrid, 1975)

Giffhorn, Hans. *Ibiza: un paraíso natural desconocido* (Ibiza, 1992)

Gil Muñoz, Carlos. *Juventud marginada* (Barcelona, 1970)

Grupo de Estudios de la Naturaleza. *La Lluita per ses Salines* (Ibiza, 1991)

Guia Ecológica de Baleares (INCAFO, Madrid, 1978)

Institut d'Estudis Eivissencs. *La Guerra Civil a Eivissa i Formentera* (Ibiza, 1985)

Institut d'Estudis Eivissencs. *Ses Salines d'Eivissa i Formentera* (Ibiza, 1983)

Irving, Clifford. *Fake!* (London, 1970)

BIBLIOGRAPHY

Joan i Mari, Bernat. *La llengua Catalana a Eivissa: situaciò i perspectivas* (Ibiza, 1982)

Lee, Laurie. *I Can't Stay Long* (London, 1977)

Macabich, Isidoro. *Historia de Ibiza* (Palma, 1966)

Martinez Genovart, Alicia. *Cuentos de Ibiza* (Barcelona, 1988)

Massacrier, Jacques. *Savoir revivre* (Paris, 1973)

Maurel/Valenti, eds. *Geografia de España*, vol. 9, Cataluña/Baleares (Barcelona, 1992)

Moreno/Pascuet, eds. *Arquitectura y espacio rural en Ibiza* (Ibiza/Palma, 1985)

Murray, Donald G. *Ses nostres cases: arquitectura tradicional de les Balears* (Palma, 1986)

Paul, Elliot. *Life and Death of a Spanish Town* (New York, 1937)

Planells, Mariano. *Diccionario de los secretos de Ibiza* (Barcelona, 1982)

Planells, ed. *Anuario de Ibiza y Formentera* (Ibiza, 1990, 1991, 1992)

Planells Ferrer, Antonio. *Ibiza y Formentera, Ayer y Hoy* (Barcelona, 1984)

Poyatos Oliver, Juan Francisco. *Cocina Popular Ibicenca* (Ibiza, 1991)

Ripoll, Luis. *Nuestra cocina* (Barcelona, 1978)

Rotthier, Philippe, and Joachim, Ferdinand. *Ibiza, le palais paysan* (Brussels, 1984)

Rotthier, Philippe, and Joachim, Ferdinand. *Maisons sur l'île d'Ibiza* Brussels, 1990)

Rozenberg, Danielle. *Ibiza, una isla para otra vida* (Centro de Investigaciones Sociológicas, 1990)

Sert, Josep Lluis. *Ibiza fuerte y luminosa* (Barcelona, 1967)

Taller d'Estudis de l'Habitat Pitius. Raoul Hausmann (Ibiza, 1991)

Terry-Thomas. *Terry-Thomas Tells Tales* (London, 1990)

Torres, Elias. *Guia de Arquitectura de Ibiza y Formentera* (Barcelona, 1981)

Wyndham, Joan. *Anything Once* (London, 1992)